FIREWALKING

The paper used in this publication meets the minimum requirements of American National Standard for Information Sciences—Permanence of Paper for Printed Library Materials, ANSI Z39.48-1984.

FIREWALKING

A New Look at an Old Enigma

Larissa Vilenskaya
Joan Steffy

Introduction by Stanley Krippner

THE
BRAMBLE
COMPANY
Connecticut

For information write to:
The Bramble Company, RFD 88 (Route 126), Falls Village, Connecticut 06031

Cover photo: Ange Stephens firewalking.

Library of Congress Cataloging-in-Publication Data
Vilenskaya, Larissa.
   Firewalking : a new look at an old enigma / Larissa Vilenskaya, Joan Steffy ; introduction by Stanley Krippner.
         p.   cm.
   Includes bibliographical references and index.
   ISBN 0-9626184-3-8 ; $14.95
   1. Fire walking. I. Steffy, Joan. II. Title.
BL619.F57V55   1991
001.9'4—dc20   91-75513
                                                                      CIP

First Printing 1991
1 3 5 7 9 10 8 6 4 2

Printed in the United States of America

Table of Contents

Joyce Quick from Seattle, Washington,
firewalking while leading her workshop
in Washington, DC, 1985.

Introduction

Stanley Krippner, Ph.D.
Professor of Psychology
Saybrook Institute

There have been tales of fire immunity from time immemorial. By 500 B.C. the tradition had been firmly established in China, Japan, Tibet, and India, eventually spreading westward. In medieval times, people in various parts of Europe walked on fire to show humility, seek purification, or demonstrate their innocence of serious crimes.

Shamans in various parts of the world have purportedly demonstrated fire immunity for tens of thousands of years, handling hot coals as well as walking on them.[1] An account of a ritual shamanic firewalk was given by William Tufts Brigham, director of the Bishop Museum of Ethnology in Honolulu. In the late 1880s, Dr. Brigham, who had grown up in Hawaii, persuaded three kahunas (or native shamans) to teach him their firewalking abilities. Brigham joined the Hawaiian practitioners as they uttered a brief prayer, then trotted over 150 feet of lava that was flowing from Mt. Kilauea. Even though his boots burned to ash, Brigham reported that there was no sensation of heat on his feet. None of the four lava walkers suffered blisters or any other injury.

Until recent years, reports of this nature were dismissed as nonsense by mainstream scientists. However, a few enterprising investigators were intrigued by these tales and began to visit firewalks, making observations and records. For example, in 1980 a team of researchers from the University of Tubingen in West Germany visited the annual festival of St. Constantine in northern

Greece, noting that the coals for the firewalk had a surface temperature that reached 932 degrees Fahrenheit. The soles of the firewalkers' feet registered a temperature of about 365 degrees, but there was no evidence of damage.[2]

When classes began to be offered to prepare individuals for group firewalks in the United States, attention could no longer be denied to firewalking and related fire immunity phenomena. From a blanket denial of the existence of firewalking, observers presented a number of explanations, many of them carefully reasoned. Consideration was given to perspiration on the feet, activation of the body's pain-blocking mechanisms, and the nature of heat conductivity itself. Various properties of human consciousness were allowed for as well as such variables as the toughness of the soles of the feet and the length of time the body was in contact with the embers.

Larissa Vilenskaya and Joan Steffy have embarked upon a challenging mission. They have surveyed the history of fire immunity and have summarized the explanatory models currently in vogue. But they have done more. Vilenskaya became a firewalk instructor, conducting many firewalking seminars herself. Steffy conducted a research study with firewalkers, using questionnaires and interviews. Their combined perspective brings a fresh dimension to the inquiry, one that calls into question the notion that most firewalkers are gullible prey for commercial entrepeneurs, or that they are naive thrill-seekers who are physically and psychologically harmed by the experience.

Firewalking: A New Look at an Old Enigma demonstrates a shift in world view on two levels. In the first place, it presents abundant evidence that the existence of firewalking is no longer in doubt; even those investigators who present conventional, naturalistic explanations for the firewalk are taking the reports seriously—and some even firewalked themselves. In the second place, interview and questionnaire data provide the provocative finding that many participants believe that firewalking has helped them to transcend the limitations of their previous beliefs.

Will firewalking in contemporary society simply be another fad that will last a few years, then give way to the next offering of "pop psychology"? Or will humanity's perennial fascination with flames revive in such a way that, again, handling and walking on fire will become a metaphor and an avenue for personal and social transformation? Vilenskaya and Steffy have vividly marked the boundaries of the present status of firewalking, and only time will tell if these borders will shrink or expand in future years.

1. Eliade, M. (1972). *Shamanism: Archaic Techniques of Ecstasy* (pp. 112, 316). Princeton, NJ: Princeton University Press.
2. Adams, R.B., Jr. (Ed.) (1988). *Mind Over Matter* (chapter 3). Richmond, VA: Time-Life Books.

Larissa Vilenskaya firewalking in Verona, Italy, 1985.

Preface

... Fire burns. The cause-effect of fire underlies the physical
world. There could be no such phenomenon as fire, did fire
not burn. But fire does not have to burn a person in this
particular case at this particular time. Neither does cancer
have to kill this particular person at this particular time;
nor do any of the other grim dragons of necessity have to
apply to this person or that person—nor to any person who
can believe in another way, or another construct.

Joseph Chilton Pearce,
The Crack in the Cosmic Egg (1971)

The above statement by Joseph Chilton Pearce[1] about the fire
that "does not have to burn a person" was made in relation to
firewalking, a wide-spread ritual in which participants demonstrate
their ability to walk over red-hot coals without injury. Since we
were introduced to firewalking, we have been attempting to answer
the question: does a change in our world view change the way we
perceive and experience the world around us? Do our thoughts, our
understanding, our concepts, our ideas of the world determine our
reality? In other words, do we create our own reality? Do our views
determine our perception of the world only for ourselves or for those
around us as well? And, if yes, to what degree? Where are the limits?
And are there any limits?

Over one thousand years before the birth of Christ, ancients wrote of priests who were able to walk through flames mysteriously and supposedly unharmed.[2] Since then, the phenomenon of firewalking has been practiced throughout the world, from Australia to Argentina, from the Himalayas to Haiti, from Thailand to Trinidad. The practitioners of old are today joined by an estimated 30,000 lay people around the world who walked across blazing coals between 1980 and 1985 in the framework of "firewalking workshops."[3] And still, for many, the mystery remains.

From ancient times to modern, scientists and theoreticians have struggled to find an answer to the questions raised by individuals traversing or dancing across fiery embers which measure over one thousand degrees Farenheit. Interested researchers have measured temperatures of the coals and have sought to answer why and how firewalking is possible. Yet, as will be seen, no single theory seems to explain satisfactorily the firewalking phenomenon.

The contemporary fad of firewalking workshops traces its roots to ancient magic and legend, with abundant anecdotal literature and remarkably scant research of a serious nature. Our review of firewalking literature encompasses both aspects, as well as current firewalking workshops and an investigation of the psychological effects of crossing the coals. To provide as broad a spectrum of understanding as possible, other unusual abilities associated with fire immunity are also discussed. The term "fire immunity" is used to denote the purported immunity of certain individuals to extreme thermal stimuli.[4] Thus, this term includes not only firewalking, but fire handling as well.

The phenomenon of fire immunity among participants of magical and religious rituals has been observed for centuries by anthropologists and world travelers. During these rituals, individuals could walk through hot infernos or expose their bodies to high temperatures without harm. In Indian and Chinese folk traditions firewalking is usually practiced as a test to prove that devotees are protected by their deity. Similarly, in Central America and other parts of North America, walking over live coals or passing unharmed through flames was used as a means of purification and for testing an accused person's innocence.[5] Throughout history firewalking has been motivated by and connected with some form of religious celebration, whether it honors a deceased saint or commemorates a once witnessed miracle of coming unscathed out of fire.[6]

Rituals involving firewalking and other kinds of reported fire immunity have been practiced in Argentina, Australia, Brazil, Bulgaria, Burma, China, Fiji, Greece, Haiti, India, Indonesia, Japan, Malaysia, New Zealand, Pakistan, the Philippines, various Polynesian islands, Singapore, Spain, Sri Lanka, and Thailand, as well as by Native Americans, several African tribes, and by Indian immigrants in Mauritius, Trinidad, and South Africa.[7]

In 1983, Larissa Vilenskaya met Tolly Burkan, a Californian who, after learning this art from a student of a Tibetan yogi, began to conduct workshops he called "Overcoming Fear and Limiting Beliefs Through Firewalking" throughout the United States and Europe. He claimed that within three to four hours he could teach any person to walk on red-hot coals unharmed. L.V. decided to explore the validity of these claims and joined one of Tolly's workshops. She was inspired to firewalk and found it to be not only an elating, exhilarating and profound experience, but also an excellent tool for healing, spiritual growth and psychological development.

Fascinated with firewalking, L.V. decided to study further with Tolly Burkan and to learn to teach firewalking seminars. After the study course (described in these pages) and several dozen workshops in the United States and Europe, L.V. decided that it was time for a change. She returned from a position of workshop leader and proponent of firewalking to that of a rigorous researcher—a modus operandi that seemed to be more appropriate to her background and experience. There were hundreds of questions: How and why is firewalking possible? Does the experience produce a change in the participants' views, perceptions, and behavior? And if it does, are these changes lasting?

L.V. was familiar enough with the scientific method to realize that her fascination with firewalking was an impediment to conducting an objective study. By serendipity, Joan Steffy, a psychologist and L.V.'s close friend, became interested in the subject and joined the study, offering her expertise, experience and unbiased approach. The result is here for you to peruse, evaluate, criticize and (we hope) enjoy.

The book consists of two approximately equal parts. The first includes an analysis of the literature and L.V.'s experiential approach to the subject. The second part presents the methodology and results of the study conducted by the authors. Chapters I and IV are written by L.V. (in the first person); Chapters V, VI and VII are written by J.S.; the rest are our joint venture.

We have intentionally preserved two distinctly diverse styles in the book, that of an experiential popular narrative as well as that of a scholarly work. First, this diversity reflects the dual approach of the authors who believe in the value of combining the scientific method and intuitive insights in the search for knowledge. Second, we believe that this structure will make the book readable for a broader audience, since the essence of our work can be easily understood without delving into the complexities and subtleties that distinguish experiential observation from scholarly investigation.

The authors gratefully acknowledge the advice, support and encouragement of Dr. Stanley Krippner, Dr. Ruth-Inge Heinze and Dr. Marilyn Rossner. We would also like to express our thanks to Martin Ebon and Rhea White who kindly lent us archival materials on firewalking. We would like to thank Elizabeth Layton for her help with the Bibliography; also Dr. Vittoria Manganas for the most interesting information about Greek fire dancers and for her kind assistance in arranging L.V.'s trip to observe their ceremony. We are grateful to all the facilitators and participants of firewalking seminars who devoted their time and effort in assisting us with this study. Our sincere thanks go to Charlotte Berney for her invaluable editorial assistance. And finally, we express our appreciation to the unseen mysterious cosmic forces of the Universe that directed us to the intriguing path of seeking knowledge and wisdom and attempting to make a modest contribution to fulfilling the ancient maxim, "Know Thyself."

In conclusion, we must warn you: this is not a how-to manual on firewalking. Perhaps in these pages firewalking appears easy, but it should *never* be attempted without proper guidance.

PART ONE

From Miracle To Science: Introduction To Firewalking

Miracles are propitious accidents,
the natural causes of which are too complicated
to be readily understood.

George Santayana,
The Ethics of Spinoza (1910).

Chapter 1
The Beginning

The distance is nothing.
It's only the first step that's important.
Mme du Deffand, Letter to d'Alembert, July 7, 1763

1. Know Thyself: The Story of a Soviet Firewalker

I have always been fascinated with what can be called "human potential." While in the Soviet Union, I read many fascinating accounts of individuals capable of supermemory, performing lightning calculation, walking on broken glass without injury and other seemingly impossible feats.

Nearly 25 years ago, when I was a first-year student at an engineering college in Moscow, a turn of events (or my fate?) brought me to a lecture by Soviet biophysicist, Dr. Yuri Kamensky, who spoke about human possibilities and parapsychology. After the lecture he and his partner, actor Karl Nikolayev, conducted a demonstration, an informal telepathy test. Suddenly I had a strange idea to conduct my own test, to "intervene" mentally and "transmit" my own image. As strange as it sounds I succeeded: Nikolayev, who was sitting in another room, described correctly both images,

Kamensky's and my own. This was the beginning of my fascination with the mysteries of the mind, which led me to study and work at the Bioinformation Laboratory in Moscow and my life-long interest in parapsychology and human possibilities.

Many interesting events followed. I met with Rosa Kuleshova, a woman from the city of Sverdlovsk in the Urals, who demonstrated "skin vision" or dermo-optic perception, as the Soviets often called it. Rosa explained to me that she learned how to perceive colors and shapes with her fingers by devoting several hours a day to this practice for about three months. I was fascinated that someone could apparently learn something as unusual as eyeless sight. I started playing with this idea myself and designed a kind of primitive training program, working with color samples and cards with large letters. Then I felt inspired to organize a small training group and to lead about a dozen volunteers in learning this skill. Soon I found that some of my volunteers no longer needed to touch the sample with their fingers. They seemed to develop a kind of extrasensory perception and were able to perceive colors and shapes by receiving the images on the "inner screen," in the mind's eye. This was a very interesting time of enthusiastic work and fascinating discoveries.

Through the years, I have encountered many other individuals with extraordinary abilities. My enthusiasm for these studies has not diminished and, time and resources permitting, I continue to travel and to peruse extensive literature to further my quest. Let me, however, return now to those years of exploration of human possibilities in Moscow where I first encountered descriptions of firewalking.

Firewalking in exotic and some not so exotic lands is occasionally discussed in the Soviet press. I cannot say that this feat or ritual is native to Russian culture. The Russians do have an old tradition of jumping over fires on the Ivan Kupala festival in summer. (Ivan Kupala is the old folk name the Slavs gave to St. John the Baptist; the word Kupala originates from the verb "kupat"—to bathe, i.e., to baptize.) The tradition is preserved in some Russian villages where on the night of July 7 (June 24 according to the old calendar) every year, large bonfires are ignited and young people jump over them. They believe in the purifying power of fire and that it can endow them with health and power. Many of them also go to the woods in search of the "fire flower" of a fern that is believed to lead to treasure and wealth. In some parts of Russia, on the day of the festival young people meet near the river and bathe till twilight, when a fire is kindled, and the boys and girls, taking each other's hands, jump over the flame, two by two. Those who do not loosen their hands while jumping are believed to become husband and wife, the same thing being predicted by a spark which comes out of the fire after them.

Soviet publications about firewalking are not, however, connected with this old tradition. Still, as soon as I came across an article on the subject, I read it carefully and placed it in a special file in my personal archives. At that time I did not know that a part of these archives (and I) was destined one day to cross the Atlantic and end up in an American town. (A part of the archives was not so fortunate, however, and was lost in this process.) To give the readers a better idea of what I am talking about, I would like to present here an abridged English translation of two of the reports.[1]

■

Way Beyond the Horizon

Igor Guberman

The phenomenon of firewalking has been encountered in several countries of the world: India, Indonesia, Japan, the Polynesian Islands of the South Pacific and several African nations. Below I present a colorful account of the firewalking ritual as recounted by an eyewitness on the island of Bali:

"In a small open area stood an open white umbrella. This meant that a priest was present. Everything necessary for the ritual stood on a small table, particularly incense in burners. Two young girls were already dressed in festive attire; the priest moved the intoxicating fumes of incense toward the girls, who began to breathe them in. They both began to go into a deeper and deeper trance state. The priest gave them fans and they, now in deep trance, began to perform an incredible dance with these fans. This was an unbelievable scene and we became somewhat frightened, since both girls had their eyes closed. Nonetheless their movements were completely in rhythm and harmony with each other.... The girls rested a little without coming out of their strange state. Then they were given the fans again, and they resumed their dance. One of the attendants lit the fire and the girls began to dance around the fire with their eyes closed. We were literally numb with fear, afraid that they would accidentally wind up in the flames. They spun in circles around the fire, approaching it closer and closer, until finally one of them ran and with bare feet leapt into the fire. The second girl followed. The girls turned round and round in the fire, stamping the burning wood and coconut husks. The dancing and the music reached its climax—I wanted to pinch myself to prove it wasn't a dream. It was hard to believe that I wasn't in a hypnotic dream along with these two girls. But at this point, a piece of coconut husk jumped out of the fire right into the crowd of spectators and the smell of burning clothing filled the air. No, it wasn't a dream, it was reality. The girls were really stamping on the fire with their bare feet, and they remained unharmed. Suddenly the dance stopped. The priest led the exhausted, trembling girls to some low benches and lit the incense again to bring them out of their trance. When we came up to see the girls, we realized that they were only children. They were both smiling weakly; there was not a single trace of any burns on them."

A scholar named Kellogg observed firewalking on the island of Tahiti. The natives there walked on a red-hot stone path 12 meters long, while spectators found it hard even to come close to the heat. When Kellogg threw a shoe on these heated stones, it burned up instantly.

It is important to note that firewalking is not just indigenous to "exotic" lands. The Bulgarian psychoneurologist Sharankov wrote a monograph in which he described in detail the ritual of firewalking as practiced by the members of the Bulgarian religious sect of "nestenaries" (after the Greek "Anastenarides").

Evidence collected by witnesses (e.g. those by British ethnographer and biologist D. Attenborough, published in *Nauka i Religiya*,

No. 1, 1967) is very convincing in the complete absence of a physiological explanation of the phenomenon. Firewalking actually exists, and is not a fraud—but it is inexplicable. Many hypotheses have attempted to explain it, but all of them have turned out to be either improbable or erroneous. Explanations about deliberately rubbing the soles of the feet with protective substances, about profuse sweating creating a "steam pillow" as a buffer, about the low sensitivity of firewalkers' calloused soles, and finally about the extreme speed of traversing the fire path have all been proven insufficient. However, one hypothesis which it is impossible to prove or disprove at present is the one about the skin's superconductivity which is made possible by changes in the nervous system. We do not understand how the skin becomes a superconductor of heat at such extreme temperatures, because the superconductivity of heat and electricity is a phenomenon occurring at extremely low temperatures. All these theories cannot explain why the protein of life cells is able to withstand temperatures many times beyond its limits, or why no burns occur.

The investigation of firewalking under laboratory conditions has completely confirmed its authenticity, but has added nothing to our understanding. And so, there remain many unsolved riddles, many questions beyond the horizon. Of course, the discoveries are also there, awaiting those enterprising investigators willing to venture into this most mysterious of realms.

(Published in *Nauka i Religiya* [Science and Religion], Moscow, No. 8, 1969.)

■

Fire Dancing

Svyatoslav Slavchev
Bulgaria

Last fall I finally had the opportunity to witness firewalking. I was staying in a resort, situated near several villages where the art of "nestenarism" has been practiced since ancient times. Every year, June 3 (the Feast Day of St. Constantine and Helen) is celebrated with a communal feast, music, and firewalking.

The night before, several adult women locked themselves up in the church in order to pray the entire night. In the morning several men arranged and lit the firewood to the sound of special music played on folk instruments. Later that day, in the evening, the men slowly raked the coals into an enormous glowing circle. When the church doors opened, the women walked out barefoot onto the coals, walking in a spiral toward the center and taking quick short steps. The women seemed to be lost in a pagan dance to the frenzied music. Then they came out of the red-hot disc unharmed. Meanwhile, everyone had gathered for the communal feast at which these women were honored as saints. In the popular imagination, only saints could perform such a miraculous feat.

After the revolution a group of young Bulgarian atheists sought to discredit the religious legends surrounding the "nestenarian" dances. In 1946 twenty-seven young men and women walked on hot coals for a whole ten minutes. Only three of them severely burned their soles; the rest were not burned. This incident was described in the proceedings of the Bulgarian Academy of Sciences.

As the evening progressed I made the acquaintance of one of the firewalkers, a young woman named Nevena. She was dressed in an embroidered shift. She told me that she had been involved in firewalking from age 12. She had once attempted it at the age of 9, but was severely burned; her grandmother spent three weeks healing her with a mixture of herbs, goat's milk, and grain husks. Nevena explained that the art was quite simple: all one had to do was to walk quickly across the coals, taking tiny quick steps, and most importantly, to curl the toes under.

At this point Todor, a Bulgarian of about 40 with sparkling black eyes, came over and gathered Nevena up into his arms and carried her over to the fire. He let her down gently into the disc of burning earth. She began to fly across the coals, her arms outstretched and her eyes half-closed, walking the way that I imagine sleep-walkers do at the edge of a roof. The music played faster, wailing even more wildly. I myself was even tempted to quickly take off my shoes and fly across the coals with the rest of the village.

After a period of time which seemed to me like hours, the ritual ended. I found Nevena sitting near the platform, and asked to see her soles. No protective ointments, no calluses, no burns on the delicate soles of her feet.

"How are you able to do this, Nevena?" I asked her.

"I don't know. As soon as the music starts, I feel the blood leaving my legs and my soles becoming numb. I feel like I am in a dream, flying over the red earth."

"How often do you do this?" "Every evening from May to November. Sometimes two or three times an evening."

"Are you afraid?"

"Why should I be afraid? I'm used to it. My brother Dimitr walks on fire with his hands. He hasn't been burned a single time."

Nevena left to change her clothes, and came back dressed in a fashionable turquoise dress and elegant suede shoes. She offered to give me a ride in her own car back to the resort. I stared at Nevena, driving back along the winding roads in the picturesque hills, and felt as if it were me snaking across the bright glowing coals to the serpentine sounds of wild music in the night.

(Published in *Tekhnika-Molodezhi* [Technology for Youth], Moscow, No. 1, 1971.)

■

Soon after my emigration to the United States, I came across another intriguing article, this time about a Soviet enthusiast of self-exploration, Valery Avdeyev. He was reported to demonstrate firewalking by crossing a 30-foot-long bonfire unharmed, acting on his firm belief in the virtually unlimited hidden human potential.[2]

Avdeyev, a graduate from the Leningrad Musical Actors Studio, is known in the Soviet Union as a performer of unusual feats. He made appearances at various educational, research, and other institutions. Among the places he performed were the Officers' Club of the Soviet Army and the Police Academy, where he elicited the following official evaluation:

"Valery Avdeyev's psychological experiments are not circus acts, but clear, scientific demonstrations of hidden capacities of the human mind and body."

Avdeyev's performances included demonstrations of lying on a thick layer of broken glass with a heavy weight resting on top of his body. He rose from his unusual "bed" without a single scratch on his back. Valery talks about his talents in his own words:

"There is nothing 'supernatural' about this. You simply block out a certain muscle, a certain part of the body at the right moment through self-suggestion. It is as if it's not there, and since it isn't, it can't be hurt, even by sharp slivers of glass. I feel that the capabilities of the human mind and body are unlimited."

When asked why he firewalked, Avdeyev recalled that in his early childhood he became interested in the human being as a phenomenon of nature. This interest gradually led him to do experiments on himself. Many questions excited him: "What am I capable of doing? How am I put together physically and psychologically?"

"I understand now that I practiced a kind of spontaneous, amateur yoga, and invented various exercises, attempted them and followed the changes taking place in me. Then suddenly one day it occurred to me that such feats as firewalking could be performed not only by yogis and fakirs, but by any healthy human being after the appropriate training (not necessarily yogic)."

"My grandfather," Avdeyev related, "possessed the ability to hypnotize. And I began to study myself in order to discover similar abilities. I devoted all my spare time to this endeavor. To give you an illustration of the kind of attempts I made in working with developing my capacities, I will relate the following incident. One summer I happened to be walking in the early morning to my village. A very large dog approached me with what I perceived as aggressive intentions. I clearly set myself the goal of dissuading it and concentrated all my energy as I walked toward it. The dog stopped in its tracks. I stretched out my hand in order to pet it, and the thought that the dog might attack me crossed my mind. The dog reacted with a shudder, jumped to one side and began to howl wildly as if he was being beaten with a stick."

Avdeyev emphasized that in his exercises he followed and noted the slightest changes in his state of mind. "No single book can give you a concrete understanding of your abilities or self-knowledge," he stated. "You need your own personal experience. I myself had to 'try it on'—does it fit or not? Books and guidelines stimulate activity and thought, but do not indicate how to go about successfully performing specific exercises for each individual. We are all different; each person has an individual nervous system and relationship to the world. And yet, in a sense we are all similar. Books, as a rule, emphasize these general similarities. And so, I had to become my own teacher in order to learn something. I feel that everyone who wishes to uncover and cultivate his abilities has to use this process."

Returning to his experience of firewalking, Avdeyev explained:

"As soon as we subject our organism to extreme conditions, in addition to instinctive protective mechanisms, other specific and subconscious defense mechanisms will be activated. So, now here I am in the woods, facing the fire. Where do I start? In this initial instant, how do I get ready for this process? I figured it out: the main thing is to overcome the psychological barrier of the fear of fire, implanted in us since childhood. And so I decided: no matter what the consequences of my experiment are, be it sizzling feet or a trip to the hospital, I will do it, I will, I must.

"This thought consumed all of me. I experienced a state of elation and excitement, fearlessness and contempt for any possible injury or even death.... In another minute I was walking on the coals. The physical sensation was unexpected, as if I were walking on hot sand — hot, very hot, but bearable nonetheless."

Avdeyev described not only his first successful attempt at firewalking, but another occasion in which he "could not bring himself to the proper state of mind" and was burned. He concluded that, "I understood that the primary factor necessary for walking on coals was to enter a state of consciousness in which this seemed possible. One could learn not only to play the violin, to run the 100 meter dash, to swim the breast-stroke, but also to desensitize oneself to fire."

Less than two years after I first read these lines I had an opportunity to see myself that he was totally right in his assertion.

2. Do You Want to Walk on Fire? My Meeting with Tolly Burkan

I always like to go through my mail: I enjoy unexpected news and surprises, and in our technological world news most often comes either by phone or by mail. Haven't you also dreamed from time to time of something wonderful and exciting happening, something that would suddenly and completely change your life? (Certainly, it would be for the better—if you're an optimist!) We all know, nevertheless, that real (and pleasant) surprises are quite rare—and the more welcome! But, I did not expect anything special when on a foggy day in San Francisco in the fall of 1983 I opened a blue airmail envelope from London. I took out a poorly xeroxed copy of a brochure and a brief typewritten note. I quickly glanced through them and was stupefied with astonishment. I made myself read them once again, slowly and carefully. There it was in black and white:

Firewalking Workshop With
Tolly Burkan

In four hours, everyone participating will be taught how to walk barefoot on hot coals without burning their feet. Information on fear and limiting beliefs will also be presented. As the classroom procedure evolves, a large fire is ignited and allowed to burn itself to coals. At the conclusion of the workshop, Tolly will demonstrate walking on the embers and anyone who desires to do so may join as well. The firewalk itself is purely **voluntary** and anyone who wishes to remain a spectator is free to do so. Tolly has taken children as young as 4 years old over the coals and emphasizes that **anyone** can do it. **Even those who participate only in the classroom procedure will receive valuable tools they can use to overcome fear and limitations in every aspect of their lives.**

The brochure, its most important words and phrases in boldface, looked impressive and very mysterious. "Is it a hoax, a joke, a mystery?" I wondered. "But, if so, why? . . ." The address and telephone number in Portland, Oregon, where one might inquire about the forthcoming firewalking workshop, was printed on the brochure and somewhat dispelled my doubts. Guy Lyon Playfair, a writer and friend from London who had sent me the brochure, wondered in his note, "It may be too late for you to go to Oregon and jump into the flames, but it would be nice one day to talk with Tolly Burkan and see what he is up to!" Too late?! No, certainly it wasn't too late—I had almost a week to the date of the workshop, plenty of time to prepare for this trip. After all, it was happening here on the West Coast, not in far-off Greece or the Philippines.

After reading numerous articles and reports on firewalking, I was more than curious and eager to see it with my own eyes. I mused again at the mysterious workings of the universe—isn't it strange to learn from London about something that is about to happen almost at home?! I recalled the words of Soviet "self-experimenter" Valery Avdeyev:

"One can learn not only to play the violin, to run the 100 meter dash, to swim the breast-stroke, but also to desensitize oneself to fire."[3]

One *could* learn... However, I was doubtful that an untrained, unprepared individual was capable of learning this skill (or art) in the course of four hours. After all, Avdeyev and others had emphasized that in order not to be burnt, a firewalker had "to enter a state of consciousness in which this seemed possible." Were four hours really enough? Would I have believed that a few days later I would be in a group of excited people, hugging each other and repeating, "We did it!" "We did it!"? No, I wouldn't have believed it at all.

The flight from San Francisco to Portland was relaxing and uneventful. After busy workdays filled with small details demanding attention, I almost lost the excitement which came over me after I read the workshop announcement. Another trip, another workshop—no big deal. In any event, I wasn't going to do anything as crazy as to walk on fire! As a writer, editor, reporter and researcher, I simply wanted to observe the unusual event, to write an article for *Psi Research*, the journal which I edit and publish, and to give my readers the most interesting, fresh, and authentic information about it. That was all.

This was what drew me on Sunday evening to a crowded room in a residential house in Beaverton, Oregon, in the suburbs of Portland. There I found two dozen people—men and women mostly in their twenties and early thirties, but also some older ones. Many of them were sitting on the floor in a very relaxed manner. (Later I learned that many had participated in a previous weekend workshop on yoga.) Soon, other participants arrived, and when their number reached between forty and fifty, a tall thin man came before the audience. At first he did not seem impressive to me; he did not look like a guru or a spiritual teacher. His face was relaxed and expressionless. This was my first encounter with Tolly Burkan. He took a guitar and began to play a song, and the audience immediately picked up the tune. I did not know the words, but the melody seemed pleasant and cheerful.

When Tolly began to speak, his seemingly unemotional face changed dramatically. He told us that for most of his life he had thought that he had a bad ear for music, that he would never be able to play an instrument or compose music. But then he learned that these abilities can be developed—and here was a song he had composed. He began playing the guitar and singing a song about how everyone has the opportunity to change, and again the audience began to sing along:

The only thing that's constant is the certainty of change
Nothing ever remains the same.

I knew a man who was lame, a year later he could run.
The past is gone, now the future has begun.
The only thing that's constant is the certainty of change.
Nothing ever remains the same...

"This is the song which we will sing after the firewalk," Tolly added. "*After* the firewalk?!" It sounded completely unreal to me, as if I were in a dream, trying in vain to wake up.

Tolly Burkan explained the procedure for the evening. First, each participant had to sign a release form (typed copies were distributed to the audience) which stated that his/her participation in the workshop was purely voluntary, that the organizers waive legal responsibility for any possible injuries, and that the participants themselves were responsible for their actions and consequences. Burkan asked that the release be signed by everyone, even those who came only as observers and had no intention of participating in the firewalk. I found this request a bit disturbing, but

12

nevertheless logical. Then he asked all participants to introduce themselves and to express what their goals were in coming to the workshop. More than half stated with clear determination, "I came to walk on fire and to show myself that nothing can stop me from doing anything I wish to do." There were a few children and teenagers with their parents who also said that they had come to walk on fire. Others (including myself) said that they came to observe and learn, but they were not certain whether they were going to participate in the actual firewalking. Some stated that they definitely were *not* going to undertake this venture.

Tolly explained that we would begin with a discussion, then go out in the yard and start the fire together, and return to continue the discussion while his wife Peggy kept the fire going. At some point we would go out and sing together, and everyone who chose to could follow him over the hot coals. It sounded a bit superficial to me, but I decided not to jump to hasty conclusions. And indeed, Tolly's lively manner of communicating with the group and his subtle humor soon turned me from a spectator into a participant.

The first point he emphasized was that in order to successfully walk on coals at a temperature of about 1,300°F (700°C), we must first move beyond our fear. "When you are standing in front of the coal bed," he told us, "you will feel a membrane of fear between you and the fire. If you can step through this membrane of fear, *if you can make this first step, you can walk on fire!*" And, to transcend our fears, we had first to understand the concept that FEAR is nothing but "False Evidence Appearing Real."

Five years ago a friend who had learned this art from a Tibetan, showed Burkan that firewalking is indeed possible. After repeating the feat a number of times, Tolly came to the conclusion that he could help others learn how to walk over hot coals unharmed and came up with the idea of the workshops. During the past five years he had conducted several hundred workshops in Sweden, Norway, Canada and the United States, with a total of about 7,000 individuals participating in firewalking under his guidance. Although so-called "scientific evidence" states that human flesh cannot withstand such a temperature, according to his experience, people can walk over red-hot coals without harming themselves. Thus, what we are dealing with here is false evidence appearing real.

To illustrate his point, Tolly offered a simple example: One day a man who is deathly afraid of snakes comes to a resort and is given an unexpected warning: please be careful, there are many poisonous snakes around. A little later the man goes to his room and sees a terrible poisonous snake on the floor. He gets so frightened that he dies of a sudden heart attack. But what was on the floor was not a snake, but a piece of rope. What killed him? An imaginary snake? A piece of real rope? Or his fear? Here it was, false evidence appearing real.

Another rule: If you want to walk on fire, learn to pay attention. He emphasized over and over again the power of concentration: if you are paying attention to something 100%, no awareness is left over for anything else. Try to listen to yourself and pay attention to your inner feelings. Your inner guidance will tell you whether or not you are ready to walk on fire.

Tolly stopped and invited us to go out and light the fire. Everyone took a few pieces of firewood from the garage and brought them to an open place in the large yard which Tolly and his wife had chosen for the fire. The excitement disappeared again, and everything seemed very ordinary. Smaller pieces of firewood were placed in the center, larger ones on the outer edge. Tolly started the fire. It was about 7 p.m., dark and cold. Joining hands, we made a circle around the kindling fire and began to repeat "OM" together—an ancient eastern tradition which is said to create harmony and penetrate into the mysterious world of subtle energies. As Tolly had coached us, we tried to attune to each other, to get into rhythm together. The flames flared up, becoming brighter and brighter in the darkness. It was powerful, hypnotic, attractive, and scary at the same time. At that moment I clearly felt how unusual and frightening this endeavor was and felt that I would not dare to walk on the coals. Certainly, this was for specially trained people, for yogis, *not* for me.

We returned to the room. Sitting so that I could see both Tolly and the faces of most of the participants, I understood that I was not the only one who was experiencing these feelings. Tolly obviously also knew this and began the next part of the evening with a very entertaining event: magic tricks. "Pay attention," he repeated, moving from one amusing and skillful trick to another, "and observe false evidence appearing real." However, he soon moved from entertainment to serious issues again: examining what fear is and how to deal with it. He noted that fear is a block, a limitation, an obstacle in our lives. There are different ways to encounter obstacles: some pretend that they do not see the obstacle, that it does not exist; some run up against it over and over again and only complain that the obstacle prevents them from moving ahead; some make a big fuss over it, complaining all the while (Tolly took a chair in his hands to illustrate the obstacle and showed symbolically how people behave in this case).

For Tolly, the first condition necessary for overcoming fear is to *acknowledge* it, to admit that it exists. Following Tolly's suggestion, we separated into pairs to discuss our fears with each other. I formed a pair with a pleasant girl and both of us, it seemed to me, kept the discussion "on the surface," observing the "rules of the game," but not trying to go into depth. We were speaking with each other for the first time, and the talk was somewhat artificial—a quality which seemed quite natural to me under the circumstances.

The second necessary condition was to *assume the worst*. What is the worst that can happen to you if you choose to walk on hot coals? Pain, agony, severe burns, going to the hospital, being crippled... What else? Close your eyes. Imagine that the worst happened to you... Could you stand it? We reluctantly closed our eyes. It was too much, I thought, I barely desired to do this ... Severe pain, agony ... *No one* would welcome it, but yet this wasn't the worst, I believe I could stand it ... burn ... burned ... but I have no time to lie in bed; if I did, who would finish the next issue of *Psi Research*? Who would do this, who would do that? ... But this is not the worst, either....

My thoughts were interrupted by Tolly's request that we open our eyes. He was moving on to the third condition: *Expect the best.* A pessimist notices that a glass is half empty, and an optimist would say that the glass is half full. "You *can* firewalk without any harm to yourself." He began to discuss the mind/body relationship, the healing potential of the mind and body, cancer therapy through visualization, and Norman Cousins' views on health and healing in his book, *The Anatomy of an Illness*. The body has much potential for self-protection and self-healing. When you are ready to walk on hot coals, he stated, something will change in your body which enables you to remain unharmed. As yet, we do not know all the laws of nature, and we do not understand all the laws of the universe.

"When you face fire, you will go through fear, much fear." Tolly continued. "When you decide that you can walk, that you are able to make the first step, this transformation will occur in your body. Therefore, *if you can take this first step*, step on the coals and keep walking. Absolutely don't run, just keep walking. You will feel heat, strong heat, but nothing more than that, it is like walking on hot sand. Do not stop—keep walking!"

"I told you that you can firewalk without any harm and it's true. But it is *you* who are taking the risk. *You* are to decide whether you choose to firewalk, whether you are ready. We have had a few cases of bad burns, and three were quite bad. In one case a man in his early forties was burned so severely that he was bedridden for five weeks. But later he said to me: 'My inner voice told me: 'Don't go.' I should have listened to it, but I chose not to. This was a very important lesson.' Listen to yourself...."

Tolly Burkan gave us a simple four-point plan: (1) Know where you are (acknowledge your fears); (2) Know where you want to go (what is your purpose/objective); (3) Choose a plan of action; (4) Follow your plan—go for it! Everything was very simple—too simple, in my opinion, to get us safely through 1,300°F coals....

Tolly explained that the plan can be different for everyone: one might simply think that he/she can walk unharmed on the coals and that there are forces in the body which protect it; others might think that God or other forces protect them, that he/she is surrounded by a white light of protection, or something else. I felt very comfortable with the fact that no particular belief system was imposed and everything was left up to us.

This "theoretical aspect" lasted slightly more than three hours. Suddenly Burkan asked everyone, even those who were not going to firewalk, to take off their shoes and socks. He explained that we would come out in silence, join hands, form a circle around the fire and begin a song-mantra:

Release your mind...
See what you find...
Bring it on home to your people....

Tolly would prepare the coals and walk over them, and then everyone is invited (but not in any way obliged) to follow. Those who choose to walk, do so only once; there should be no attempts made to repeat the walk. Everyone would have time to listen to oneself and to choose whether or not to walk. He added that sometimes it requires more courage to choose not to walk when others do so, and that whatever decision one makes, it would be the right decision and a useful experience. However, there would not be endless time for contemplating, for making this decision. At some point Tolly would say: one minute left, and whoever wants to use this opportunity to walk is welcome to do so. Then he would announce: thirty seconds left, fifteen seconds left, and finally he would extinguish the fire.

It was chilly to go outside from the warm room, and stepping barefoot out onto the cold, wet grass was awful! The fire still looked powerful in the darkness, though it was not as impressive as before. As we made a circle and began to sing, Tolly took something which looked like a rake and leveled the glowing coals, making a "run-way" of about 6-7 feet. There it was, the hellish path, shining and glowing. On either side of the path there were larger pieces of firewood, which were still burning. Tolly took a few steps away from the fire. His face was strangely, unexpectedly calm, lit by the gleam of flame... Then with few words of a song or prayer, he stepped forward ... towards the glowing embers ... onto them ... His face was still calm—smiling!—and illuminated by an inner light, his arms stretched forward in a beautiful gesture. One, two, three steps ... and he was on the other side of the glowing path....

Before the workshop I asked one of the organizers whether taking pictures was allowed. The answer was that I could take a picture of Tolly but no one else. Yet I was so fascinated and excited during his firewalk that I forgot about the small camera I had in my hands! Then, when someone else left the circle and headed towards the fire I decided to try to take a picture. But the camera (the simplest I could find for such an event) shook in my hands, and after a couple of attempts Tolly came up to me and whispered that I'd better not do this because the flash might disturb the concentration of the walkers. So, my "duty as a reporter" was over, and looking at those who dared to venture along this path, I understood that now I had nothing left to do but to make my choice... Listen to yourself, I remembered. But what was I listening to: my true self, or my fear? Can I understand this? ...

The song continued... Someone left the circle, made a few steps across the coals and joined the circle again. A few seconds (or minutes?) later, another person did the same. How long did this last? I had no idea—I had lost all sense of time. I was standing as if frozen, and nothing could move me from this spot, towards the fire... "One minute left," Tolly announced. "Now or never?" was my thought at this moment, and suddenly I felt that I could do it, I would! Something strange happened in me: my fear changed into determination, energy, and confidence: I can! I will! Before I could think of anything else, I found myself stepping onto the coals. It was not frightening—to the contrary, it was a great relief, a relief from the stress of indecision. At first I did not feel anything at all, a moment of numbness, then heat, but it was quite bearable, not painful, really like walking over hot sand. Another step, then another, just three or four altogether. It turned out to be simple, incredibly, ridiculously simple! And it was over!

Suddenly a powerful feeling of satisfaction and happiness overtook me—"I did it, I did!" I returned to my place in the circle and a girl took my hand with a reassuring grip. How much a simple touch of the hand can tell! I was not a stranger here anymore, I became an inseparable part of this group. We were singing together, caring for each other, for others, for the whole planet. It was an even more powerful feeling!

A few others crossed the path, and Tolly announced the 15 second deadline, and momentarily a gush of water from the hose killed the fire. Then I found myself inside the house, singing the simple melody with the others about our opportunity for change, but it sounded quite different! Again we divided in pairs to share our experiences. Talking with a young man, I felt that it was no longer artificial to share my feelings with a stranger, but completely natural. And we were not strangers anymore, for this powerful experience had instantly united us.

Only four or five participants did not firewalk. One of them explained that it was a useful lesson for her to choose not to walk, as she always used to be and strived to be the first in any group. Of those who walked (more than forty individuals, among them—two children, 9 and 12 years old); only five or six got small blisters on the soles of their feet, while the others were completely unharmed. (Later, back in the hotel, I carefully examined my feet—there was nothing, no trace of burns or cuts or anything else, as if I had walked on cotton and not over hot coals!)

Closing the workshop, Tolly led us into an integration of the experience. "The fire was a model: if you walked on fire you will be able to overcome fear in your life. There will be many other situations in your life when you will experience fear, but it will not stop you from action;" this was the meaning of his conclusion. He presented everyone of us with a yellow card and asked us to write on it: "I walked on fire! I can do anything I choose!"

Now I could turn from feelings to analysis. In the final analysis, what happened? Firewalking without long preparation and special rituals—how and why was it possible? Certainly, one might assume that most of the participants were "yogis," but I know at least that I myself am not a yogi. One might also assume that most of them had walked barefoot all their lives and had such thick calluses on their soles that they were protected, but again this was not so in my case. And I definitely was not in any kind of trance or similar state. Then what?

Was it Tolly's personal power which protected us, or the mutual "energy field" created by the group, or the power of personal belief alone which created some special condition in our bodies? From my own experience, the only answer I had was: at the instant of making the decision, "I will go," I found the way to "turn off" my conscious controls and rely on the "secret wisdom" of my subconscious mind and body, allowing them to find the best way "to do the work." And they did it beautifully! In fact, the whole lesson was: We (our conscious control) can't help the body to do this, all we can do is *not* to impose negative thoughts and beliefs, *not* to prevent, *not* to interfere.

After the workshop was over, Tolly reminded me that now it was time for our prearranged interview. To my surprise, I found by that time most of my questions had been answered. What could I ask, after all that had happened? However, I quickly turned on my tape recorder. Here is our brief interview:

Tolly Burkan: This [firewalking] is a demonstration of what it is to use more of our potential than we usually use. I mentioned that we use a very small percentage of our brains, but tonight people made a leap and started using parts of their brains that they usually don't use. Here we see the potential: We see we can do so many things we thought are impossible.

LV: What, in your opinion, can lead us to use our potential to a greater extent, in a more creative way?

TB: For me the bottom line is knowing who we really are. When we realize that we are not separate from the source of creation, we then realize that all the power of the universe is at our disposal through our minds, because we are connected to everything. We sit around thinking about a friend, and all of a sudden the phone rings and the friend calls us, because we are all connected, everything is connected. And when you realize the powers within you, you can experience incredible miracles like healings; miracles such as the terminal illnesses that have been healed through the power of the mind. These have actually been documented and now researchers are trying to figure out why it's possible, *if* it's possible. We know it *is* possible. Now we are trying to understand the process.

You saw what happened tonight. There were almost fifty people here and they all, except the four or five who did not walk, were able to do what seemed impossible.... Even the children... it was great to see the kids walking!

LV: Perhaps for children it's even easier to overcome these inner barriers, because they are not conditioned that it's "impossible" to such an extent as adults. And my last question: If you wrote about your workshops yourself, what would you say to the readers in the shortest possible way?

TB: Nothing else I have ever experienced in life has caused so much change in me in such a short period of time.

I positively agree with Tolly. Anyone who has spent the four hours with him would not be the same and would never forget the experience. But I still don't understand, Tolly, what you have done to us and how you achieved this—after only three hours of talking and singing together, 90% of the audience easily, unquestionably followed you into the fire!

Leaving Portland the next day, I knew for certain: I wanted to study with Tolly Burkan; I wanted to really understand the ancient art of firewalking. To do so, I had to first delve into extensive literature about fire, ancient traditions of fire-worshipping and fire-immunity.

3. Symbolism of Light and Fire in Ancient and Modern Spiritual Teachings

When encountering something as unusual as firewalking seminars, a question inevitably arises: Why firewalking? Why would anyone do something so strange (or foolish) as to walk on fire? Why would anyone encourage people to take risks by inviting them to step onto red-hot coals? In part, these questions are answered by universal beliefs about fire.

Throughout human history, fire has had spiritual significance to all nations of the earth. Fire is the symbol of creation, energy, inspiration, passion, purification, divinity, and the visionary state. In the pantheon of numerous gods were those of flame—Narasamsah Agni of the Parsees, Camaxtli of the Aztecs, Nusku of the Assyrians, Svarog of the Slavs, Ulu Tojon of the Yakuts, Vahagn of the Armenians, Verethraghna of the Persians, Pele of the Hawaiians, Hephaestus of the Greeks, and Vulcanus of the Romans, to name but a few. Eternal fires burned upon their altars. And today in shrines dedicated to modern concepts of God, from humble homes in the East to the great cathedrals of the West, lights and candles burn on and on, remembering the dead, and seeking divine favors for the living. Lights illuminate pagan temples, Christian altars, the Holy

Ark of the synagogue and the crescents of mosques. When one has the light of faith within, one lights a consecrated fire.[4]

In Jewish mysticism (Kabbala), God is described as projecting from himself ten Sefiroth, or channels of light, by which the divine existence became perceptible and comprehensible. The last of the Sefiroth is Shechinah, "indwelling," the presence of God in individuals, communities and places.[5]

Throughout the Old Testament, fire was spoken of as an emblematic token of the divine presence: "And the angel of the Lord appeared unto him [Moses] in a flame of fire out of the midst of a bush: and he looked, and, behold, the bush burned with fire, and the bush was not consumed." (Exodus 3:2)

"And Mount Sinai was altogether on a smoke, because the Lord descended upon it in fire: and the smoke thereof ascended as the smoke of a furnace, and the whole mount quaked greatly." (Exodus 3:18)

"... The hand of the Lord God fell ... upon me [Ezekiel]. Then I beheld, and lo a likeness as the appearance of fire: from the appearance of his loins even downward, fire; and from his loins even upward, as the appearance of brightness, as the color of amber. And he put forth the form of a hand, and took me by a lock of mine head; and the spirit lifted me up between the earth and the heaven, and brought me in the visions of God...." (Ezekiel, 8:1-3)

So holy was the sacred fire considered to be in ancient Rome that an early writer says it was believed to betoken the Godhead. Fire, or heat, proceeds from Divine Love, whose essence is life; wherefore, in the world, the sun is emblematic of self-existent Being.

Francis Quarles, a Protestant mystic, invokes the image of fire to emphasize the union of God and human:

E'en so we met; and after long pursuit E'en so we join'd, we both became entire;
No need for either to renew a suit, For I was flax, and he was flames of fire.
Our firm united souls did more than twine; So I my best beloved's am; so he is mine.[6]

Fire was extensively and prominently employed in China as a sacred medium, between the Ultimate Cause and human beings, and had a presiding deity. The Egyptians regarded this element as a voracious animal devouring whatever it seizes, and, when, satiated, expiring with the object consumed. In Zoroastrianism, fire is the earthly form of the heavenly light, the eternal, infinite, divine. The life of all creatures is vital fire.[7]

The Parsees of India worshipped the four elements (fire, water, earth, and air), but gave prominence to fire. Fire was supposed by the Hindu to be presided over by a spirit, called Agni, to whom prayers were addressed. The final hymn of a treasure of Hindu wisdom, the *Rig-Veda Samhita*, is offered to Agni, the God of Fire, the Divine Fire, the Divine Will and Love that unites the wise in their common striving to live and speak the Truth:

You take possession, Divine Fire;
Of all that the devoted bring—
On the altar you are kindled.
Bring us the priceless treasure....
Let your aim be one and single;
Let your hearts be joined in one—
The mind at rest in unison—
At peace with all, so may you be.[8]

According to some spiritual teachers, Agni is one of the few guides mortals can trust, for he is the Master of the Universe.

The other two chief deities in the *Rig Veda* were Indra, god of the rain, and Surya, god of the sun. The most distinct of several Hindu sun gods, Surya is described as short, with a burnished copper body, riding through the sky in a chariot drawn by seven ruddy horses. When Surya's wife Sanjna, overpowered by his radiance, fled as a mare to the shade of a forest and studied meditation, the sun god came to her as a stallion. Later her father, Visva-karma, reduced Surya's brilliant rays by cutting away one-eighth of his substance, the fiery trimmings falling to earth, among other things, as the disc of Vishnu and the trident of Shiva. Worship of Surya can be found in Bihar and Tamiland, where his benevolence is invoked for the healing of the sick.[9]

Among the Brahmanical writings the following expression was

used: "Truth constantly reveals itself by its own inward Light, and the divine fire continually burning in the soul is sufficient worship"—an idea agreeable to the philosopher's explanation, since divine fire symbolizes divine love, the kindling flame of immortal souls.

"From the substance of that supreme spirit are diffused, like sparks from fire, innumerable vital spirits, which perpetually give motion to creatures exalted or base." Such is the statement of a Hindu sage, which is but an elaborate expression of the Indian's idea of the human soul, or the essence of life.

It is stated that the Persians worshipped fire with peculiar reverence, because it represented the original fire from Ormuzd, whose dwelling place was in the sun. In the Zend Avesta of the Persians, the following expression is found: "Kings are animated by a more ethereal fire than other mortals, such fire as exists in upper spheres."

Many Finno-Ugric and Siberian peoples anthropomorphize fire in their myths and legends. The attitude to fire as a living being can be found among all peoples of the arctic and subarctic regions and their neighbors. The Ostiaks (a Finno-Ugric ethnic minority in Russia) call the fire "Fire girl" or "Fire woman" in their prayers, as do Cheremiss and other Volga peoples. The Mordvins say: "The Fire mother 'flames,' " the Ostiaks speak of "many-tongued Fire mother," and in a Cheremiss prayer the passage occurs: "Fire mother, thou whose smoke is long and whose tongue is sharp."[10]

Among the Nganasans the cult of *Tu-njami*, "Mother fire," occupied an exclusive place. Fire in the Nganasan conceptions was a female divinity. Mother Fire protected the home, assisted in childbirth, chased off diseases, purified people who violated some sacred establishment. In incantations they appealed to *Tu-njami*, just as they did also to Mother Earth—*imidima* "Mother's Mother." Judged from the formulas of their appeals, the ideas entertained by the Enets, Nenets, Yukagirs and Saams were identical with those of the Nganasans. Mother Fire was imagined as a woman who continually gave birth to girls in the form of tongues of flame.[11]

The Enets and Nenets especially worshipped the fire: "Earlier the supreme belief was in the fire, without fire no one can live because there is great strength in the fire." The fire's mistress was a woman, *tu e* (Enets) or *tu nebe* (Nenets), "fire's mother." "She warms the fire as the mother warms her child," the Enets explained.[12] Because of its numerous flames Altaic shamans call fire the "thirty-headed mother, the forty-headed virgin-mother." In the prayers of the Chuvash there appears beside the "Mother fire" a "Father fire." In the tales of Ostiaks, the "Fire spirit" can even take a human form. In Yukagirs' beliefs Mother Fire looks like a naked small girl. Mother Fire is also believed by the Yukagirs to protect the family to which the fireplace belongs. The Yakuts in Siberia see the Fire god in the form of a "grey old man." To a certain Buriat he appeared as a great, red, and therefore flame-colored, man.[13] Many Siberian peoples maintain that the Fire god or the Master of Fire who, according to the Yakuts, "lives right in the flames,"[14] may appear to people before a disastrous fire or other catastrophe which threatens the home.[15]

According to old Hawaiian lore, the goddess Pele, who is especially connected with fire and lives in the volcano, also will appear to someone in a human form shortly before each major volcanic eruption. Hawaiians believe that Pele "has been seen as a woman covered with flames, or even as if she were flame in the shape of a woman."[16] They also believe that a "soul [of a person who made the transition called death] might be transfigured into a volcanic flame."[17] Some of Pele's brothers and sisters are also connected with fire, such as Pele-Hiiaka i Keahi-enaena and Hiiaka i Ka Poli o Pele. Fire can heal, a Hawaiian priest reminds us, talking about working with the four elements, but it can also burn with a fierce temper.[18] These ancestral spirits, *'aumakua*, that are of vital importance in the Hawaiian spiritual tradition rule the fire element and the spirits of fire. Since ancient times, Hawaiians believe in the purifying force of fire.[19]

Fire was viewed as a mystery by the American Indians.[20] Regarding it as a kind of connecting link between the natural and supernatural worlds, they believed, as do the Muslims, that spirits were able to dwell in it. Fire was believed to be the heart of being; upon it depended all existence, corporeal and spiritual. The breath of life was identical with fire. It was alive. It breathed and ate. Fire was used by Indians in their sacrificial feasts as an emblem of purity.

Fire is believed to be endowed with the faculty of sight. The Menominee tribes of Indians in the Eastern Woodlands (the Wisconsin and Upper Michigan region) in North America call comets "sko-tie-nah-mo-kin,"—the Seeing Fire. "Know," said a native American seer and medicine man, Shawnee Jossakeed, "that the fire in your body and the fire of your hearth are one and the same thing, and that both proceed from the same source."[21]

In the pictography of the Ojibway Indians a bear is seen represented with a line running from the mouth to the heart. The heart, in most cases, is depicted in its natural position in the body of man or animal. Under the figure is the parallelogram denoting fire.

A-she-mang guit-to iah-na ish-ko-tang.
A-she-nahng guit-to iah-na,

(I made myself look like fire),

is an Indian song, sung with many repetions and little variation. "This," explains John Tanner, a researcher of Native American traditions, pointing to the figure, "is a medicine-man, disguised in the skin of a bear. The small parallelogram, under the bear, signifies fire."[22] Does it mean that a medicine man is a person who has ignited his inner fire of faith and spirituality?

In the Ojibway dialect the sun is called Ka-no-waw-bum-min-uk (He that sees us). The Indian pictured both a serpent and a bird, in connection with his symbol of the sun, as did the Egyptian. The origin of the use of the serpent was probably from observation of the appearance of natural phenomena—the forked lightning and the radiant coil of the halo, both equally giving origin to the sacred image.[23]

Among both Indians and Hindu we find the serpent occupying a place in the story of creation; it is used in divination, and worshipped at the sacred feast. It is probable that this reverence arose from their belief in a spirit of fire; and the fiery dart, in the form of a serpent, dropping to the earth, would appear to be representative of the power of the Source of life, or that life itself, in a divine degree. It appears that in accordance with the belief of the descent of a divine serpent of fire, that spiral fire was arranged as part of the worship in the rotunda of a town, built and inhabited by the Cherokee tribes. It is also related that the Creek tribes had a structure built in the form of a rotunda, and composed of three circular lines, within which was constantly kept a fire burning, guarded by the priests. This fire was newly-kindled on the occasion of the Feast of

First Fruits. None but priests attended or renewed the fire. There was in the interior a spiral fire, curiously flaming up at an appointed time.[24]

The serpent has great significance in mystical teachings. According to Helena Blavatsky, a Russian mystic and Theosophist, Jesus accepted the serpent as a synonym of Wisdom, and this formed part of his teaching: "Be ye wise as serpents," he says. "In the beginning, before Mother became Mother-Father, the fiery Dragon moved in the infinitudes alone." Blavatsky further describes the "fiery Dragon" as a long trail of Cosmic dust (or fire mist) which moved and writhed like a serpent in space. The spirit of God moving upon Chaos was symbolized by some nations in the shape of a fiery serpent breathing fire and light upon the primordial waters.[25]

An esoteric text "channeled" and published in Denmark in 1920, also describes the role of Light in creation:

Through all eternity Darkness was everywhere. In the Darkness was the Light; in the Light were *Thought* and *Will*. But Thought and Will *were not in the Darkness*. In the Light was the seed of all that is good.... Unknown eternities passed. Slowly, Thought and Will were drawn toward each other. Slowly, the Light spread, it became brighter and purer. *It was dawn.*[26]

We can find some similarities in Polynesian myths of the creation of the Cosmos. At the beginning there was a Void, Nothingness, Chaos, Immensity, Space, Night or Darkness. It was called *Po*, the passive element. *Ao*, light, was the active element. It is through the union of Po and Ao that the world was created. The Maori hypnotic-sounding creation chant describes the process in abstract terms:

From the conception the increase; From the increase the swelling; From the swelling the thought; From the thought the remembrance;
From the remembrance the consciousness, the desire.[27]

After a brief excursion into creation myths, let us return to
Blavatsky's views. In explaining occult cosmology, she refers to the
"Sea of Fire" which she defines as the "Super-Astral (i.e., noumenal)
Light, the first radiation from the *Root*, the Mulaprakriti, the
undifferentiated Cosmic Substance, which becomes *Astral* Matter." It is also called the "Fiery Serpent." According to Blavatsky,
all Kabalists and mystics, eastern and western, recognize "(a) the
identity of 'Father-Mother' with primordial *Aether* or *Akasa* (Astral
Light); and (b) its homogeneity before the evolution of the 'Son,'
cosmically *Fohat*, for it is Cosmic Electricity."²⁸

Referring to ancient teachings, Blavatsky states: "Light is cold
flame, and flame is fire, and the fire produces heat, which yields
water, the water of life in the Great Mother (Chaos)." She indicates
that the words "Light," "Flame," "Hot," "Fire," "Heat," "Water,"
and the "water of life" are all, on our plane, the progeny; or as a
modern physicist would say, the "correlations of electricity" (a
contemporary writer would probably substitute the more general
word "energy" for Blavatsky's "electricity"). She looks at "electricity" (energy) as "sacred progeny; of Fire—the creator, the preserver
and the destroyer; of Light—the essence of our divine ancestors; of
Flame—the Soul of things."²⁹

The Tibetan Book of the Dead speaks about "the Clear Light,"³⁰
"the Divine Body of Truth, the Incomprehensible, Boundless
Light."³¹ Describing death rites in Tibet, it states, "... As the
cremation ceremonies end, the priests and the mourners visualize
the spirit of the departed as being purged of all karmic obscurations
by the fire which is Amitabha, the Incomprehensible Light."³²
Amitabha, "infinite light," represents the primordial, self-existent
Buddha. Avalokitesvaro, a manifestation of the underlying essence
of the six "meditation Buddhas," sprang from a lotus and cease-
lessly stretches out to aid the weak and faltering. He vowed that he
would refuse personal salvation unless he should gain the power to
cause any being who appealed to him to be reborn in the pure land,
the Western Paradise, immediately after death. All that is asked of
the would-be saint is worship or uttering the holy formula of
Amitabha's name. On the lips of the dying for countless genera-
tions, therefore, has been the name of Buddha of the "immeasurable
enlightening splendour."³³

The serpent is also often viewed as a symbol of the "inner fire," awakening of inner life energy, the mysterious Kundalini, described so vividly in many spiritual teachings. The earliest references to it can be found in the most ancient scriptures of India, the Vedas. This ancient knowledge formed the basis for the later esoteric teachings as expounded in the Upanishads, Agamas, Tantras, and Samhitas, and especially the many texts belonging to the Hatha Yoga tradition. One of the best discriptions of the Kundalini can found in writings by Gopi Krishna:

Words are hardly adequate to express the staggering magnitude of the traditional concept of Kundalini, as presented in the tantras and shakti shastras. Her other name is Prana Shakti, the creatrix of the universe. As a small sample of the tributes paid to her as Prana Shakti or cosmic life energy, the following ... verses from *Panchastavi* will be illustrative of what I mean:

Thou art luster in the moon, radiance in the sun, intelligence in man, force in the wind, taste in water, and heat in fire. Without Thee, O Goddess, the whole universe would be devoid of its substance.

Those starry hosts that roam the sky, this atmosphere which gives birth to water, this Shesh-nag [a mystical serpent] which supports the earth, the air which moves, the fire which shines bright with leaping flames, they all, O Mother, exist only by Thy command.

... Sings *Panchastavi*,

O Goddess, Thou art the Shakti [power] of Shiva [the creator], who has the moon on His forehead, Thou art His body, the senses, the mind, the intellect, the power of action, and doer of deeds. Thou art desire, rulership, and also delusion. Thou art His refuge as also the veil that hides the reality. What is there that doth not spring from Thee?[34]

Gopi Krishna describes his own experience of Kundalini awakening as a "jet of an extremely subtle and brilliant substance rising through the spine" and a "luminous glow within and outside [his] head," perceived by his mental eye.[35] To get an almost instant understanding of what Kundalini is, short of having the experience, one need only read the descriptions he wrote of his own state of consciousness. Up until the age of thirty-four, he was just like any other normal human being. But on Christmas in 1937, everything changed, and he was never to be the same again. What follows, in an abbreviated form, is his own account of the awakening of Kundalini:

I sat steadily, unmoving and erect [in meditation].... My whole being was so engrossed in the contemplation of the lotus that for several minutes at a time I lost touch with my body and surroundings. During such intervals I used to feel as if I were poised in midair, without any feeling of a body around them.

During one such spell of intense concentration I suddenly felt a strange sensation below the spine....The sensation....extended upward, growing in intensity, and I felt myself wavering; but with a great effort I kept my attention centered around the lotus.

Suddenly, with a roar like that of a waterfall, I felt a stream of liquid light entering my brain through the spinal cord.

Entirely unprepared for such a development, I was completely taken by surprise.... The illumination grew brighter and brighter, the roaring louder, I experienced a rocking sensation and then felt myself slipping out of my body, entirely enveloped in a halo of light. It is impossible to describe the experience accurately. I felt the point of consciousness that was myself growing wider, surrounded by waves of light. It grew wider and wider, spreading outward while the body, normally the immediate object of its perception, appeared to have receded into the distance until I became entirely unconscious of it. I was now all consciousness without any outline, without any idea of a corporeal appendage, without any feeling or sensation coming from the senses, immersed in a sea of light simultaneously conscious and aware of every point, spread out, as it were, in all directions without any barrier or material obstruction.

I was no longer myself, or to be more accurate, no longer as I knew myself to be, a small point of light and in a state of awareness confined in a body, but instead was a vast circle of consciousness in which the body was but a point, bathed in light and in a state of exaltation and happiness impossible to describe.[36]

Swami Muktananda describes a similar phenomenon:

I looked all around. The flames of a vast conflagration were raging in all directions. The entire cosmos was on fire....I saw a dazzling brightness in my head and was terrified.[37]

The experience of light can be called a universal constant of spiritual or mystical experience. It is no accident that the highest mystical realization is generally referred to as "illumination" or "enlightenment." Mystics of all ages have spoken of the "radiance" aspect of their spiritual state, which is a literal experience for them.

The experience of "inner fire" and "inner light" is an integral part of shamanism. Thus the Eskimos know of a mystical condition that they call *angakoq* or *qaumaneq*, meaning "lightning" or "illumination," without which a person cannot become a shaman. This strange light fills the shaman's head and body, and it is thought to enable him to see at great distances, in the dark, and even into the future.[38]

It is interesting to note that the Russian word *svet* means both "light" and the "world." I do not know the etymology of this connection, but allow me to fantasize a little: An enlightened person who has found "light" within may also be able to see, to perceive, to know the whole world without leaving his or her own room! Incidentally, there is more to this symbolism of the Russian language: another word for world, *mir*, also means "peace," i.e., peace is a prerequisite for the world to continue its existence.

According to the *Lalita-Vistara*, a traditional biography of the

Buddha, a ray of light would arise from the crown of Gautama's head whenever he sat absorbed in deepest meditation. This reminds one of a verse in the fourteenth chapter of the *Bhagavad Gita*, which states that when there is a real knowledge, or wisdom, the body emanates light:

> Sattva, Rajas, Tamas—light, fire, and darkness—are the three constituents of nature. They appear to limit in finite bodies the liberty of the infinite Spirit.

> Of these Sattva, because it is pure, and it gives light and is the health of life, binds to earthly happiness and to lower knowledge.

> Rajas is of the nature of passion, the source of thirst and attachment. It binds the soul of man to action....

> When the light of wisdom shines from the portals of the body's dwelling, then we know that Sattva is in power.[39]

In the famous eleventh chapter of the *Bhagavad Gita* there is a beautiful description of Prince Arjuna's enlightenment experience. He was overwhelmed by a vision of the radiant glory of God Krishna, symbolizing the ultimate reality:

> When Krishna, the God of Yoga, had ... spoken, O King, he appeared then to Arjuna in his supreme divine form. And Arjuna saw in that form countless visions of wonder: eyes from innumerable faces, numerous celestial ornaments....

> If the light of a thousand suns suddenly arose in the sky, that splendour might be compared to the radiance of the Supreme Spirit.

> And Arjuna saw in that radiance the whole universe in its variety, standing in a vast unity in the body of the God of Gods.

Trembling with awe and wonder, Arjuna bowed his head, and joining the hands in adoration, he thus spoke to his God.

Arjuna:

I see in thee all the Gods, O my God; and the infinity of the beings of thy creation. I see god Brahma on his throne of lotus, and all the seers and serpents of light....

I see the splendour of an infinite beauty which illumines the whole universe. It is thee! with thy crown and sceptre and circle. How difficult thou art to see! But I see thee: as fire, as the sun, blinding, incomprehensible.[40]

The Hawaiian word *aka* means a halo of light around the moon or sun, or a circle of light extending from the moon or sun before it rises above the horizon. The same word is also used to describe the "shadowy body," a luminous extension away from the human body.[41]

In early Christianity the rite of baptism was known as *photismos* or "illumination." The Holy Ghost came to be represented as a flame. As Christian legend has it, when Jesus was baptized in the river Jordan, the water was set on fire. According to an ancient tradition, a true monk literally shines with the "light of grace." Many stories are told of monks who, absorbed in prayer, would radiate light.[42]

The legend about the phoenix, the wonderful bird that renewed itself in fire, was used in the second century after Christ as an argument for Christian resurrection. The later Christian poet Dracontius (fifth century A.D.) argues in the following way: the non-Christian who believes that the phoenix is reborn out of its own ashes has no grounds for reproach against the Christian who holds the same belief about the decayed body. And life can be rekindled, just as a slaked fire can flare up again, or, to use Dracontius's words, "The phoenix's perfect youth God renews with fire."[43]

Da Love-Ananda, a contemporary Western mystic, speaks about awakening the "fire of the spiritual process."[44] The spiritual fire is the subjective sense of catharsis, of being gradually purified of all presumptions, opinions, illusions, and delusions as well as all attachments and preferences—that is to say, every single movement within our own consciousness by which we deny or hide from spiritual reality.[45]

■

Parapsychology has long been studying so-called poltergeist phenomena when some objects (at times quite heavy) move without apparent reason, and other strange forces manifest themselves. Often researchers were able to find a "focus" of the poltergeist, i.e., a person (often a teenager) in whose presence all (or most) of these phenomena seem to happen. These mysterious occurrences sometimes include "spontaneous combustion." Dr. Andrade from the Brazilian Institute for Psychobiophysical Research in São Paulo reported such phenomena in the Brazilian town of Suzano in 1970.[46] Some of the events were witnessed by police officers. Similar cases were reported in the United States[47] and in the Soviet Union.[48] The latter happened in the Ukraine, in the town of Yenakiyevo, Donetsk province in 1986. The "focus" of the case discussed in several Soviet newspapers is most likely a 13-year-old teenager named Alexander (Sasha).

In this case, along with the spontaneous movement of objects (as heavy as a cupboard, refrigerator and washing machine), numerous cases of spontaneous combustion were observed. Some of them took place in the presence of police and firemen. As usual, tricks were suspected, but none were discovered. Spontaneous fires continued to erupt in the boy's apartment, and fuses and electric bulbs to blow up (even those which were not connected to the electric circuit). A round hole of unknown origin appeared in the window glass, with its edges melted as if it were made by a blow torch.

The boy's parents were in despair: nine large fires and many small ones occurred in the apartment. When the family temporarily moved to the apartment of relatives, the fires continued there. Once the boy's favorite brief-case caught fire while at school, and everyone—the teacher and students—had to struggle to put the fire out. The police could not find the "magicians" and "tricksters" whose participation they suspected. They turned to the scientists.

34

Alexander was studied at the Department of Theoretical Problems of the U.S.S.R. Academy of Sciences. The scientists, although familiar with the terms "spontaneous telekinesis" and "poltergeist," could not explain the phenomena. Another researcher, M. Dmitriyev, Professor of Chemistry from the Laboratory of Physico-Chemical and Radiological Studies in Moscow, came up with the idea that the nature of the forces causing the spontaneous combustion is close to that associated with ball lightning. Then the opinions divided: while some believed that these forces were triggered by a specific mental state of the boy and some kind of "psychic energy" associated with it, others maintained that the phenomena of spontaneous combustion were caused by ordinary ball lightning, without any connection with the human mind. However, they could not explain how ball lightning could cause movement of heavy objects and again had to resort to the "hypothesis" of "tricksters"— and the discussion came to a dead end.

It is interesting to note that some of those who experienced the awakening of Kundalini report an actual sensation of heat, which at times has a strong (even painful) physical manifestation. Such a sensation of heat is reported by a modern Western mystic, Irina Tweedie, who was an apprentice of an Indian Sufi teacher. In her autobiography she has the following diary entry:

> Burning currents of fire inside; cold shivers running outside, along the spine, wave after wave, over legs, arms, abdomen, making all the hair rise. It is as if the whole frame were full of electricity.[49]

Another diary entry reads:

> The power inside my body did not abate all night and I could not sleep. I noticed something completely new. My blood was getting luminous and I saw its circulation throughout the body. I soon then became aware that it was not the blood; a light, a bluish-white light was running along another system.... The light came out of the body and re-entered it again at different points. Observing closely, I

could see that there were countless points of light like a luminous web encircling the body inside and out. It was very beautiful. No bones existed; the body was built on the web of light.

Soon however, I became aware that the body seemed to be on fire. This liquid light was cold but it was burning me, as if currents of hot lava were flowing through every nerve and every fibre, more and more unbearable and luminous, faster and faster. Shimmering, fluctuating, expanding and contracting, I could do nothing but lie there watching helplessly as the suffering and intense heat increased with every second ... Burned alive.[50]

Heat, as psychosomatic heat, makes its appearance in numerous religious and spiritual traditions of the world. As the well-known researcher of shamanism, Mircea Eliade, observed:

A great many "primitive" tribes conceive the magico-religious power as "burning" and express it by terms that signify "heat," "burn," "very hot" etc.[51]

Eliade further noted:

It must be remembered, too, that all over the world shamans and sorcerers are reputedly "masters of fire," and swallow burning embers, handle red-hot iron and walk over fire. On the other hand they exhibit great resistance to cold. The shamans of the Arctic regions, as well as the ascetics of the Himalayas, thanks to their "magical heat," perform feats of resistance to cold that passes imagination."[52]

Thus, perhaps it was believed in some cultures that the development of "inner fire" may help in mastering real fire. On the other hand, it was probably believed that one could become closer to "hidden realities" and attain "illumination" and enlightenment by achieving the unity with the fire itself, a symbol of purification and cleansing, transformation and alchemical transmutation. We do not know for certain whether or not the majority of people who performed firewalking throughout ancient and modern history, have ever consciously considered or referred to such a rationale. Nevertheless, we believe that this is probably the last (although, as they say, not the least) factor that led us to further explore the mysteries of firewalking and fire-immunity.

Chapter 2
Throughout Ancient and Modern History

Wonder is the beginning of wisdom.
Greek Proverb

1. In the Mist of the Past: Historical Evidence

The phenomenon of firewalking has been known as far back as written history extends. The earliest reference to such a practice is found in the ancient (c. 1200 B.C.) Indian story of two priests who resorted to a walk through fire to determine who was "the better Brahman." One of the contestants, it is said, vindicated his claim to superior holiness by emerging from the ordeal without so much as a singed hair.[1]

Pliny the Elder (A.D. 23-79) traced the strange practice of firewalking to ancient Roman families, known as the Hirpi Sorani or "Wolves of Sora" of Mount Soracte, and tells us that, "at the yearly sacrifice to Apollo, performed on Mount Soracte, [they] walk over a charred pile of logs without being scorched." They enjoyed, by Senate decree, perpetual exemption from all taxes and military service, because, as Virgil makes Aruns say, "strong in

39

faith we walk through the midst of the fire, and press our footsteps in the glowing mass."[2]

Three Biblical passages are believed to be related to fire-immunity: Isaiah 43:2 ("When thou walkest through the fire, thou shalt not be burned; neither shall the flame kindle upon thee"); Hebrews 11:34 ("Faith ... quenched the violence of fire"); and Daniel 3:20-27, which relates the deliverance of Shadrach, Meshach, and Abednego from the "fiery furnace."

The firewalk was also known in Medieval Europe. In 1062 a Florentine monk named Peter Aldobrandini walked barefoot over smoldering coals, and if contemporary accounts are to be believed, sustained not the slightest injury. He was later canonized as St. Peter Igneus in commemoration of the feat.[3] In Spain firewalkers were wisely employed to help put out fires. D'Alembert's account of the Earl Marischal, related by Lang, stated:

> There is a family or caste in Spain, who, from father to son, have the power of going into the flames without being burned, and who, by dint of charms permitted by the Inquisition, can extinguish fires.[4]

There is a widespread tradition that fire cannot harm saintly individuals. One such story refers to early Jesuits who were engaged in a theological controversy with members of another religious order. Failing to get the better of their opponents through verbal argument, one of the Jesuits filled his hands with red-hot coals and challenged his opponent to do the same. This feat so impressed the audience that the Jesuits won their point.[5] Another account tells of the martyrdom of St. Polycarp, who was sentenced to be burned alive. Although the fire was lighted all around him, it is claimed that the flames did not consume his body, but merely enclosed him in an incandescent globe, within which he could be seen to be quite unharmed. Finally, the executioner was ordered to kill him with a sword.[6]

For ages the "mastery of fire" or defiance of fire represented the strength of the spirit over the weakness of the flesh—a test of faith or the demonstration of a power within man greater than flame. Ordeals by fire, to establish the guilt or innocence of a suspected person, have been historical customs and still exist today in certain cultures. According to Sir William Blackstone, the famed English legal writer, the ordeal of the Middle Ages consisted of either picking up a piece of red-hot iron, or walking barefoot and blindfolded over red-hot ploughshares laid lengthwise at unequal distances. If the subject was burned, he was judged guilty; if unhurt, he was innocent.[7] In the ancient Indian epic, *Ramayana*, after appealing to the fire-god to attest to her innocence by not injuring her, Sita, the wife of Rama, passed through fire and was not burned.[8]

Firewalking and fire-handling have been an inherent part of various shamanic practices. It was believed among Arctic peoples that neither fire nor water could destroy a great shaman. According to old legends, he could even seat himself naked on a glowing fireplace and scatter fire and burning cinders over his body without the least danger. Native North Americans not only were said to have walked through flames and on glowing coals, but also immersed their arms in cauldrons of boiling water and handled red-hot coals and stones. Occasionally live coals were rubbed over the body and placed in the mouth.[9] Grim[10] described American Indian shamans of the Ojibway tribe who manipulated fire in order to interpret dreams and heal the sick. After using some herbal preparations, it is claimed that they were able to handle glowing coals without being burned.

Around the world, fire immunity is considered to be a sign of spiritual connection, as in Balinese trance dancing, when the little *sangian* dancers trip across hot coals or remain impassive when hot coals fall onto their skin.[11] In Sumatra, spirit mediums are said to fill their mouths with burning coals,[12] while red-hot iron bars reputedly are handled in Haitian voodoo ceremonies.[13] The shamans of northern Asia are celebrated for their "mastery over fire," and dervishes in Egypt and Algeria are alleged to swallow hot coals. Also in Algeria Muslim fakirs supposedly withstand the application of red-hot iron to their bare flesh without apparent pain or injury.[14]

As fire is a natural means of purification and is regarded as defense against evil spirits, one of the early forms of firewalking was to ward off and cleanse from evil. Fire was also believed to protect from sickness, and a firewalk over glowing stones or embers has often been undertaken to bring about healing to the ritual participants and even the whole community.

2. "*J Saw Jt With My Own Eyes*": Eyewitness Testimonies

Beginning with the last century, many Westerners observed firewalking rituals in exotic far-away lands. Basil Thomson,[15] an anthropologist and a British official in Fiji, described a ceremony called Vilavilairevo in which he claimed that members of the clan "Ivilankata" on Mbenga Island of the Fiji archipelago were able to walk over red-hot stones due to their "mastery over fire." According to Thomson, the Fiji firewalkers dug a ditch 19 feet long, where at the beginning of the ceremony burning-hot wooden stumps and large round hot stones were placed in the ditch, soon becoming a "white-hot mass, shooting out little tongues of the flame." During the next part of the ceremony the participants leveled the surface and began to walk over it, planting "their feet squarely and firmly on each stone." The researcher came up to a stone, on which a clan member was walking, and dropped a handkerchief upon it. The kerchief instantly flamed and burned. After the ceremony, however, the feet of the participants "were cool and showed no trace of scorching." The Fijian firewalkers claimed that they could transfer their fire-immunity to others.

Hocken[16] observed the same phenomenon on Fiji and gave more detailed information about firewalkers there. Roth[17] noted that during a firewalking ceremony in Fiji the temperature of the stones was so high that the wooden sticks which the participants used to level the stones became black from the heat.

Another eye-witness account of a Fijian firewalking ceremony comes from Sebi Breci, an American military man who served in the South Pacific in 1942-1943. He describes a ceremony which included about 20 firewalkers in the vicinity of Nandi Airport:

> As if in a state of wild possession, the walkers approached the hot pit, which they circled a few times.... Then, screaming something unintelligible ..., they stepped one by one into the fire and walked quickly across the embers to the other side of the pit. Once across, they dropped to the ground in front of a small statue, then fell over on their faces, apparently unconscious.[18]

Colonel Gudgeon[19] observed firewalking at Rarotonga Island of the Cook Archipelago and joined a firewalking (Umu-Ti) ceremony himself, together with some of his European friends. Gudgeon remarked that the local priest (called "tohunga" in the local dialect) and his disciple came to the Europeans, and the disciple handed one of them a branch of the Ti plant (*Dracaena*) as the priest said to him: "I hand my mana (power) over to you; lead your friends across."[20] Gudgeon and other four Europeans walked, and only one of them was burned.

The rite of firewalking did not form a part of the older Polynesian culture. It was introduced around 1850 from Fiji and spread to many of the South Pacific Islands and New Zealand.[21] Henry[22] describes firewalking in Polynesia, in which some Europeans participated. In Hawaii, firewalking rituals are similar to those observed in Polynesia, although in the neighborhood of active volcanoes in Hawaii, firewalking has been done on lava overflows when they had hardened sufficiently to bear a person's weight.[23]

Sayce[24] observed some episodes of fire immunity in Natal (South Africa) and claimed that the ability could be conveyed to others. Muslims in Southern India were reported not only being able to walk unharmed over glowing coals, but also to pass through flames with impunity. A witness, the Bishop of Mysore, Monsignor Despartes, described the ceremony: "There must have been 200 people who passed over the embers, and 100 who went right through the middle of the flames."[25]

Rajendra Pathak, an Indian physicist with a long acquaintance with Indian customs living in Germany, described devtia dances near Padli, a small village in the Himalayan foothills about 200 miles from New Delhi. These dances and their firewalking ceremonies can be seen every year between June and October. The devtia have many deities, although it is common for people to have a single patron deity called an *Isht*. Devtias have their Isht come into and act through them at certain times. Drummers beat out a hypnotic rhythm and the devtia gradually enters an altered state of consciousness. "While the devtia remains in trance he is oblivious to his surroundings and absolutely immune to pain."[26] A huge fire, 6 feet long and 3 feet wide, is lit, and a special drum, called a *hurka* gives a strange tone, like an ordinary drum beaten under water. The characteristic beat of the hurka is one beat followed by a double beat, and they are accompanied by metal plates beaten with a wooden stick. The devtias' bodies jerk to the rhythm, shiver, and shake into frenzied involuntary movements, followed by the devtia prescribing remedies and sacrifices. During the dance, a devtia traverses a pit of glowing coals and rubs a red-hot iron spoon over his chest and back. They are also reported to be able to walk through flames.

In Japan a firewalk was witnessed by a Westerner, Colonel Andrew Haggard, in 1899, in which the fire was 6 yards (18 feet) long by 6 feet wide, and the rite was conducted in honor of a mountain god. After some waving of wands and sprinkling of salt, people of all ages (including a six-year-old boy) walked over red-hot charcoal. Colonel Haggard "examined their feet afterwards, they were quite soft, and not a trace of fire upon them."[27] More recently, a *hiwatari* firewalking ceremony at Mount Takao, Japan, has been conducted annually for the purpose of training *yamabushi* or mountain priests who belong to the Shingon sect of Buddhism. About 200 believers, priests, townsfolk, farmers, and house-wives cross a 20-foot pit of orange-red coals during the ceremony.[28]

Andrija Puharich, a physician, related an account of Joseph Campbell, the eminent scholar, who experienced firewalking in the great Shinto temple in Kyoto, Japan:

He [Campbell] was observing monks performing the firewalking ceremony, standing in his bare feet while the ceremony was going on. He relates that one of the monks took him by the hand and requested him to walk over the glowing coals. Following the monk and stepping quickly, and as he thought, lightly, over the coals, he was able to pass through the long pit without suffering any burns. In fact, he says that the sensation on the soles of his feet was one of coolness, rather than of heat.[29]

E.G. Stephenson, a professor of English literature, attended a Shinto ceremony in Tokyo during which a 90-foot blazing trench was prepared. Professor Stephenson asked if he might try. The officiating priest took him to a temple nearby and sprinkled salt over his head, after which the professor "strolled over the trench in quite a leisurely way," feeling only a "faint tingling" in the soles of his feet.[30]

Leonard Feinberg[31] of Iowa State College and Gilbert Grosvenor[32] of the National Geographic Society described the annual firewalking ceremony conducted by Hindu devotees in honor of the Hindu god Kataragama in Sri Lanka. Here, more than a hundred devotees, both Buddhists and Hindus, walk over a 20-foot pit of blazing coals. Although occasional burns have been reported, most participants reputedly survive the ordeal unharmed.

The writer Arthur C. Clarke photographed a firewalking ceremony at the Sri Lankan village of Udappawa in which a pile of glowing embers was banked into a mass about 12 feet long and 2 inches deep. Nearly all of the several hundred participants walked or danced across the glowing firebed. The procession was accompanied by an ear-splitting symphony of shouting and drum beating. The walkers, who sank into the flickering embers up to their ankles, seemed to be in an altered state, and none of them showed signs of pain.[33] Another eyewitness describes the Udappawa ceremony:

Preceded by flutists and drummers, the leader of the procession bursts into the arena, his face lit eerily by the red glow of the coals.... He does a high, goatish jig around the pit, balancing on his head a wooden throne or casket. His eyes roll in his head. After one turn around the arena he veers and prances into the glowing pit, neither slowing his step nor speeding up. Sparks shoot up into the air. The line of villagers ... follow him across the fire. Two priests who have stationed themselves at the entrance to the pit, chanting and clapping, seize each firewalker as he approaches, clasp his hands above his head and shout an incantation at him.... They [the firewalkers] are mostly younger men, many carrying infants in their arms. Every sixth or seventh marcher is a boy or girl between ten and fifteen.... The expressions of the firewalkers range from the trancelike ecstasy of their leader to stoical indifference.... Each marcher walks the pit at his own pace. Some lope across it in three or four strides, others loiter, as if to test their will, until they are pushed from behind. Two grinning youths re-enter the line for a second walk, evidently treating it as a contest between themselves.[34]

In Karachi, Pakistan, Muslim worshipers march through a bed of glowing coals fanned by attendants. Each year, during the Islamic month of Moharrum, many members of the Shia sect walk through the searing coals to honor the Prophet Mohammed's grandson, Hussain, who was martyred in the burning desert of Karbala in the 7th century.[35]

Numerous travelers and researchers have observed and studied firewalking in Greece among the Anastenarides, a religious sect whose origins are lost in legends.[36] Reports dated as early as 1257 describe events in the village of Kosti in Northern Thracia. Legend tells that a fire suddenly broke out in a small church honoring Saint Constantine. While inhabitants of the village observed the flames gradually destroying the church, they heard strange sounds, as if people within were crying. Since all of the villagers were present, they decided that these sounds were created by the icons in the church. Concluding that the icons left in the flaming church had called for help, several villagers threw themselves into the flames, removed eight icons, and left the church without any burns. These icons became the property of those who saved them, and the legend states that from this time on, these individuals had the ability of fire-immunity, which was passed down from one generation to the next.[37]

Cassoli[38] described a ceremony of fire dancing among the Anastenarides as follows:

A bed of red-hot coals 10-15 cm thick was spread on an 14 x 12 foot area. In the darkness, the coals glowed so brightly that one could see the faces of those who participated in the ceremony. I saw an individual kick off his shoes.... Several others also took off their shoes and socks. Then I saw him walking with a very calm and rhythmic step, like dancing, on the coals. Seven steps were required to cross the surface covered by the coals. He was followed by a woman who stepped on the fire and her feet even plunged into the burning coals as they touched the external surface of her feet. She walked slowly, making six steps to cross the fire.[39]

The Greek tradition continues in contemporary Bulgaria. Like the Spanish and Greek firewalkers, the Bulgarian Nestenaries regard the faculty as hereditary. The tradition came to Bulgaria from Greece, and the ritual is very similar to that performed by the Greek Anastenarides.[40] A Bulgarian eyewitness, Svyatoslav Slavchev,[41] wrote that the night before the ceremony, several adult women lock themselves in the church in order to pray the entire night. They spend the night and the next day in preparation for the event. In the evening the men slowly rake the coals into a large glowing circle. When the church doors open, the women walk out barefoot onto the coals, continuing in a spiral toward the center taking quick, short steps. The women, seemingly lost in a pagan dance to frenzied music, emerge from the red-hot disc unharmed.

Gaddis[42] summarized some of the earlier observations of "mastery over fire" in his attempt to find common features among the reported instances of fire immunity. He claimed that many participants were in an altered state of consciousness, and cited instances in which the immunity reputedly was transferred by the adept to someone else, not accomplished in the art, such as a bystander, an observer or the author of the account. Although space limitations do not allow us to continue this enumeration of observations and sources, the interested reader can find useful references to other noteworthy reviews and bibliographies in our notes to this chapter.[43]

Ruth-Inge Heinze, an anthropologist from California, reported her observations of the Timiti (firewalking) ceremony performed by Tamil devotees in Singapore, who call it Pookulittal, "walking on a bed of flowers."[44] On October 23, 1978, she saw over 800 people cross an 8 by 20 foot pit of glowing coals at the Tiru Mariamman Temple on South Bridge Road in Singapore. Devotees believe that if they are pure in body and mind, the fire cannot harm them, and in Heinze's observations, less than 5%, i.e., about 40, were burned. She "could predict whether people would survive the ordeal by looking at their faces before they entered the pit: in particular, doubt appeared on the faces of some white-collar workers, and they got burned, sinking into the coals up to their ankles."[45]

A Taiwanese magazine, *Echo*, gave a detailed description of a firewalking ceremony on the island of Taiwan in which, following extensive chanting and ritual preparation, hundreds of individuals walked over a bed of red-hot coals carrying statues of Taoist gods.

Witnesses stated that in some of the ceremonies, the coals were piled over a foot high, and the firewalkers were up to their ankles in hot coals, yet most of them suffered no burns.[46]

Sometimes the "mastery of fire" is demonstrated not through firewalking, but by putting the hands and/or feet in flames and escaping injury. Dr. Marcus Bach, of the School of Religion of the University of Iowa, observed and described exotic Voodoo rites of Haiti where he witnessed the mastery of fire, the *bruler zin, Kanzo*—the fire ceremony. There was the beat of the drums, an invocation, chanting. Suddenly

> ... two men thrust their hands into the flames. They held them there deliberately, as if to prove to us that this was real. They did not flinch. They made no cry. They showed no sign of pain. Time stopped while we were watching this spectacle. It seemed like an eternity before they drew away from the crackling fire, only to fall back on their shoulders and put their feet into the flames. I closed my eyes to bring myself back to reality. I looked again and saw the men on their knees holding out their unscarred hands to the *mambo* [priestess].[47]

Later Marcus Bach learned that his guide, Reser, had also participated in *kanzo*, the ritual of fire-immunity.

> "Isn't it true that anyone who takes *kanzo* is well on his way to becoming a Voodoo priest?" Bach asked.
> "That's right," he [Reser] agreed.... "The outward ceremony," he was saying, "is the visible form of the inner reality. There is a baptism of fire that spectators do not see. That is the real thing. Putting one's hands in the fire is only the symbol of putting one's life into harmony with the unseen. Always look for the secret of Voodoo *within*."
> "Within what?" Bach asked. "Wthin the outward signs ... within the inner life."[48]

Richard Gunther, a businessman from Los Angeles, and his son, a medical student at the University of California, Los Angeles, joined a firewalking ceremony in São Paulo, Brazil, which was organized by members of the local Japanese colony in celebration of the Buddha's birthday. Gunther describes the ceremony:

> There was a pit with red-hot coals giving off a terrific blast of heat. The priests and other participants went through an elaborate ceremony with swords, sticks, and pinches of salt. In the audience were about three hundred people, half of Japanese extraction, half more traditionally Brazilian. There were old men, old women, women carrying babies, everybody laughing and chatting as if they were at a carnival.

> The priests walked across. And then some of the older men began to get up from the audience and walk across—and they walked, they didn't run; in fact, some of them were grinding their feet into the fire.[49]

Gunther, his son, and several members of the American TV crew also walked across the coals. Although the temperature of the coals was measured to be 350°C (about 650°F), only one woman in the camera crew was burned.

Finally, closer to home, Ambrose Worrall, a well-known American healer, tells a story of his introduction to fire-immunity. In 1920, he participated in a 12-member spiritual "developing circle" with John E. Cockerill, the local YMCA secretary in Barrow-in-Furness, Lancashire, England, who was not a professional medium. During the seance, Cockerill assumed the appearance of a Chinese man, took red-hot coals from the fireplace and showed them to everyone as he walked around the room while the group sang. Then, Worrall recalls, "Mr. Cockerill was holding my left hand between his hands directly in the flames…. My hand was thrust into the red-hot coals and held there for about two minutes."[50]

Many individuals interested in psychic phenomena are familiar with the alleged capacities of Daniel Dunglas Home, a famous American medium of the last century, who also demonstrated fire-handling through his purported ability to hold hot coals without harm to himself. There were some reports that he also was able to transfer this ability to mediumistic seance participants.[51] Zorab, the biographer of the medium, described numerous documented cases of this type.[52]

Thus, from its roots in magic and legend, firewalking can be traced from ancient times into the present. It is a phenomenon well-documented in anecdotal literature throughout the world. Yet, to date, fire immunity has received little serious study.

3. Is Seeing Believing? From Observations to Controlled Studies

The first experimental tests of firewalking were conducted by the University of London Council for Psychical Investigation under the direction of Harry Price.[53] In his initial report, Price discussed two sessions which were held with Kuda Bux, a Mohammedan fakir from India.[54] Before a large audience of reporters and scientists, Kuda Bux walked over a 12-foot pit of burning coals. During one demonstration on a windy day, the surface temperature of the fire was measured at 430°C (806°F), while the body of the fire was 1,400°C (2,552°F). Kuda Bux took four steps across the pit and suffered no burns. The test indicated that firewalking was not a trick and that it was performed with chemically untreated feet. The entire event was recorded on film, which showed that no portion of the firewalker's skin was in contact with the hot embers for as long as half a second.[55] Price concluded that the firewalker's quick, even steps allowed for fire immunity.

Kuda Bux claimed that he could convey immunity to other individuals who followed him across the coals. This was not the case, however, during the first set of experiments. All other individuals who followed him over the coals suffered minor burns.[56] The weight of all the participants was determined, and Price concluded that weight had some bearing on firewalking, adding that a very heavy person would be unwise to attempt the feat.

A second series of experiments conducted by Price with another fakir from India, Ahmed Hussain, seemed to confirm this point of view.[57] Hussain showed approximately the same ability as Kuda Bux by crossing a trench 12.5 feet long, 4 feet wide, and 15 inches deep. The surface temperature of the fire was 575°C (1,067°F), and in the interior it was 700°C (1,292°F). Interestingly enough, the temperature on his feet was found to be 10°F *lower* after the firewalk than before,[58] indicating a certain amount of autonomic physiological regulation, although the significance of this fact somehow escaped Price's attention. However, when the length of the trench was increased to 20 feet, Hussain also suffered burns. Furthermore, several amateurs found that they could walk across the 12-foot fire-trench without suffering burns.

These tests led Price[59] to conclude that fire-immunity was somewhat limited, since the test participants could walk a maximum distance of 12 feet over the coals, taking four or fewer steps. He ruled out the significance of any special preparations to induce the immunity:

Any person with the requisite determination, confidence, and steadiness, can walk unharmed over a fire as hot as 800° Centigrade. The experiments proved once and for all that no occult or psychic power, or a specially induced mental state, is necessary in a firewalker.[60]

Jeffrey Mishlove,[61] a parapsychologist who participated in a firewalking ritual with a group of Kailas Shugendo Buddhists in San Francisco, appears to agree with this conclusion. Charles W. Kenn,[62] however, opposes it on the basis of a study conducted by the University of Hawaii. The study included four firewalks in which 567 individuals, led by kahunas (Hawaiian magico-religious practitioners), who, after incantations and prayers, walked over hot stones with temperatures of 210-610°C (410-1130°F). For most of them, it took five to eight seconds to traverse the 15-foot-long path. While for many firewalkers the time of contact between the foot and the stones was about 3/4 second, the chief firewalker (a kahuna) was observed to stand with both feet resting upon the stone for 1.5 seconds. From 567 participants, about 50 firewalkers suffered burns ranging from the slightest blisters to burns of a serious nature. At least three individuals required hospitalization, and a half dozen were treated by emergency stations and sent to their personal physicians. Since the majority passed "the test of fire" unharmed, Kenn (who safely firewalked during the ceremony) emphasized that the stones of the walk were sufficiently hot to burn, and concluded that some nebulous psychological element aroused an "unidentified force" which prevented the firewalkers from being burned except in certain circumstances.

In 1960, a committee of the Argentine Institute of Parapsychology observed a quasi-religious firewalking ceremony in the town of Abasto, about 40 miles from Buenos Aires. After four or five of the local people had walked across the bed of red-hot embers, Luis A. Boschi, a Committee member, persuaded the organizers of the ceremony to let him try it. They did so reluctantly, warning him that he might be seriously burned. Boschi crossed the 7-foot bed of live coals twice, taking three steps in each direction. He reported feeling no pain—only a slight tingling sensation. Another member of the committee examined Boschi's feet and reported they were perfectly normal excerpt for tiny greyish areas—not inflamed or painful to the touch—on the arch of the foot and between the first two toes. In August 1960, three volunteers from the Institute of Parapsychology crossed a bed of live coals 15 feet long without any ceremony or special preparation. Subsequent examination showed small blistered spots on the feet of all three experimenters.[63]

Friedbert Karger, a West German nuclear physicist and a member of the Max Plank Institute for Plasma Physics in Munich, went to the Fiji Islands in 1974 and filmed a firewalking demonstration by 20 natives on the island of Viti Levu. Before the ceremony began, he daubed temperature-sensitive paints, which change color when certain temperatures are reached, on the feet of one of the participants. Karger's color film shows his subject walking over hot rocks for 4 seconds and standing directly on one of them for seven seconds. When Karger poured his special paint on that rock, it registered over 320°C (600°F). Despite the intense heat, the feet of Karger's native subject suffered no damage whatsoever and did not become hotter than 65°C (150°F).[64]

Mayne Reid Coe, a chemist, successfully attempted not only firewalking, but other "related behaviors," which he described as follows:

Touched red-hot iron with my fingers.
Touched red-hot iron with my tongue.
Touched molten iron with my tongue. (No sensation! Can't feel it!)

Bent red-hot steel bars by stamping them with my bare feet.
Ran barefoot on red-hot iron.
Walked on red-hot rocks.
Plunged my fingers into molten lead, brass, and iron.
Took a small quantity of molten lead in my mouth and spat
    in out immediately. (Once I allowed it to solidify
    in my mouth and almost was burned.)
Carried red-hot coals around in my hands.
Popped red-hot coals into my mouth.
Chewed charcoal off burning sticks. (This is easy if done
    quickly enough.)
Walked on beds of red-hot coals, taking eight steps to cross
    a fourteen foot pit.
Placed my fingers, hands and feet in candle flames until
    covered with carbon black. (No burns! Not hot!
    Only warm!)
Held my face, hands, and feet in fire for a short time.[65]

Coe believes that during a short time of contact with the hot surface, the natural moisture of the skin seems to form a thin layer of water vapor between the skin and the hot surface, which protect the skin from injury. Later he also stated that mental states can aid in conferring immunity to burn, since he has claimed that he enters into a state of altered consciousness while attempting such feats.[66]

Despite the antiquity of firewalking, it is paid more attention by anthropologists than by medical researchers. One exception, however, is Loring Mandell Danforth,[67] who conducted a comprehensive study of Anastenaria—a ritual involving trance, possession and firewalking performed in villages and towns in Northern Greece and Bulgaria. While numerous observations of Anastenarides' fire dancing have been reported previously,[68] Danforth not only presents a detailed firsthand account of the ritual, but also analyzes the Anastenaria as a diagnostic and therapeutic system.

A group of researchers in Greece[69] reported the results of their 10-year studies of the fire dances (Anastenarides) of Langada (Salonika), using Tele-EEG, Tele-EKG, blood tests, and other physiological and neurological tests and filming in order to measure the times of contact of the feet with the burning coals. Temperatures of the coals were taken by a Philips' Thermocoax Miniature

Thermoelement and ranged from 180°C and 450°C. The EEG showed low voltage theta rhythms during the preparation stages, but normal ones during the fire dance proper. The theta rhythms were not comparable to those referred to in the literature for yoga states and Schultz's autogenic training. EKGs were normal with changes of cardiac rhythms from 80 to 120/sec. Neurological, psychiatric examinations, and general lab tests (blood, urine electrolytes) were in the normal range. Anastenarides never lost contact with the environment, and only an emotional lability, specifically, rapid fluctuations in intensity and modality of emotions, was observed.

Reviewing these investigations, Manganas emphasized that "Anastenarides have been subjected to almost all current medical and psychiatric tests, even injections of endorphin antagonists, without conclusive results."[70] In her study, she used high-frequency (Kirlian) photography to photograph the hands and feet of Anastenarides (a total of 11 subjects) during preparation, while fire dancing, and during their everyday life for a three month period following the firewalk. The images were compared with those before and during special states—obtained by Manganas in earlier studies[71]—such as hypnosis, yogic meditation, and autogenic training (AT). In all the above conditions, including fire dancing, an increase of the corona discharge was observed, when compared to the corresponding rest conditions.[72] In the high-frequency images of the hands during fire dancing, a pattern similar to those seen in intense emotional arousal was noticed, different from the color and pattern of relaxation states (hypnosis, yoga, AT). The Kirlian photos of the feet after fire dancing showed a "remarkable increase of the length and density of the streamers and sparks of different colors."[73] However, due to the scant research and controversial nature of high-frequency photography, as well as the difference in heat as the circulation changes, these findings are difficult to interpret.

For 16 months between 1972 and 1976 the anthropologist Steven M. Kane[74] carried out field research of fire-handling performances of Free Pentecostal Holiness Church snake handlers in Southern Appalachia. Kane relates his observations of believers handling torches as follows:

The torches used consist of soda pop bottles or brake fluid cans filled at least half-way with "coal oil" (kerosine) and provided with tightly twisted, cotton rag wicks. They give a very sooty, bright orange-yellow flame 6 to 20 inches high. At the emotional peak of a religious gathering, amidst the din of vigorously strummed guitars, clashing cymbals and tambourines, shouting, and singing, communicants light the torches and put the flames to various body parts and articles of clothing....

I observed many successful instances of torch handling in the course of my field work. On two separate occasions, an elderly Kentucky preacher seized a burning torch with his right hand and slowly rotated his outstretched open left hand in the flame for about 10 seconds.... In two different services, a West Virginia man, said by his fellow communicants to have "good victory over fire," alternately held each hand stationary in the midpoint of a flame for 10 to 15 seconds....

At the conclusion of the services, the fire handlers cleaned the soot from their hands and permitted me to inspect them carefully. They claimed the flames had not caused them the slightest degree of pain or discomfort, and in no case did I detect blistering, tactile hypersensitivity, erythema, edema, or other indicators of thermal injury. Nor was their any sign that clothing which appeared to have been in direct contact with flames had received damage.... Once, after a meeting, I myself attempted to handle a torch in order to have some basis for assessing the risk of physical injury involved. Painful singeing of the hand occurred almost instantaneously, and I involuntarily jerked it away from the flame before I had even reached the midpoint or hottest part.[75]

Kane noted that the fire handlers used not only "coal oil" torches, but also miners' carbide lights, blowtorches, kerosine lanterns (both the flame and the hot glass chimney), and red-hot coals. He also related instances in which unbelievers, convinced that the rite was a trick that could be duplicated by anyone, attempted to handle a torch and suffered serious burns. Kane noted that many worshipers while handling fire are likely to be "in an altered state of consciousness commonly designated "trance" in the literature."[76]

A number of observations of fire-handling among the "saints" of the Free Pentecostal Holiness Church were also reported by the psychiatrist Berthold E. Schwarz. He witnessed the following incidents:

> Twice, at separate times, one of the "most faithful of the saints" slowly moved the palmar and lateral aspects of one hand and the fifth finger in the midpoint and tip of an acetylene [high-temperature] flame ... for more then four seconds, and then repeated the procedure, using the other hand.... Once this saint, when in a relatively calm mood, turned to a coal fire of an hour's duration, picked up a flaming "stone-coal" the size of a hen's egg and held it in the palms of his hands for 65 seconds while he walked among the congregation. As a control, the author could not touch a piece of burning charcoal for less than one second without developing a painful blister.[77]

He also surmised that the fire-handlers were in altered states of consciousness.

Concluding this review on home territory, it is appropriate to mention Jack Schwarz of Selma, Oregon, who performed a fire immunity test before physicians of the Los Angeles County medical and hypnosis associations. After examination by the doctors, Schwarz put his hands into a large brazier of burning coals, picked some up, and carried them around the room. Subsequent examination showed no burns or other signs of heat on his hands.[78]

4. Factors and Rituals Involved in the Preparation for Firewalking—Then and Now

Throughout the firewalking literature, various rituals are mentioned which prepare the participants for their feat. Although the rituals vary, in all cases, from the fadists of Los Angeles to the devotees in India and Sri Lanka, firewalkers must prepare themselves for the coals. Hindu firewalkers, for example, emphasize the observance of a strict vegetarian diet, the abstinence from all stimulants (including cigarettes, coffee, tea, and narcotics), and celibacy.[79] Tamil devotees in Singapore who have taken the vow to participate in firewalking spend several days and nights in the temple, praying and fasting.[80] Buddhist devotees in Japan prepare themselves in a similar way to the firewalk in Mount Takao ceremony:

> Few of the religious members of the ... group had eaten anything since the day before. Each, in his own way, had spent the evening alone with his thoughts, his meditations or his prayers. And, for the two hours prior to the test, they had marched together slowly, zombie-like around the burning pyre, chanting a short repetitious prayer to their Buddhist god. Thus, they had freed their minds to swim in the persistent flood of sounds from the conch shells clutched in sweating hands and the hypnotizing symphony of hundreds of tiny brass bells. The smooth but commanding incantations of their elder priests had reassured them.

Breci, who observed firewalking in Fiji, was told: "They [firewalkers] would come to the pit as soon as they had 'readied their minds and bodies.' "[81] A Fijian explains:

> It's a learned ability.... There are no drugs, just endless incantations until each man is prepared to do just about anything. It's like hypnosis. Why, even you could persuade yourself you could walk through the fire. Once you do, you can—and emerge unscathed.[82]

Horn observed a firewalking ritual in Tahiti and asked the chief priest about his preparation for firewalking:

> He [the priest] told us that in older times the priests went into strict seclusion in the marae [sacred place] for several days to prepare their minds and bodies for the ordeal.

However, in recent times this period of preparation has been lessened to one night before the trial. Chief Titi, as his people familiarly call him, was reticent about just what his preparation consisted of. But he did insist on one thing as of paramount importance: ... "I must *know* that the fire—the heat of the stones—cannot harm anyone." And he said it was necessary for him to repeat with absolute accuracy his invocation at the fire-pit before crossing.[83]

For the Greek Anastenarides, the basic preparation may take years, and more specifically begins about a month before the celebration with strict adherence to moral principles, moderate food intake (generally without meat), and abstinence from sex.[84] They reinforce the preparation before the fire dance by means of rituals, special day-long dancing (always to the same monotonous music), and techniques to enhance group dynamics. In the preparatory stage, prior to the fire dancing, they enact a kind of psychodrama that includes their personal and minority-group conflicts and problems, and reach a highly charged emotional state.[85] Danforth described the preparatory dance as follows:

> The atmosphere ... is one of intense and anxious expectation. Soon one or more Anastenarides begins to show signs of entering trance and beginning to dance. An Anastenarissa may begin to tremble, to rock back and forth in her seat pounding her knees with her fist, or she may jump up with a cry and begin to dance. At this point the lyre player begins to play a much faster, much more rhythmic tune known as "the tune of the dance," or "the tune of the fire." Soon the lyre player is joined by the drum player who begins to beat out a loud 2/4 rhythm which gradually becomes faster and more intense.[86]

After a short time, an Anastenaris who has begun to dance is given an icon of Saint Constantine, Saint Helen, or another sacred object (e.g., a large red kerchief) which is believed to possess the supernatural power of Saint Constantine and to enable the dancing Anastenarides to perform a firewalk unharmed. Anastenarides are convinced that those whose faith is strong are protected.[87]

Thus, the preparation may involve seclusion, diet and fasting, prayer and meditation, chanting and singing, and dancing to the sound of drums or the specially selected music which may lead to entering into altered conscious states. Another common variable emphasized by most firewalkers from the earliest times[88] is the *power of belief*. In many parts of the world, as on the South Pacific Islands, firewalking is a manifestation of "fire within," of "inner fire" of faith. While the rest of the world favors firewalking on red-hot embers, the islanders prefer hot stones. There is, however, one exception. Max Freedom Long related the story of Dr. William Tufts Brigham from the Bishop Museum who while in Hawaii firewalked on hot lava under protection of three kahunas (Hawaiian priests). The ceremony was conducted as soon as the lava was hard enough to bear a person's weight. When Brigham was invited to join the kahunas in walking on lava he was advised to take off his boots and socks. "The goddess Pele hadn't agreed to keep boots from burning," he was told. Brigham refused, thinking that heavy leather soles of his boots would protect him from heat. After the kahunas chanted long incantations, and Brigham walked and ran over the unbearably hot lava, he found the soles of his boots and socks burned to a crisp, but his feet were completely unharmed.[89]

Charles W. Kenn who became a kahuna and received the Hawaiian name of Arii-Peu Tama-Iti, describes the training that kahuna had to go through in order to become a "firewalking chief" and protect others who follow him over hot stones or lava. Kenn himself underwent part of this training:

> The [kahuna] training was extremely strenuous. The student had to undergo hardships and suffer privations. He had to learn the invocations, the proper methods of caring for, installing, or empowering the deities. He learned through a process of 'mental absorption,' observation, close contact with the spiritual forces, and strict adherence to rules and regulations. Some of his practices were based on the Polynesian theory that through constant invocations, using the same words and tone of voice, eventually the deities become accustomed (hoomau) to the calls, and will respond readily, willingly, and promptly. But, to neglect

them by not calling upon them frequently, will cause them to 'die' (desert the kahuna).

Furthermore, it was the belief of the kahunas that as the invocations were handed down, the later kahunas became more and more powerful. This was because they have a longer line of direct ancestors, all of whom have acquired *mana* (power) in great amounts, which is, in turn, passed on down the line.[90]

The incantations talk about "dark cool heat" and "light cool heat" thereby expressing desire of the kahunas to make the heat "cool" and not harmful to the participants. "O ka pule ka mea nui," say the Hawaiians: "Prayer is the most essential thing." The meaning is that "prayer conditions a person to receive the blessings he seeks, and faith and understanding are the essential qualifications."[91]

"There IS some invisible form of consciousness," Kenn concludes, "using some form of energy, and probably some form of matter, to produce fire-immunity in the firewalk."[92]

Thus, our search in the realm of fire brought us to "enlightenment," "illumination," and the ability of mortals to defy fire. Some of those who show the feats of "fire-immunity," however, believe that the underlying reason for the immunity is not "defying" fire, but rather establishing some kind of connection with the flame, invisible and intangible, and becoming one with the seemingly destructive force.[93] Then, in this alternative reality, the fire within, the inner fire of faith and the outer fire unite in protecting a human, extremely vulnerable and mighty powerful at the same time.

This power of belief and faith has been recently translated into the popular form of a "firewalking workshop."

5. Firewalking Workshops

There have been reports by or about individuals who performed firewalking and similar feats outside of a ritual,[94] and thus were precursors to firewalking workshops.

In the late 1970s, the Californian entrepreneur Tolly Burkan started conducting firewalking workshops throughout the United States and later in Canada, Norway, and Sweden. Burkan, who claimed that he learned the art of firewalking from a friend who had studied with a Tibetan, maintains that he has demonstrated at his seminars that everyone can successfully, without being burned, walk over 6 to 10-foot-long beds of red-hot coals after just two to three hours of preparation. According to Burkan, if people *believe* that dieting/fasting or any other component of the ritual is necessary for firewalking, then it *is* necessary for them. The only truly essential component is the *belief* itself.[95] In other words, from the numerous variables involved in shamanic and other ritual firewalking ceremonies, enthusiasts of contemporary firewalking have singled out the only imperative component as the power of belief.

Other factors to which a majority of successful seminar participants attributed their success were: group energy, the power and charisma of the leader, and visualization of successful walking.[96] To this list, the present study adds the power of the mind over matter, to which a significant number of firewalkers attributed their success. It is still unclear whether these factors simply reinforce the individual's power of belief or are significant beyond this.[97] McClenon has used similar techniques (group dynamics, chanting, hypnotic induction procedure, and guided imagery exercise) to conduct firewalks in Okinawa, Japan.[98]

Among students and followers of Burkan, the most well-known is Tony Robbins who, in addition to Burkan's techniques, uses elements of hypnotic induction and neuro-linguistic programming to lead seminar participants through a firewalk.[99] Burkan, Robbins, and other "firewalk instructors" maintain that (a) firewalking can help the participants to overcome fear and transform it into personal power; (b) each walker must assume responsibility for his own "walk" in order to walk successfully (i.e., without "burning"); and (c) one must go into a certain "resourceful state" of consciousness in order to move beyond fear and walk unharmed.[100]

Interviewing facilitators of firewalking workshops, Vilenskaya found that between 1980 and 1985 no less than 25,000 to 30,000 individuals had participated in such seminars, and most of them took part in actual firewalks.[101] Surprisingly, although some of the participants suffered minor burns or small blisters, she found no more than a dozen who were burned seriously enough to require medical attention.

To conclude this section, we would like to share with the readers impressions of Beverly Calicoat who attended a firewalking seminar and described her perceptions both as a first-time participant and a student of Huna, an ancient Hawaiian spiritual teaching.[102] Before the firewalk she compared the seminar leader's explanation about some kind of "protective mechanism" that would allow the participants to firewalk safely, to similar concepts in Huna:

In Huna we know that the High Self is not limited by anything in this dimension. When the High Self enters into the physical body...the body is also unaffected by anything negative or harmful.[103]

The seminar leader clearly laid out the conditions under which the "protection" would be created:

Whatever the explanation, something occurs which alters the body chemistry and causes it to be impervious to heat. However, this brain-activated chemical reaction does not happen:
(1) if there is little or no emotion;
(2) if we fail to *pay attention* to the danger or situation; or
(3) if we allow negative thoughts to enter into our minds.[104]

Calicoat was the first of the students to step forward and walk toward the coals:

I took a deep breath and became very calm. Fear was incredible and like a wall. My intention to walk safely opened a door in that wall of fear and I stepped through. The embers felt crunchy...and I thought the words "cool, cool moss" whenever the awareness of heat was experienced. The heat travelled up and through me as if I was not there. And then it was over.

... I felt no pain and was not burned. Stunned, disbelieving, I decided to walk again.... I knew that this was a very powerful physical stimulus to convince my subconscious mind ... to trust me and my (our) High Self completely. I walked three times. Each time, it passed through me, fooled by my neutrality. I thanked it and thanked my High Self. I came out of the Silence.[105]

There was, however, one more lesson for Beverly to learn that night:

Lest I think that fire was "cool," my High Self allowed me to experience a smoldering, *wet* coal as we were putting out the fire. I hopped off of it *quickly*, but it was too late. I had burned my foot *immediately*....Moments ago, in the right mindset, I had hotfooted it over *hundreds* of red-hot coals safely and in an instant. Stepping on a small ember out of the right mindset, I had been burned. And the burn was from a blackened, wet and cooled ember![106]

Calicoat concludes by relating her conviction in the importance of the experience:

I think that this activity has transformed me to a different level of being. Irrational, psychological fears and real fears still exist. I pay them attention, but I *manage* them more effectively. Common sense is still needed. But my subconscious mind now looks to me for guidance regarding the irrational fears. And I always look to my High Self for the right path....[107]

6. Fire-Immunity and Other Reported Extraordinary Abilities

Some of those who participate in firewalking and fire-handling rituals are known to perform other "extraordinary" feats. Hindu firewalkers reputedly demonstrate their apparent immunity to pain by perforating their cheeks with pins, walking on nails, thrusting skewers through their arms and cheeks, or imbedding meathooks into their naked shoulders and pulling with them heavy carts along a pitted dirt road.[108]

Another reported ability of some firewalkers is a high degree of self-regulation which enables them to voluntarily raise the skin temperature and "sit for a long time, in winter, immersed in ice-cold water, without feeling the cold in the least,"[109] similar to the tum-mo yogis in Tibet.[110]

In Manchuria, on the Russian-Mongolian border, the shaman initiation ceremony included the candidate's walking over burning coals. If the apprentice had at his command the spirits that he claimed to possess, he could walk on fire without injury. The Manchu shamans also had another initiatory ordeal. In winter nine holes were made in the ice. The candidate had to dive into the first hole and come out through the second, and so on to the ninth hole, thus demonstrating his ability to defy extreme cold, similarly to Tibetan yogis. Eskimo shamans also had to prove their magical powers by resisting the most severe cold and demonstrating their insensitivity to fire.[111]

The fire-handlers of the Free Pentecostal Holiness Church handle venomous rattlesnakes and copperheads. During the worship ceremonies, one to four poisonous snakes are held in the hands, around the neck, on the head, or close to the lips of the members. The serpents often "appear to be cataleptic," show no response, and usually do not bite the handlers who, as a rule, are said to be in an altered state. When a Holiness member is bitten, medical treatment is refused, but the level of recovery seems to be much greater than among ordinary individuals.[112] The mental preparation seems to be specific in each case, i.e., a person will incur injury if he or she is prepared ("anointed") to handle a snake, but picks up a torch instead.[113] Some members of the sect were also reported to be able to consume dangerous poisons (e.g., strychnine) without harm to themselves.[114] Other phenomena claimed by various members of Holiness have been the "power of prophecy," so-called "clairvoyance," prolonged fasting, and even the "levitation" of "a bearded patriarch."[115]

Kuda Bux, who participated in Price's study of firewalking,[116] claimed the ability to "see with the inner eye" and gave demonstrations of reading while blindfolded. The authenticity of his "eyeless sight" and alleged ESP was questioned, however, since some researchers believed that the blindfolds allowed a line of vision along the side of the nose.[117]

The Bulgarian Nestenaries are reported to dance on the embers and "utter prophecies."[118] Greek Anastenarides while in trance are believed to possess "dinami—spiritual or supernatural power to perform miracles," which enables them not only to firewalk, but to "gain access to supernatural knowledge" and perform diagnosis and healing.[119]

There are numerous such instances of a relationship between firewalking and healing. The Anastenarides are considered healers who are able to diagnose and cure many illnesses.[120] They believe that the fire they lit and walked on, "was for good health. It burned all the sickness"[121] and that the power given them by Saint Constantine can bring about a cure. There are accounts that they have suggested some sick individuals join in their dance, and after fire dancing the individuals were reportedly healed.[122] The Anastenarides also "consider themselves healers of all the community,"[123] who perform the ritual "for the good of all"—for health, success, and prosperity.[124] Similarly, it is claimed that a *devtia* in India "has the power to help people who are troubled by things for which there seems to be no proper explanation or treatment—especially by unaccountable illnesses."[125]

Members of the Free Pentecostal Holiness Church whose fire-handling feats are described above,[126] are also known for their healing powers.

> If a member of the congregation claims he is ill or knows of someone who is ailing ..., the members gather around the afflicted, anoint with olive oil, "lay on" their hands and loudly pray for divine intercession and healing.... In their vivid descriptions and testimonials the Holiness people claim to have cured diseases that physicians had diagnosed as hopeless: cases of what might have been tuberculosis, carcinomatosis, breast tumors, "skin cancer of the jaw," acute adenitis, poliomyelitis, other forms of paralysis, "sleeping sickness," and convulsive disorders.[127]

Weil further indicates a clear connection between firewalking and healing:

I agree with the firewalkers of Greece that the *power that protects them from burns can also cure disease* [emphasis added]. The mind holds the key to healing, and healing is as extraordinary as firewalking. It may also make use of some nervous pathways and mechanisms.[128]

Referring to Pearce and Weil, Blake and Vilenskaya discuss further possible interconnections between firewalking and "innate healing" as well as mental ("psychic") healing.[129] Finally, a link between firewalking and healing is corroborated by Norman Cousins[130] who noted that the mental state of firewalkers—which he characterized as "blazing determination"—"is real and has untapped curative potential."

7. Psychological Effects of Firewalking

Both ancient literature and contemporary accounts abound with testimonials of the effects of firewalking. In Greece and Fiji firewalkers say their experience has enhanced their lives and given it meaning.[131] The Greek Anastenarides maintain that they are "chosen" to be immune to fire and they "feel worthy" because of being given this power.[132] They are noted for their courage and sometimes explicitly compared to soldiers entering the "fire of battle."[133] It is contended that,

the firewalk of the Anastenarides ... is not only a rite of cleansing, purification, and separation, involving a transition from bad to good, but also a miracle proving that the Anastenarides are in possession of the supernatural powers of Saint Constantine, the very power through which this transition is brought about.[134]

Images of fire and heat are often associated with feelings of anxiety, and through fire dancing Anastenarides are also believed to overcome anxiety.[135]

This tradition continues in firewalking workshops in which the participants are led to overcome anxiety and fear.[136] Many believe that firewalking is an "excellent tool for healing, spiritual growth and psychological development."[137] They also have pointed out implications of firewalking seminars for psychological and spiritual transformation and growth. While in earlier rituals firewalking has been primarily used in initiation and purification ceremonies, contemporary enthusiasts of "firewalking workshops" attempt to use the firewalk as a tool, as a metaphor for overcoming fears, limiting beliefs, and psychological problems. "If you can walk on fire, you can do anything you choose," states Tolly Burkan and his followers.[138]

These subjective opinions and anecdotal reports of the significance of firewalking have recently been confirmed by Julianne Blake. Using the State-Trait Anxiety Inventory, the Internal-External Locus of Control, the Personal Orientation Inventory and in-depth follow up interviews of participants of firewalking seminars, she came to the conclusion, "Firewalking is empowering!"[139] She found that firewalking successfully led individuals to a discounting of the influence of "powerful others" and reinforced the belief in the controllability of life.

A final aspect of the psychological effects of firewalking was emphasized by Richard Gunther, an American businessman who participated in a firewalking ceremony in Brazil.[140] He emphasized that firewalking may be an example of how we limit our potential with our limiting beliefs. He wrote:

If we can change our assumptions enough to walk over hot coals without injury, what other assumptions might we change? What powers might we possess that are never used, or are undeveloped? What are we humans capable of doing, and of being?

... From our firewalk we learned that the limit to our experience was the limit that we had created—i.e., "I can't walk on those hot coals without burning my feet." But when we transcended that limiting belief a new experience was available to us... If we decline to remain tied to specious views of the possible, if we open ourselves to a higher vision of what humans can accomplish, the old boundaries on human potential will disappear, and the world could become a more humane, compassionate and hopeful place in which to live.[141]

Thus, the plethora of published material on firewalking is in dramatic contrast to the dirth of controlled observations of firewalking, providing a literature of testimony and anecdote. Both anecdotal evidence and research findings confirm the objective existence of firewalking and its significance in religious and cultural contexts in various parts of the world. Examining the accounts and scant empirical literature, we find that firewalkers throughout the world generally claim to be empowered by their participation, be they ritual dancers in Greece or Fiji, or Americans walking on fire in the parking lot of the Holiday Inn. Stillings has pointed out a far-reaching significance of firewalking:

The image of firewalking is that of daring to make a dangerous passage involving fire. Certainly the entire world is currently in a dangerous transition period involving fire—and involving fear. By generating an enthusiasm among ordinary people to walk on the small, microscopic fire of the firewalk, it appears that something is trying to reveal a message through this collective symbolic act, namely, that if one accepts the fire, accepts its consequences and reality, and gives oneself over to it, *something interrupts the "normal" expected outcome*. I do not care if the firewalk be explained in terms of known science; this important image, this symbol, remains, and is one worth meditating on. The firewalk is a kind of ritual dance we enter into that puts us in touch with the cosmic fire of transformation. Passing through the alchemical fires of transformation is an old theme. The firewalking format is indeed presented as a potential personal transformative experience. However, the fact that firewalking has become a widespread movement involving thousands of people points to a transformative process taking place on the collective level.[142]

Therefore, we return to the question of Gunther, "What are we humans capable of doing, and of being?"[143] Additional studies of the phenomenon are needed for understanding the mind/matter and mind/body relationships and their possible significance for healing and human potential. Before discussing these issues, however, we would like to review scientific views of the nature of firewalking and fire-immunity.

Chapter 3
What Does Science Say?
Existing Hypotheses

What is now proved was once only imagined.
William Blake, *The Marriage of Heaven and Hell*

1. How is Firewalking Possible?
Our Approach to the Mystery

While the ancients as well as many contemporary firewalkers have attributed their abilities to spiritual powers, scientists look to commonly understood properties of human physiology and the physical universe to explain the mystery. Recent studies in physics and psychophysiology provide additional insights into the nature of firewalking. Five major hypotheses offer avenues for further research: they include: (1) those which deal with firewalking as mere trickery or deception; (2) firewalking explained within the laws of physics and known properties of human physiology; (3) hypotheses surrounding the psychophysiological changes induced in an altered state of consciousness; (4) firewalking as a function of belief; and (5) firewalking as an expression of "mind over matter." Utilizing such a structure of hypotheses, we can begin to examine the phenomenon and separate anecdote from actuality.

Firewalking has long been surrounded by an aura of fascination and mystery which can be attributed to the fact that it appears to defy rational explanation. Yet, despite the numbers of descriptive publications, there have been surprisingly few attempts at scientific research to answer a major question: How is firewalking possible? There are difficulties inherent in researching the nature of this phenomenon, for we must, on the one hand, avoid reductionistic approaches and, on the other hand, avoid simplistic "esoteric" assumptions. The existing literature contains examples of both. This phenomenon can be formulated as follows: Certain individuals apparently possess immunity to the influence of sufficiently high temperatures as to be *normally* detrimental for the human organism. The tissues of mammals cannot stand temperatures higher than 60°C (140°F), since protein begins breaking down, and skin exposed to a temperature of 75°C (167°F) will blister within one second of contact. At a temperature of 250°C, the effect on the protein, muscles, fatty tissue, and nerves of the foot would be devastating in only a fraction of a second.

A few decades ago, firewalking was seen as simply a magic trick performed by professional fakirs. More recent, but equally simplistic explanations of the phenomenon have included the insensitivity of the callused feet of native Indian and Fijian firewalkers who walk barefoot all their lives, or the "primitive" nervous system of natives which enables a higher tolerance to heat.[1] The experience of numerous Europeans and Americans who have successfully participated in various firewalking ceremonies, however, suggests the need for a more complex explanation.[2] In recent years numerous observations have also indicated it is a complicated phenomenon.[3]

While most research to date has examined the physical aspects of the phenomenon[4] and advanced physiological hypotheses,[5] over the years alternative ideas have been advanced to explain the phenomenon of firewalking. These hypotheses concerning firewalking and fire immunity include psychological, psychophysiological, and religious theories, and must be thoughtfully considered.

A scientifically valid hypothesis must explain all observable phenomena as well as all the variations of the phenomena under question. Therefore, each hypothesis will be followed by a discussion which will include problematic issues and unanswered questions.

2. Hypothesis One: Trickery and Deception

One hypothetical approach to explain firewalking is to attribute the phenomenon to fakery and deception: that either it is simply an illusion or trick conducted by stage magicians, or that the participants do not report their true injuries and thus deceive researchers.

Early researchers attempted to explain away firewalking by contending that it is simply a magic trick, claiming that firewalkers treat their feet with special ointments which toughen the skin or smear them with ashes.[6] However, since the beginning of the century, numerous observations have indicated that this is not the case.[7] Hocken, after observing a Fijian firewalk and examining the participants, wrote:

> The skin, legs and feet [of the firewalkers] were free from any apparent applications. I assured myself of this by touch, smell, and taste, not hesitating to apply my tongue as a corroborative. The foot soles were comparatively soft and flexible.[8]

Many observers believe that firewalkers distract the attention of observers in order to deceive them. Such purported trickery involves dragging the feet on the earth at the edge of the fire.[9] Similarly, in demonstrations of handling red-hot coals, "a charred piece of white pine, introduced among the burning coals in a fireplace, may be handled with ease."[10]

Although trickery must be acknowledged as a possibility in any particular firewalk, there have been numerous carefully controlled observations, in which researchers made certain that the pit was filled evenly with red-hot coals and no special preparations were applied to the feet.[11] Although the deception by legerdemain is facilitated by distance, in most of these controlled studies the observers remained at the edge of the pit, far closer than a "stage show" audience.

The likelihood of such deceptive tricks can now be ruled out, since among the people who have successfully performed firewalking are not only "professionals" (e.g., shamans, members of esoteric, magical, and religious sects), but also the thousands of ordinary individuals who have participated in firewalking workshops and ceremonies.[12]

Other advocates of the theories of deception believe that burns during firewalking and fire-handling ceremonies are frequent, but the participants prefer to hide the fact that they were burned because they do not want to admit their failures.[13] Such "deception" on the part of participants is attributed to psychological weakness, and particularly applies to contemporary firewalking workshops. In a seminar which claims that firewalking transforms "fear into power," for example, a participant without blisters is recognized as "powerful." To acknowledge pain, on the other hand, is to admit a lack of personal power.

Once again, there have been several controlled observations, including photographs of the walkers' feet, which refute this hypothesis. Blake, for example, studying participants of firewalking workshops, used the most conservative indicators of burning or "blistering," considering even a *slight discoloration of the skin* to be "blistering." Nevertheless, 64.1% of all walkers she studied showed no evidence at all of exposure to high temperatures.[14]

3. Hypothesis Two: The Laws of Physics

Within the framework of classical physics, there are three primary avenues to explain firewalking. The first, and most simplistic belief, is that the firewalkers have callouses on their feet. Second, the surface across which individuals pass during firewalking ceremonies (hot stones or the hot coals of a wood fire) provides low heat conductivity, and therefore any individual making quick, even steps can perform a short firewalk without injury.[15] A final position is that the natural moisture of the foot protects the individual while passing across the coals.[16]

Some researchers emphasize that individuals who participate in firewalking ceremonies have usually walked barefoot from early childhood and have calluses on the soles of their feet which protect them during firewalking.[17] Since these individuals make only a few quick steps on the fire, they do not get burned. Others reject this explanation pointing out that there were a number of Europeans with non-calloused feet who participated in similar ceremonies without harm to themselves.[18] Furthermore, although some participants may walk quickly and take only a few steps, this appears to be insufficient to explain the lack of burns given the extremely high temperatures involved,[19] and the fact that 60-feet-long firewalks have been performed without injuries to the participants.[20]

There are two characteristic forms of firewalking: walking on hot stones, which is the practice throughout Polynesia; and walking on hot coals or embers, which is the practice in many other parts of the world.[21] One explanation which has been offered for the success of the ritual firewalk is the assumption that the basaltic stones used for these rites are poor conductors of heat.

Fulton[22] and Roth[23] observed firewalking during a Vilavilairevo ceremony in Fiji and attempted to explain the phenomenon of fire immunity through the specific physical properties of the stones used to prepare the place for firewalking. In their opinion, these stones possessed large thermal heat capacity but small heat emission. However, others have counteracted this assumption. Kenn pointed out that in a firewalk lasting 17 minutes during which 167 people walked, the heat-measured stone "lost 35 degrees [Centigrade] of heat during that time, which shows fairly well that its porous nature did not prevent its sending out heat—a supposedly non-conducting characteristic offered to explain away fire immunity."[24] In addition, after the firewalk "four pieces of steak were broiled on the stones."[25]

Additional data concerning this hypothesis appeared in a pilot study conducted at the University of Hawaii. During four firewalking ceremonies in Honolulu and Maui, some 567 people walked on the same type of basaltic stones used in Polynesia. The pit was 15 feet long and 6 feet wide. While the temperature of the pit before the walk was 920°C, and the temperature of the stones averaged 610°C, the first stone was only 210°C. For the majority of the firewalkers, the time of contact of each foot with the stones averaged 3/4 seconds, as documented by a 16-mm film taken during one of the ceremonies. However, the "chief firewalker" stood with both feet resting flatly upon the stone for 1.5 seconds. From 567 participants, "about 50 suffered burns" ranging from slight blisters to "burns of a serious nature" and, among them, "at least three individuals required hospitalization," with the chief firewalker not among them.[26]

Another investigation was carried out by the University of London Council of Psychical Investigation.[27] It included three experiments, in which two experienced firewalkers from India, Kuda Bux and Hussain, walked through a 12-foot-trench filled with coals whose surface temperature ranged from 806°F to 1,472°F. Each was able to take four strides through the pit and suffered no burns. In addition, several untrained volunteers also performed the firewalk. The first few times they walked over the coals, their feet were burned "to a varying, but slight, degree,"[28] but some of them were eventually able to successfully duplicate feats of the experienced Indian firewalkers. The most successful of them, Reginald Adcock, believed that the reason for his success was that his "former attempts had given him confidence to walk steadily."[29] Ingalls summarized the results:

> Kuda Bux, Hussain, and Adcock, weighing respectively 120, 126, and 160 pounds, walked distances of 11, 12, and 12 feet, taking 4, 4, and 3 steps, in 2.2, 1.6, and 1.8 seconds, in minimum time of contact per step of .55, .40, and .60 seconds, over surface temperatures of 806 and 1,472 degrees, Fahrenheit.... Both Hussain and Adcock [a volunteer] exceeded Kuda Bux's performance by walking on a fire of nearly twice the surface temperature. Further it is remarkable that Adcock should have survived, without injury to his feet, the greatest minimum mean time of contact.[30]

From an earlier experiment, Price drew the conclusion that the weight of the firewalkers might be an issue, but when Adcock, who weighed more than Bux, did not sustain injury despite a longer time of contact on the hot surface—twice as hot as the surface than Bux walked on—this suggestion could not be considered valid.[31] Kenn[32] and Stillings[33] further emphasized that up to 250 pounds, weight was unimportant. They surmised that above this considerable size, the increased pressure alone would lead to burns. Nevertheless, many who cite Price's experiments still question the possible importance of weight.

Of interest, human flesh scorches at a lower temperature than cotton fabric, and Price's experiments with a wooden shoe covered with calico cloth indicated scorching in less than a second when placed on the hot embers.[34] The experimenters noticed, however, that no portion of the skin was in contact with the hot embers for as long as half a second. From the three experiments Price and his colleagues drew the following conclusion:

> The low thermal conductivity of smoldering wood prevents damage to normal skin and other objects if the time of contact is below about half a second and the number of contacts is not too great.... Facts of a purely physical nature—namely, brief contact, few contacts, and a poor conductor of heat—seem sufficient to account for the ability to do firewalking.[35]

Many of those who cite these conclusions,[36] fail to notice an important point: while the longest walk was reported as to be 2.2 seconds, in the same report Ingalls stated that during the second experiment, Kuda Bux traversed in "four strides" an 11-foot trench in 4.5 seconds.[37] If "four strides" mean that Bux's foot touched the fire a total of 5 times, this gives an average duration of contact of .9 second per step; if there were 4 contacts, it would mean 1.1 seconds per contact, using the same calculation which resulted in .55 second contact in 4 steps during 2.2 seconds walk.

Furthermore, although Price[38] concluded that a firewalker cannot take more than 4 steps over a firebed without getting burned, Fonseka documented a walk over an 18 by 4 foot pit, 6 inches deep, having a surface temperature of 430°C, with 10 steps taken, without injury.[39] Coe took 60 continuous steps across a pit that had reached a temperature of 1,200°F,[40] and anthropological literature contains information about 60-foot-long firewalks.[41]

The low thermal conductivity hypothesis has been recently revived and widely publicized in terms understandable by non-physicists.[42] The main proponents, Leikind and McCarthy,[43] stress the distinction between thermal conductivity and heat, explaining that even though the coals seem hot, the firewalkers will be burned only over an extended period of time, not instantaneously, due to the low thermal conductivity of the coals. Leikind and McCarthy have not, however, submitted quantitative data to suggest the minimum of this period of time.

Thus, difficulties of testing and a lack of quantifiable data to test the hypothesis of low thermal conductivity have arisen in several studies. Coe walked on hot iron, a surface which is a much better conductor of heat than basaltic stones or wood coals, without injury.[44] Karger, who studied firewalking in Fiji using temperature sensitive paints, found that a firewalker stood for 7 seconds on a rock with a temperature over 600°F.[45] Kane during his study of fire-handlers, observed instances when a person held each hand stationary at a midpoint of the torch flame for ten to fifteen seconds, without injury.[46] Such reports provide evidence which refute the hypothesis of low thermal conductivity as the major explanation of fire immunity.

The auxiliary hypothesis of classical physics, that the feet of firewalkers are protected due to natural moisture on them, is often referred to as the "Leidenfrost Effect."[47] The name derives from the 18th-century physician Johann Leidenfrost, who noted that at temperatures lower than 200°C water droplets on a smooth, heated surface will evaporate quickly. At higher temperatures a vapor barrier builds up around each droplet, and it vaporizes much more slowly. At temperatures above 500°C, the droplets again vanish rapidly.

Enlisting this information to explain firewalking, proponents state that the natural moisture on the walker's feet partially vaporizes at high temperatures and provides a primary protection. This depends on the ability of water to achieve a "spheroid state."[48] The phenomenon is encountered by the breakfast chef, who sprinkles water on the pancake griddle, knowing that when the temperature is high the droplets do not vaporize immediately, but turn to spheres and remain a moment "dancing" on the griddle. (One can easily surmise, however, that a coal bed is a far cry from the smooth, nonporous "griddle" surface required for such effects.[49]) According to this theory, the sweat on the feet of the firewalker enters the "spheroid state" of water. In so doing, the sweat does not vaporize instantaneously, but instead serves to protect the firewalker from burn.

Yet, since the Leidenfrost effect is stated to occur only within a fixed temperature range, how can we explain successful firewalks outside of that temperature range? The temperature of the coal bed (ranging from 100°C to 800°C) has been both above and below the Leidenfrost range, without the occurrence of burns.[50] Temperatures at the lower end of the Leidenfrost range for water or sweat (about 200°C) are still more than sufficient to quickly produce a painful burn in a very short time. Furthermore, burns have occurred within the Leidenfrost range.[51] McClenon pointed out that the Leidenfrost effect does not occur at temperatures lower than 200°C (390°F). Since this temperature is still high enough to cause burns, it does not explain firewalks performed over "cool" firebeds—including one firewalk performed by McClenon during cold and rainy weather in Japan.[52] As far as the higher end of the Leidenfrost range is concerned, the *Guinness Book of World Records* indicates that during the firewalk of "Komar" (Vernon E. Craig) of Wooster, Ohio, performed at the International Festival of Yoga and Esoteric Sciences, Maidenhead, England, on August 14, 1976, the temperature of the coals recorded by a pyrometer was 1,494°F (812°C). A group of 11 people led by Steven Neil Bisyak of Redmond, Washington, participated in a firewalk with an average temperature of 1,546°F (841°C) on December 19, 1987 at Redmond.[53]

In discussing the Leidenfrost hypothesis, Ingalls pointed out that moisture on the feet would present a disadvantage: it would cause hot embers to adhere to the soles, increasing the time of contact with the hot surface and the danger of injury.[54] Ironically, James Randi, who is known for his debunking of extraordinary phenomena, also notes that Sri Lankan firewalkers believe that foot moisture causes embers to stick, and carefully dry their feet before walking.[55]

Jearl Walker from the Department of Physics of Cleveland State University, has been a proponent of the Leidenfrost hypothesis of firewalking. Walker himself attempted firewalking several times until he suffered third degree burns on both feet. Walker warned that his explanation is sufficient for a short firewalk "unless the walker has an unusual tolerance for pain."[56] He did not specify, however, how short the "short" is. Therefore, one has no way to tell whether *standing* on a hot surface for seven seconds, observed by

Karger[57] or holding a hand *stationary* in a torch flame for 10 to 15 seconds[58] falls into this "short" category.

In addition, the Leidenfrost hypothesis requires that the "steps not be too fast," so that sufficient sweat can build up on the foot while in the air, mid-stride. As the literature documents, the time range of steps varies considerably between, for example, the fire dancers of Greece and the firewalkers of America.[59] An account of fire dancing in Greece emphasized that the time of contact of fire dancers' feet with the burning coals was "extremely variable."[60] Another account stated that, "Thracian firewalkers somehow dance over ... white-hot beds, and sometimes kneel down in the center for several minutes."[61]

Finally, the laws of physics do not, by themselves, satisfactorily explain the numerous cases in which some firewalkers have been burned, while others remained unharmed.[62] Feinberg, for example, describes a mass firewalk in Sri Lanka (Kataragama), where about 100 devotees crossed a 20-by-6-foot fire pit:

> On the night we watched the firewalking at Kataragama, twelve people were burned badly enough to go to the hospital, and one of them died....A young English clergy-man who visited Ceylon a few years ago...volunteered to walk the fire with others. He...spent the next six months in a hospital, where doctors barely managed to save his life.[63]

The hypothesis which explains firewalking strictly according to known physical properties then, cannot give a satisfactory answer as to why some people are burned during the same firewalk when others are not.[64]

4. Hypothesis Three: Psychophysiological Changes Induced in an Altered State of Consciousness

The notion of a "trance" or hypnotically induced altered state of consciousness is frequently relied upon to explain the mysteries of firewalking. Such states are hypothesized to include the psychophysiological changes induced in hypnotic or other kinds of altered states.

Hypnotic states are known to alter the body's ability to respond to heat, and thus provide a possible explanation for firewalking. Over half a century ago, the British physician J. Arthur Hadfield carried out some interesting hypnosis experiments which studied the influence of the power of suggestion on the inflammatory response. Hadfield was not only able to cause a burn in the absence of a noxious stimulus, but also to partially alleviate the response to a noxious stimulus. In one of his experiments, he burned a hypnotized subject with the end of a steel pencil-case heated in a Bunsen flame, suggesting that there would be "no pain" in consequence of the burns. The result was as follows:

> There was no pain either when the skin was touched or afterwards. But the remarkable thing was that in these burns there was *no hyperaemia* around. Round each of the two spots, which themselves presented the ordinary appearance of blisters, there was a thin red line and nothing more. These blisters healed very rapidly and never gave any sign of inflammation or pain.[65]

Similar and more recent studies were conducted by Ullman and by Chapman, Goodell, and Wolff, in which hypnotically induced anesthesia successfully lessened the visible damage induced by a thermal stimulus applied to the subject's arm.[66] Plethysmographic and skin temperature recordings made during these experiments indicated vasoconstriction in the arm suggested to be anesthetic. Thus, the power of hypnotic suggestion can indeed be employed to repress an inflammatory response.

The contention that firewalkers and fire-handlers are in "trance" or, more precisely, in an altered state of consciousness, has been frequently expressed in the literature.[67] However, there have been very few attempts to assess experimentally the states of consciousness involved. Interviewing participants of firewalking workshops, Blake found that of 52 respondents, 38% reported perceptions inconsistent with consensual reality (i.e., the coals felt cool or wet), 67% described their experience as euphoric, 54% expressed a feeling of timelessness, and 81% described a shift in their energy while firewalking.[68]

Stillings suggests that simply looking at the hot coals glowing bright orange and knowing that one will step on them in a few seconds can lead to an altered state of consciousness, as this action is outside of our ordinary behavior.[69] The underlying issue in this case concerns those factors which cause an individual to enter an altered state, and how radical a shift in attention must be before one's state is considered to have been "altered."

Another explanation concerning the induction of an altered state of consciousness in firewalking concerns the interaction of group members. A firewalking workshop which includes collective singing, "*aum*ing," chanting and other kinds of group interaction may shift the conscious state of most or all group participants.

Some healers claim to be able to conduct mass healing sessions in which they work with a group of individuals and focus the "group energy field" on a single individual. One of the healers discusses this idea as follows:

> All the actions in which human beings participate can be subdivided into individual and collective. "Collective" suggests three or more people. When it is only two, it's still a personal act. In primitive societies, it is assumed that a collective, "team" consciousness has a greater degree of power and influence. This is all based on a relatively well known statement that a thought is an action. This confronts one of the basic questions of philosophy, "what is an action?" Does the concept or idea of an action correspond to the action itself? ... If so, we can possibly explain the phenomena and visions that occur in team healing or team praying. It is known that a person can influence the actions of a group of people, consciously or subconsciously. Similarly, a group of people can influence the actions of an individual.[70]

Yet, group effects are not necessary in every case of firewalking. Coe[71] and McClenon[72] performed solitary firewalking without the presence of a group. In both cases, however, this was not the initial firewalk. To date, there are no data on anyone who has attempted a first firewalk alone and the significance of the group for first-timers remains an issue for study.

An unusual aspect of the hypothesis of altered states is to consider that it is not the ability of fire-immunity that is transferred, but rather the altered state.[73] This assumption may explain why the phenomenon of fire immunity reportedly has occurred during mediumistic seances, in which the medium, who claimed to be in "trance," purportedly "transmitted" this ability to other participants.[74] Rather than a "transfer" of fire immunity *per se*, the medium could have altered the group's awareness. Fire immunity could have been one of several effects of this shift in consciousness.

Recent attempts to understand the interrelationship of mind and body have begun to shed light on the phenomenon of altered states of consciousness and fire immunity. Andrew Weil summarized a psychophysiological perspective as follows:

> Several different mechanisms may take part. Changes in blood circulation might help conduct heat away from body surfaces or reduce the flow of heat to vulnerable tissues. Changes in the functions of local nerves might suppress the activity of neurochemicals that mediate pain and inflammatory reaction to strong stimulation.... A more hypothetical possibility is some as-yet-undiscovered capacity of the nervous system to absorb potentially harmful forms of energy, transform them, and conduct them away from the body surface.
>
> ... I think the abilities are quite natural, the results of using the mind in certain ways (or not using it in ordinary ways) and so allowing the brain and nerves to alter the body's responsiveness to heat.[75]

In Weil's opinion, psychoneurological mechanisms which may contribute to successful firewalking include the following: (a) absence of fear, or any effort at defense which produces neuromuscular tension; (b) deep relaxation; (c) the presence of someone experienced and unafraid; (d) concentration, produced by techniques such as chanting or hypnosis.[76] In the present research, within these categories, only (c) the presence of an experienced firewalker, and (d) concentration, were apparent in a significant measure.

The emergence of the relatively new field of psychoneuroimmunology may augment knowledge of the mind/body interaction as it relates to fire-immunity. Recent research has documented correlations among psychological events, endocrine secretion, and modulation of immunity.[77] The studies indicate a connection between the hypothalamus, the limbic system, and the most evolved part of the cortex, the frontal lobes, which may effect certain aspects of immunity.[78] Such findings may lead to further information about an interface between the mind/body interaction and extraordinary practices such as firewalking.

Since there have been insufficient studies of the relationship between firewalking and altered states of consciousness, however, the role of hypnosis, trance and other kinds of altered states remains a topic for further study.

5. Hypothesis Four: Power of Belief

The power of belief refers to the individual relinquishing some degree of personal power to forces greater than oneself, be they the natural forces of the universe, the power of a placebo, or the power of God. While contemporary firewalk instructors strengthen "the power of belief" in the possibility of safety, "No firewalk instructor that I know of," Stillings has stated, "claims that any one belief system is necessary for success."[79] Thus, *which* belief system is held by the firewalker is not so important as that there *is* a belief system.

One example of the power of belief is Leikind, who gave a physics lecture about "low thermal conductivity of the coals" and led a group of people through the firewalk unharmed.[80] In this case Leikind utilized a well-ensconced belief system with appropriate imagery, "a system with some 300 years of paradigm support behind it."[81] In other words, Leikind acted as a "firewalk instructor" using the same basic belief principle of firewalk preparation: belief in the laws of physics.

In the realm of belief, the most common reason given by participants is the attribution of their firewalking to a belief in the power of God or 'friendly spirits' that protect the participant. Similar to the magical thinking found in the literature of anthropology and mythology,[82] the literature of firewalking contains numerous references to the beliefs of firewalking adepts in mysterious forces and supernatural powers that protect them from ordinary harmful external influences.

In India, for example, the devtias who perform firewalking claim to be protected by their personal deity, or Isht, who is invited to come into and act through them during the firewalk.[83] In Greece, the fire-dancing Anastenarides are believed to possess "dinami— spiritual or supernatural power to perform miracles," which enables them both to firewalk and to "gain access to supernatural knowledge" and perform diagnosis and healing.[84] It is believed that,

> the firewalk of the Anastenarides...is not only a rite of cleansing, purification, and separation,...but also a miracle proving that the Anastenarides are in possession of the supernatural powers of Saint Constantine, the very power through which this transition is brought about.[85]

A Greek fire dancer explains:

> If the Saint calls you to go into the fire, then you don't feel the fire as if it were your enemy, but you feel it as it were your husband or your wife. You feel love for the fire....You go into the fire freely....When the Saint gives you courage, you feel love for the fire. You feel hope. You have a longing to enter the fire.[86]

Within our own culture, devotees of the Free Pentecostal Holiness Church who participate in numerous feats of fire-handling,[87] evoke a Biblical passage to explain the use of fire without harm in their rituals, "When thou walkest through the fire, thou shalt not be burned; neither shall the flame kindle upon thee" (Isaiah 43:2). The essential concept is the belief that the Holy Ghost "moves" into the worshipers and takes possession of their faculties, rendering them capable of carrying out one or more of the works of God, that is, fire handling, snake handling, healing the sick, prophecy, and so forth.

Fire-handling devotees claim to achieve the state of "anointing" which they describe as follows: "It makes a different person out of you"; "I about lose sight of the world for awhile"; "It's like a good cold shower"; "You feel just like your hands are in a block of ice. I've had it all over me"; "You feel queer all over, like you stick your finger in electricity"; "It's like a bolt of lightnin' goes through you"; "It's so wonderful. You can feel it in your flesh. You're conscious, but everything looks just beautiful to you."[88]

Such spiritual beliefs can be considered in a contemporary scientific context as well, and result in an overlap between states of consciousness, the mind/body interaction and the power of belief. Physician Andrew Weil says that "extraordinary" abilities are natural to all human beings, and that the question of how mind and body interact is the next frontier of medical research.[89] Yet, both Weil and Pearce conclude that *belief* is the key—that the power of belief accounts for all the anomalies of innate healing, the placebo effect, and such extraordinary phenomena as firewalking.[90] Weil specifies that:

> Belief that counts is gut-level belief that stirs emotions and connects to the body through the centers of the deep brain. It is based on experience as well as thought and must be psychosomatic to begin with, bridging the barrier between modern cortex and primitive brainstem.[91]

In addition, Weil addresses the universal human tendency to externalize belief in saints and deities, rather than recognizing one's own spiritual power. He postulates that we may actually need to project belief onto external objects, such as placebos or gods, in order to reap the benefits of our innate power since there is an apparent barrier between the cortex and the deep brain centers that control psychosomatic events.[92]

Regardless of the universality of the power of belief or the belief system utilized to protect one from injury, however, Evaggelou suggests that this hypothesis may not pertain to noninjurious firewalks by non-believers.[93] But Evaggelou does not consider that belief in natural forces may be as effective as belief in deities. One might conjecture that every firewalker believes in *something*, regardless how disparate the belief systems may be.

6. Hypothesis Five: Mind Over Matter

The hypothesis of mind over matter, however loosely defined, is associated with both advocates of of psychokinesis and those writers who postulate that physical reality is mutable, and that individuals, through their minds, are reputedly capable of changing physical laws around them.[94] Psychics have been touting this approach for ages. In contemporary terms, psychokinesis (PK) is defined by parapsychologists as, "the direct influence of mind on a physical system without the mediation of any known physical energy or instrumentation—that is, the extramotor aspect of psi."[95] Schmeidler, for example, reported that when she asked the psychic Ingo Swann to change the temperature inside a distant thermos, significant continuous changes on automatic temperature recorders were repeatedly produced.[96]

Other researchers go further in speaking of the PK-created superconductivity of the skin to heat,[97] or the PK-mediated resistance to injury.[98] Some even refer to so-called "levitation" by noting that many native firewalkers, particularly in Fiji, "maintain they are "lifted" over the [hot] rocks."[99] Pearce went so far as to make an assumption that, through PK, people are capable of modifying physical effects in the limited space around their bodies.[100] This possibility has been considered by those who believe, as is sometimes reported,[101] that not only the skin of the "fire immune" individuals was unharmed, but also articles of clothing they wore during the firewalk were not singed.

Another aspect of the purported mind over matter is that a heretofore undiscovered electrostatic cooling effect might be involved. Stillings points out that known cooling effects produced by strong electrostatic fields can be quite dramatic, as in the cool winds which reputedly may blow across the seance table. He believes "that the mind and body, in certain altered states, are capable of mentally producing strong electrostatic fields surrounding the legs and feet of firewalkers and can then protect the subject by cooling the coals."[102] Interestingly enough, many firewalkers report tingling sensations, like slight electric shocks, on the bottom of their feet during and after firewalking.[103]

Although one of the possible mechanisms may be the creation of anomalous electrostatic fields which cause or provide a cooling effect, there has been no research reported to date and no known attempts to measure such fields during firewalking or fire-handling.

Some observers are attempting to explain firewalking phenomena by appealing to recent developments in physics. As Pearce conjectures,

> The [firewalking] action itself is a transfer of imagery. We have an image of people walking [on] fire, and extract from this the essence behind it, the blueprint of that action. We then fill in this blueprint with the content of our own action.... The changed image changes reality.... We can change the interaction between self and world, as in firewalking, or change aspects of the world itself, as in metal-bending. We can change our notion of physical laws over and over.[104]

Pearce considers at length the implications of quantum mechanics and Bell's theorem for the performance of anomalous behaviors. He concludes that human beings sometimes are the creators of their own, mutable reality (as yogis and mystics have claimed for ages), noting,

> The brain/mind is the median, the interface between possibility and its expression. Our outer field is limited and restricted, but contains specific models that give the direction our inner fields can take to shape our experience.[105]

Similarly, LeShan emphasizes that firewalking seems to be impossible by our cultural—and therefore our personal—definition of reality. Nevertheless,

> The only possible way out of this that I can see is that there are other, equally valid, definitions of reality, and in one of these this procedure of "firewalking" is possible. The careful psychological preparation by the participants thus becomes a procedure for changing their definition of reality. It is clear that not only do other definitions exist, but that these others include some that are very different from our ordinary definition.[106]

We can see that the hypotheses which have been advanced through the ages to account for the phenomenon of firewalking range from the esoteric to the mundane, and come full circle with the overlap between ancient spiritual beliefs and contemporary parapsychological hypotheses. Hypothesis-builders tend to fall into two general categories: (1) those who explain firewalking within a framework defined by the presently understood properties of the known physical universe; and, (2) those who hypothesize outside of the commonly accepted scientific laws. In the latter category are found those who ascribe the mysterious phenomenon to external agencies, and those who believe that the human mind is capable of powers that are yet to be fully understood. Needless to say, controversy abounds and further research is necessary.

Several writers use natural processes to explain what might allow for individuals to cross burning coals unharmed: the low conductivity of the embers which will radiate heat without actually burning skin; the protection offered by sweat on the feet; magical tricks and deceit. Psychologists often postulate a fear of failure which inhibits firewalkers from reporting blisters they sustained while firewalking.

Psychophysiologists, meanwhile, frequently study the mind-body relationship, sometimes professing the power of an altered state of consciousness to provide protection—whether that state is provided by the hypnotic skills of a firewalk leader or the social reinforcement of the group. They may also study the role of endorphins, the hypothalamus, and the limbic system in fire immunity.

The power of belief constitutes the most widespread position, as seen in the efficacy of the belief in spirits and deities to protect the faithful. Here, psychologists, anthro-pologists, and contemporary firewalking instructors agree on the important role taken by the power and necessity of belief.

There is also a strong possibility that several factors may operate simultaneously. A Fijian firewalker, who believes that it is his spiritual deity who protects him from the fire adeptly summarizes the overlapping of several hypotheses:

It's really mind over matter…. There are … endless incantations until each man is prepared to do just about anything. It's like hypnosis.[107]

Spiritual and physical hypotheses for firewalking may blend, each gracefully allowing for and including the precepts of the other. If so, the basis for a multi-level explanation of this phenomenon emerges: Belief can build upon some natural phenomenon and can evoke other natural processes. Further research is needed, but, from what is already known about fire immunity, we must take seriously the conclusion of Kane who emphasized that "there appears to be more than a little objective truth in the communicants' assertion that 'it takes faith' to handle fire."[108]

Chapter 4
Learning To Walk On Fire

It is the mind that maketh good or ill,
That maketh wretch or happy, rich or poor.

Edmund Spencer, *The Faerie Queene*

1. Three Weeks Beyond the Limits:
I Become a Firewalking Instructor

"Do I want to become a firewalking instructor?" I asked myself when I received a brochure from Tolly and Peggy Burkan entitled, "WANTED: FIREWALKING INSTRUCTORS." In the brochure Tolly explained that he wants to work with individuals who are ready to break through their own limitations and learn to conduct firewalking workshops. Three weeks (May 5-25, 1984), he promised, will be sufficient to master this new "profession."

Despite the strange nature of this proposal, my first impulse was "yes!". Then all of my rational objections came in: time constraints, financial problems, etc., etc. After a few hours thinking over these matters and meditating on the idea, I decided: Something like this can happen only once in a lifetime. I should not miss this opportunity. If Tolly accepts me, I will undertake this endeavor. Like he sometimes puts it, I was ready to "go for it." After many years of studying human potential I believed it was time to explore my own potential. I also wanted to better understand firewalking: What is ultimately going on? What are we dealing with—ordinary physical laws, striking manifestations of ordinary psychophysiological mechanisms of adaptation, or something yet completely unknown? I am offered this chance to peek into the unexplored.... Why should I neglect it?

There was not much time to think of these problems, since I was soon leaving for Europe. All of my arrangements had been made, all lectures and talks scheduled. I wrote Tolly asking him to accept me for his training, and shortly I left for Italy.

When I came back after a month of traveling, I found Tolly's letter in a huge pile of mail. It started with the word "CONGRATU-LATIONS" in capital letters and informed me that I was accepted into the course and had to be in Sacramento, California, before noon May 5. So, here it was, the beginning of my "journey beyond the limits."

Because the specific topic of firewalking workshops is over-coming fear and limitations through firewalking, we, 11 trainees (including three women) were first invited to break through our own limitations. To do this, Tolly proposed spelunking in California's largest cavern (which began by lowering ourselves 200 feet down on a rope), parachute jumping, spending a night alone in the forest, and similar "tests." Although some of them required a certain degree of physical fitness (which I lacked, but still had to meet the challenge), they seemed to be completely unrelated to the mysteries of firewalking. Breathing exercises, an American Indian sweat lodge, purification procedures and psychological group processing also did not seem directly related to our future "career." The course included logistics pertaining to organizing and conducting the workshops, as well as some public relations skills.

We participated in 10 firewalking workshops and, during the last week of the course, conducted some of them together as a team with Tolly. However, there were not many opportunities for re-search. At one of the workshops, the temperature of the embers was measured by a pyrometer to be 1,230°F. Therefore, we had an opportunity to convince ourselves that the figure usually cited by Tolly during the workshops (1,200-1,300°F) was not exaggerated.

After participating in 12 firewalking workshops (ten as a part of the course and two previously) I realized that there were no two identical firewalks in terms of subjective feelings and perceptions. Sometimes the coals felt quite hot, while at times the heat was virtually imperceptible. Twice the coals even felt cold as snow. Sometimes it was quite easy to step on the embers, and at other times I again went through a self-analysis, through my own fears and doubts, like before the very first walk: "Am I ready?"

I found that most of my lessons from this training course were not in the realm of mastering specific skills, but rather learning to view differently some familiar things and appreciate subtleties. For example, for some time I was quite preoccupied with the question of why some firewalkers get minor burns (blisters) while others emerged from the firebed completely unharmed. There was no obvious, easily detectible difference: The same individuals (e.g., members of our training group) who firewalked without getting blistered during one workshop blistered at another one. The only tendency I could pinpoint was that those who walked more confidently (not necessarily faster, often quite the opposite) got blisters more rarely. When I asked Peggy Burkan whether she had an "anti-blistering" technique, her answer was immediate: "Sometimes I get blisters, too. Most important, don't go onto the fire casually! When I started getting blisters, I had to upgrade my energy." She continued emphasizing not some mechanistic factors like walking quickly or slowly, but rather such intangible variables as "energy," "attitude," and "state of mind."

I learned one more lesson during our "graduation ceremony" on the last day of the course. The ceremony included an ancient American Indian ritual with feathers. While Tolly was putting sage on burning charcoal and praying, Peggy asked us to come up to her, one by one, as she moved the ritual feathers around the person, whispering something which was barely audible to the rest of the group. When I came up to her, I did not have any preconceptions or expectations as to what was supposed to happen—in fact, I respected the ritual but did not expect anything special. However, standing with my eyes closed, as was required, I felt a tremendous surge of energy through my body—the intensity of which I've never before experienced in my life. And then I heard Peggy's words: "Take the power!"

I realize that this sounds subjective and "unscientific," but I went to the training to experience it and to describe my experience, to seek and understand. Therefore, I feel it necessary to be detailed, thorough and honest in presenting my account.

After completing the training for becoming a firewalking instructor, I realized that I failed to find the sought-for answers concerning the nature of fire immunity. However, I did not consider this a failure: I *could* walk on fire myself, and I could conduct these workshops. My "journey beyond the limits" was not over!

After studying with Tolly, I have conducted a number of firewalking seminars not only in California, but also in Switzerland and Italy. I found that my tours in Europe were probably a more valuable education for me than for my students.

During my trips, I soon discovered that Europe is not like California. Although many had heard of firewalking in India or Greece, virtually no one had heard of firewalking workshops for ordinary people. Everyone was extremely cautious and talked about insurance and possible complications. At the same time, the idea stirred tremendous interest and curiosity. In this situation, I would first conduct a demonstration, at which I would describe major points of the workshop, show a video tape and then walk 2-3 times over a 8-10-foot coal bed. As a rule, after such a demonstration, which was extensively followed up in the press, I had an opportunity to conduct actual seminars on "Overcoming Fear and Limiting Beliefs Through Firewalking." In the press, I often was portrayed as someone who possesses "psychic" powers or unusual gifts which allegedly permit me to walk on fire. I strongly opposed these speculations, emphasizing that I can teach anyone to do the same, but most reporters preferred to preserve some veil of mystery around it.

To my surprise, most of the European participants in firewalking workshops were quite open to accepting this startling human ability and had little difficulty in incorporating it into their world view. It must be noted, however, that a number of the participants had some acquaintance with psychic phenomena and/or psychic healing. Some were extremely interested in discussing and exploring the spiritual implications of firewalking and regarded the seminar as a profound spiritual experience.

I have come to prefer smaller seminars (from 10 to 20 individuals), in which all the participants can relax and explore their fears, problems, and goals, and the ways to achieve them. My purpose is not to get as many individuals as possible to participate in the actual firewalk, but rather to lead them to explore their limitations and psychological problems and to understand their potential. On the contrary, I try almost to discourage them from firewalking, making it clear that if at the end of the evening I am the only one who traverses the coals, I will be not disappointed or offended. In this framework, a firewalk becomes an emotional peak of the evening, but not its objective. In my European seminars usually about half of the participants (unlike over 80% in the United States) chose to firewalk and became almost as excited and exhilarated as Californians. I do not have exact statistics, but I found that many fewer participants were getting blisters. In one case, a small blister appeared two days after the firewalk, when the person was convinced by his friends that it was impossible not to get burned.

I am glad to see that the interest in firewalking around the world is continually growing. Ilyas Abdulkhakimov, a Soviet engineer from the town of Grozny (north of the Caucasus region), decided to repeat this feat after he learned of Valery Avdeyev's firewalking demonstrations. Later he commented about his attempt as follows:

> When you have a fairly clear picture about the human organism, you realize that the peak of our physical and mental potential most often manifests in extreme situations. I hold Valery Avdeyev in high regard for his courage in deciding to master the ancient art of walking on hot coals... And so, here I stand before the glowing coals... In order to attain the necessary psychophysiological state, I repeat lines of verse which I have specially chosen for this purpose. I persuade myself that I will be successful. I am so convinced of a positive outcome that I feel little emotion at the end of these experiments.[1]

I firewalked many times but I still feel much more than "little emotion" after crossing the fire. My thoughts often return to the chant that I heard several years after I had completed the "firewalking training":

We are a new people
We are an old people
We are the same people
Deeper than before.

Have I changed as a result of my "firewalking journeys"? ... I
feel in some ways I certainly did. But don't we all change as we go
through life? In this connection I would like to conclude this section
with an excerpt from my personal diary written several years after
my introduction to firewalking and containing my reflections on the
issue of psychological change:

"... Some authors believe that such experiences and practices as firewalking lead people to psychological change
and growth. Others object that this is a misconception, that
a grown-up person cannot change: If people talk about
'change,' it is all superficial and nothing more than their
wishful thinking. I believe that perhaps these views are not
as opposing as they sound. Could it be that, as opposite as
they seem, both are right nonetheless? The inner core of a
person, what we call inner Self, True Self, never changes.
But do we really know our True Self? What we do know is
our everyday personality with all the thick 'layers of
conditioning,' of trying to adapt, to please, to be loved; the
layers of worry, doubt, fear and guilt so readily acquired
throughout the life in this world. Actually, what we are
familiar with, not just in others, but ourselves as well, is
only a 'false personality,' as called by Georges Gurdjieff.

"... Once in my childhood I saw in the yard, under a bench,
two rubles apparently dropped accidentally by someone. I
did not pick them up and was somehow totally confident
that this person would remember where he had lost them
and return to look for them. When I mentioned this to my
mother she was shocked. 'Why didn't you take them?' she
asked with reproach. 'How could I take them? They aren't
mine....' My answer was probably as surprising to her as
her response was to me. I could not comprehend how I
could take something that did not belong to me—I just

couldn't! I remember this now not to remind myself of how 'good' I was, but with great regret: where has this little girl gone? ... I certainly did change. Oh, I don't steal and still have difficulty to being evasive or not completely truthful for the sake of 'politeness,' but I'm far gone from that girl who could not make herself to pick up the two rubles which at that point in time belonged to no one!

"I feel, however, that although I probably lost something I definitely gained considerably more. Instead of childish naivete I have life experience and knowledge of the higher purpose. And if I still continue to trust people, despite some bitter experiences in the past, this is not because I am still naive but because I want to believe in people, in a divine spark in their souls, in all of us, in each and everyone living on the planet called Earth."

2. Fear into Power: The Firewalking Experience

After studying with Tolly Burkan and conducting many firewalking seminars myself, I realized that my accounts of firewalking would be incomplete if I did not learn and write about another well-known firewalking instructor, Tony Robbins. An opportunity presented itself quite soon, in Spring of 1985, since Tony was coming to San Francisco with his famous "Fear into Power: The Firewalk Experience" seminar. I decided to come and play along. Although I did not make a secret of the fact that I myself teach firewalking seminars, I thought it would be better if I came as a writer and editor of *Psi Research* and try to participate fully with an open mind, as I had at Tolly Burkan's workshop.

The more than one hundred participants constituted quite a diverse group, the youngest being a 6-year old boy and the oldest a 64-year-old woman, with the majority in their early and middle 30's. Waiting for the ceremony to begin, most tried to hide their anxiety, some meditated sitting on the floor of the hotel hall, and only a few looked quite casual, as if just coming to watch a movie. Many did not look like the kind of people who ordinarily attend self-development seminars. As I learned later, quite a number were concerned that the seminar was being videotaped, since they did not want anyone to know that they went to such an unusual and "stupid" event.

After the audience showed a growing impatience, 25-year-old Tony impetuously appeared on the stage, radiating energy and confidence and instantly creating the impression of a charismatic leader. After a brief introduction he went into an explanation of Neuro-Linguistic Programming (NLP) techniques. This system of knowledge about human communication, developed by John Grinder, a Ph.D. in linguistics, and Richard Bandler, a computer expert with a background in Gestalt therapy, and widely known under the abbreviation of NLP, has been described in detail elsewhere.[2] Hence I will only outline some techniques as they were explained by Tony.

One of these, called *modeling*, means systematic duplication of human behavior, thereby affording the opportunity to duplicate any form of human excellence. According to Tony, in order to achieve what has been achieved by a successful person, one should: (1) duplicate the person's belief system ("whether you believe you can, or whether you believe you can't, you are right"); (2) duplicate the person's "mental syntax" (which can be assessed, among other factors, through observation of the person's eye movements); and (3) duplicate the person's physiology (in particular, one can change his/her physiology through breathing).

Another method, *Ericksonian embedded (subliminal) commands*, represents a technique of covert hypnosis: while pronouncing certain words (commands), the speaker makes a specific sign or gesture which is supposed to influence the participants' unconscious mind, ultimately leading to automatic implementation of the commands in response to this gesture. Throughout the evening, Tony made this 'covert' gesture very obviously (deliberately, I believe, so as to enforce the participants' belief that they had received something that would aid them in firewalking successfully). Examples of commands I found being used and emphasized in this way were: "totally responsible," "totally committed," "totally congruent," "I have so much power," and "change" (perhaps I missed some others).

Tony used another method called *anchoring* in the preparation. According to this concept, a repeated display of a specific sign or gesture in response to another individual's particular mental state will subsequently trigger this state every time the gesture is made. If the individual himself or herself makes a specific gesture several times (e.g., clenches his/her right fist) while in a particular state, then repeating this gesture will invariably put the individual in the same state.

Interspersing a semi-scholarly/semi-entertaining narrative with typical elements of a "human potential" seminar (with the participants creating a "massage train," hugging each other, dancing and handclapping), Tony led the audience to an understanding of how one can achieve the state which he calls "congruency" ("the inner and the outer is aligned")—in my opinion, the same state of deep concentration that Tolly Burkan calls "paying attention 100%." To illustrate how powerful this state can be, Tony did an impressive demonstration of board-breaking.

Although we started at 7 p.m., the actual time of the firewalk was after midnight. Three coal beds, 12 feet long, were prepared very thoroughly, which, in my observation, is an important factor for a safe firewalk, especially for first-time walkers. To the sound of drums reminiscent of traditional firewalking ceremonies, Tony took several deep breaths and strolled across one of the coal beds. Then he and his two assistants started working with people (who, as instructed, had already formed three lines) checking to see whether the participants about to walk were "in state": breathing deep, eyes rolled upward, right fist clenched.

Despite the fact that I have firewalked more than 50 times (I stopped counting my firewalks after 50 a while ago), I found these recommendations to concentrate on breathing and look upward to be a bit distracting. Usually, before stepping onto the coals, I first look down for a moment, then directly ahead and experience a "letting go" feeling, surrendering to the "inner wisdom of my mind and body," as I often put it. At this moment I do not feel like paying conscious attention to any aspect of my bodily processes, including breathing. I just stand in front of the pit until I feel an increase in energy and a sudden inner impulse, "You are ready, go!" Usually it is almost impossible for me to assess how much time passes from when I come into "position" in front of the coals until I step onto them, but my friends have assured me that "my state of timelessness" does not usually last more than a few seconds.

When I came to the front of the "firewalking line," a girl, Robbins' assistant, shouted at me, "You are not 'in state'!" I tried to reassure her, "I've done this before!" "No, I can't let you go!" she insisted. I decided that there was no point in arguing with her— "When in Rome..." Okay, I'd try to play by these rules and use the split second between her word "go!" and my actually stepping onto the coals to create my "state of timelessness."

"Go!" I went—perfect; my confidence returned, the coals felt cool and smooth. But other than that, I didn't lose touch with the surrounding world, whereas others, chanting "cool moss" and walking blindly with their eyes upward, fists clenched, and wild facial expressions, stopped only when they were told by an assistant to do so; it looked as if some of them did not even feel that they were already off the coals.

Although Tony remarked that the use of NLP techniques reduces the risk of being burned during a firewalk, I would like to emphasize the conclusion of Julianne Blake in her excellent study: *The differences in techniques used by Burkan and Robbins "did not make any difference in the number of people who blistered."* [3] In fact, I think that overemphasis of a particular technique may even be dangerous: If one *believes* that firewalking with a facilitator who does not use NLP is unsafe, but still chooses to firewalk, one can be burned. Tony claims that, using NLP techniques, he can easily manipulate people. Nevertheless, he could not convince me by the use of these techniques that NLP was essential for a successful firewalk. In addition, I would like to cite Tolly Burkan's note published in his newsletter, *The Sundoor*:

NLP and Firewalking

Tony Robbins learned firewalking from Tolly Burkan and is one of several dozen firewalking instructors who teach it using the format of "overcoming fear and limiting beliefs" developed by Tolly and Peggy Dylan. What makes Tony's firewalks different is that he also includes information on Neuro-Linguistic Programming. People have contacted us asking if NLP is responsible for people not getting burned at a firewalk. Based on research conducted over the past two years, it seems that NLP in no way reduces the risk of getting burned. In fact, several people have been badly burned using the NLP approach. Scientists have not yet discovered a bottom-line explanation for the firewalking phenomenon, but we know that any claims for NLP being responsible are not true. At one firewalk, a renowned Neuro-Linguistic Professional used NLP techniques to traverse the coals and was the only person burned. No one else at the firewalk used NLP and no one else was burned. We trust that in the future scientists will unravel the mystery of firewalking. If you are aware of any new research in this area, please let us know.

■

I am now totally convinced that the crucial point in firewalking is the person's belief system: If one *believes* in the Leidenfrost principle, one can firewalk safely; if one believes in NLP that would certainly do; and if one totally, unconditionally believes in the protective and healing power of the mind and body (the "gut-level" belief emphasized by Julianne Blake after Dr. Andrew Weil[4])—one *can* walk on fire!

I'd like to make one more point. In Tolly Burkan's seminars a person firewalks when he or she feels they are ready. Tony's approach is different: Either he or his assistants say "go" when they feel that the person is ready. Among the common obstacles preventing people from succeeding is not only fear, but doubt and indecision. I believe that Tony's seminars, as powerful as they are, do not give people an opportunity to deal with these issues: Who will be there to tell us "go!" in a real life situation? It is true that the person first has an opportunity to decide whether to walk or not when he/she chooses to join the line. But there's still a difference between getting in line ("about as exciting as a cafeteria line," as one of the participans, Dennis Stillings,[5] mentioned) and actually making the decision to step onto the coals without someone telling you that you are "in state" and you can firewalk safely.

What about the results of the seminar? A lengthy article in *Life* magazine quotes Norma Barretta, a San Pedro, California, psychotherapist who claims that she "has treated more than two dozen fire-walk graduates" of Tony's seminars. "His hyperbole—'You can make someone fall in love with you in five minutes'—fosters grandiose expectations." "It stirs up a tremendous amount that some people are not equipped to handle," Barretta points out. "That can be devastating."[6] I believe that these overexpectations could appear only as a result of a serious misunderstanding, for Tony repeatedly emphasized, "To be successful you should learn how to handle frustration and how to handle rejection." In other words, he does not advise participants to expect immediate success; perhaps success will come only after a hundredth or even thousandth attempt, but it will certainly come if we are persistent, have energy and skill to pursue our goals and do not allow fear to stop us from doing what we want to do. Robbins Research Institute, directed by Tony, proclaims its objective (or, as they call it, "mission") as follows:

To free and empower the largest number of people in the shortest period of time to know and demonstrate that they are in complete control of their living experience now.

Tony Robbins has described some of his ideas (which, in his "modest" opinion, are intended to change the world) in his book, *Unlimited Power*.[7] An ambitious young fellow, Tony does not hide that he uses firewalking to promote NLP ("The Firewalk Experience" is the first part of "The Mind Revolution" seminar which deals with the fundamentals of neuro-linguistic programming) and to generate income for himself and those who are working with him. His firewalks no longer take place in back yards of private houses, but rather at fashionable hotels.

... The evening is over. Almost everyone has been literally "touched by fire" and looks that way. In the midst of the elated crowd, however, I notice a woman in her middle forties, looking sad and disappointed. "Did you walk?" I ask. "No," she answers curtly and does not appear willing to elaborate further. Nevertheless, while not suppressing alternative opinions or my negative attitude toward the overt commercialism surrounding Tony's gatherings, I do not want to understate the value of what Tony Robbins does. Almost everyone with whom I spoke after the seminar radiated exhilaration and happiness, expressing a feeling of having accomplished something very significant and made a giant step forward towards a happy and successful life.

After participating in Tony Robbins' seminar, I decided that it was time for me to witness one of the traditional firewalking rituals. A year later I went to Greece to observe an ancient fire-dancing ceremony.

3. Fire Dancing in Greece: Personal Encounters

Langadas, May 23, 1986

"The phenomenon [of fire dancing] ... is not new and unique to a group of people known as '*anastenarides*.' Its roots may be found in pre-Christian and Byzantine Christian times....

"... [These] individuals ... use their religious belief system to protect the skin of their feet from burning and they are persuaded that nothing will happen to them as long as their faith lasts. Faith to whatever thing, living entity or supreme being may work miracles for those who possess it.

"The magic of believing has been known throughout ages to enable individuals to perform extraordinary acts that seem impossible for the powers that man is known to have. Faith and belief may become a dynamo which propels individuals through meditation, contemplation, suggestion on oneself and on others to harness the unlimited energies (we all have) of our subconscious minds in order to achieve 'just about anything' we seek as a goal.

"... Besides faith, the anastenarides undergo a conditioning through certain movements, by playing their music, by inhaling incense, through specific verbal and nonverbal expressions, by participating in the procession of animal sacrifice, by using the power of autosuggestion, heterosuggestion and collective suggestion and other. This type of ingroup solidarity and unity that characterizes the anastenarides facilitates the development of specific group psychology and dynamics among themselves and serves as mysticism, exaltation and ecstasy for all the members. All the above conditioning assists the anastenarides in reaching a transcendental state and triggers certain internal states in their psychological dimension which apparently ... [cause them] not to feel the pain and not to burn their skin....

"The phenomenon of firewalking by anastenarides ... still continues to be a scientific enigma and challenge for scientists of all fields for further study, analysis and interpretation."

George Flouris, Ph.D.
Visiting Professor of the University of Crete[8]

■

After an exhausting 6-hour drive from Athens, we came to the main square of Langadas (a small town 10 miles away from Saloniki) around seven in the evening. "We" refers to the three of us, including my two guides and translators—Mr. Costopoulus Nicos, the owner of *Nea Prooptiki* (New Perspectives) magazine from Athens, and a reporter from this magazine.

Langadas is the only Greek town which has held the firewalking/ fire-dancing ceremonies publicly and continuously since 1947. On the square, preparations for lighting the fire are in progress: kindling is placed first, followed by larger pieces of wood on the top. The fire is expected to be started around 7:30 p.m. and left to burn for about two hours, forming a large mound of hot coals.

We were in Langadas to see the ancient ritual of fire dancing (anastenaria) and to talk to anastenarides—those who follow this old tradition. The Archianastenaris (chief fire dancer), Stamatis Liuros, met us near his house. A quiet man in his early 40's, he radiates an aura of calm and self-assurance. Although I am well familiar with the ritual from literature, I turn to Liuros, asking him to explain what is going on at the moment and what will happen later.

Stamatis Liuros: At this point, all the anastenarides are getting together at my house, which is called the *konaki*. They will dance and pray, so that later they can participate in the ceremony. This dance may last 10 minutes, 15 minutes, half an hour, or an hour, depending on the desire of the chief of the anastenarides. The dance is in honor of the Saints Constantine and Helen. It's not a dance for fun, it's a dance expressing their faith in the saints.

When they finish dancing [in the konaki], the dance will continue into the street, and to the special place where the fire dancing will take place. At first during the fire dancing they dance with the music of their instruments, but then they continue dancing when the music stops. They will come back for some period of rest and later, around midnight, they have a feast in the honor of the saints. That's it, until the next year.

I started fire dancing when I was 19 years old. First I was just looking at the dance. My father was an anastenaris.... One day I suddenly found myself dancing on the fire and did not get burned. The only thing you must have is *faith*—that's about it, nothing else, *nothing else*, works.

Later I learned from Dr. Vittoria Manganas, a Greek psychiatrist who has been conducting extensive research of fire dancing for many years, that Stamatis' first fire dance was not as spontaneous an event as he chose to present it, because his mother was a renowned anastenarissa and his father as well. He already knew everything about the ritual and had all the training from his family. For many years his parents were trying to encourage him to dance, but he didn't choose to do so until he was 19.

Since I studied firewalking and had anticipated this opportunity to come to Greece for a long time, I had another question to ask:

LV: Can anyone else, a Greek or a foreigner, dance on fire, if he/she has the desire and the faith— for example, someone like me?

Stamatis Liuros: If one is a good Christian and one believes very strongly, he/she may do it. The problem here is that we dance on fire because we have faith. If you dance, it would probably not be exactly faith, but you concentrate within yourself, you get the power not to get burned, and that's it. There is quite a difference between you and me.

LV: I agree with you that the most important factor is faith. And although our faiths may not be identical, we all have the same God and live on one Earth with the same God.

SL: Of course there is only one God, and you and I believe in the same God. The only difference is that my faith starts with Saint Constantine. In addition, we have a special way of dancing that you don't know. It's not simple—the temperature of the fire is about 400°C. If I were dancing alone, I would agree to take you, but the others would be against it—you will be considered a foreign body within the total body of faith.

LV: I certainly won't insist, and I don't want to intrude in your ritual. And yet, if someone wants to dance could you give your power of protection? In this case, it's not that someone who is not an anastenaria follower would be able to dance on fire, but it's *you* who would protect the dancer only for this special night.

SL: I agree that the extension of power from me to you is available, and I have no problem with it.

The only problem is that the rest of the people wouldn't accept you. In addition, if a foreigner dances, it will take longer for the fire to go out than it usually takes. And what is the reason that *you* want to walk on that *special* fire, at this special place here in Greece?

LV: Because I believe this is one of the oldest places where people walk and dance on fire. I first heard about firewalking and dancing as performed in Bulgaria and in Greece. I feel that I want to share this very special tradition. But at the same time I feel that if it's meant to happen, it would happen. If not, I will never insist since something like this can't be forced.

SL: You are a scientist. I am a simple human being. If you were a common person, it wouldn't be a problem for me.

LV: I *am* a common person, because what scientists do is seek—they want to understand. Furthermore, there is a difference between rigid, narrow-minded scientists who only look at their numbers, and people like me who search and want to understand what nature is, what the world is, and how to come closer to God.

SL: Belief is not searched for, it comes from the Holy Bible, and this is the only explanation. I don't believe any scientist would be able to dance on fire. Scientists sometimes believe they are better than other people.

Our tradition is very old and has a special meaning for us. All the songs we sing before the dance are war songs, in honor of the victories we had in combating the Byzantine empire. We celebrate these victories.

My family came from Eastern Rumelia. All the people who came from there were not slaves for 400 years like the rest of Greeks, but for 600 years.... The custom of fire dancing started there slowly, and then it moved down here. Dr. Tanagras, the first President of the Greek Society for Psychical Research, went to Bulgaria and found the custom there, and then he traced the people here, in Langadas. First fire dancing was done secretly, because they did not know how people would react, and then when Dr. Tanagras brought them out, they are doing it openly in the square.

The dancers are called anastenarides [those who sigh] because sometimes in the dance someone would say aaahh!—not from pain, but in relief. It's the name given to them, but it doesn't represent them. I would call myself "pyrovatis"—the one who walks on fire.

LV: Fire dancing is quite an old tradition, and it is surprising to me that, as far as I know, throughout the ages women have always participated in this ceremony, although I have an impression that in former times women were not allowed to do anything of importance.

SL: Yes, but we believe that the first one who started it was a woman—Saint Helen. The custom of fire dancing is not a religious custom but also a philosophical and national one. It's our national pride.

In the konaki, the anastenarides are dancing to the powerful, inspiring music of a three-stringed Thracian lyre, a bagpipe, and a large two-headed drum. As they dance, some of them are holding icons of Saint Constantine in their hands or large red kerchiefs known as *simadia* (literally "sign" or "mark"). Some of the dancers, with very peculiar looks on their faces, are apparently in a trancelike, ecstatic state; some look like crying or close to crying.

About half an hour later the dancers are leaving the house, and I am introduced to anthropologist Maria Dede. Our conversation returns to the question I asked earlier—whether others, including foreigners, can or may participate in the ceremony:

Maria Dede: We do not deny that others can walk on fire. But this fire is especially for the believers in Saints Constantine and Helen. Others don't know the special way they must dance in order to coordinate with the rest of the dancers and not to disturb them. Whenever a foreigner joins the group, the whole thing is turned into a circus—everybody starts laughing. And trying to do it on your own, without being in rhythm with the others—you weren't trained this way—you may get burned. Fire is fire—it's 400-600°C.

I cannot see well, I don't have the speed they have, and I know that I may create a problem for them. That's the reason I don't dance. I've been here every year for 18 years. I like them—I know everyone of them and everything, I believe. I am a researcher but I also am a believer—although I don't know how these two things can match.

LV: I think they can match quite well!

MD: I still feel that the anastenarides have their own, special way of doing it. Last year we had a man from Poland who danced on fire, but he upset the rest of the dancers—they started crying and they were very upset and distressed.

Later Dr. Manganas emphasized that, in her opinion, most likely Dede, who felt very strongly against the participation of non-Greeks in the ritual, to a large extent imposed her own attitude on the anastenarides. I believe this is perhaps an exaggeration since many fire dancers have had similar opinions on the issue for quite a long time:

The anastenarides believe that Saint Constantine ordains who is to become a firewalker. They do not actively seek new members. In fact they become upset when outsiders try to firewalk.[9]

■

In the square at the center of Langadas, the atmosphere is one of excited and joyful expectation on this warm spring evening in Northern Greece. The fire is burning not on a flat surface, but on a small elevation—something which I have never seen in a firewalk. Dozens and dozens of people are coming, looking for the most comfortable places to sit down and observe the ceremony.

My guide-reporter asks a 7-year-old boy why the fire dancers are not burned. His answer was immediate: "They trap the fire. The fire is burned in the trap, and it can't harm them, they are safe." Such a statement seems to be quite consistent with the opinions of those who believe that firewalkers may exert a kind of psychokinetic influence over the fire.

The reporter also asks opinions of other spectators. One replied, "It's not the power of God, it's not the power of Christ, it's not the power of Saint Constantine—it's their own power that protects them." (This is closer to what I believe to be true.) The intrepid reporter related yet another observation of the villagers: "During and after the dance the dancers' hands and feet are ice cold." This is an interesting confirmation of my assumption that firewalkers and dancers achieve, intuitively or purposefully, a certain degree of self-regulation—similar to some firewalkers in the United States who imagine that they walk not on red-hot embers, but on pieces of ice which cannot burn them. Dr. Manganas stated that it is the belief of many anastenarides that Saint Helen or the Virgin Mary pours ice-cold water in front of them on the fire before they start dancing on the coals.

The reporter turned to me with another question. We first saw dancers in the konaki apparently in a special, altered state of mind, in ecstasy. Then most of them broke this state—they chatted with the spectators, explained, gave directions. How can they go onto hot coals afterward? I expressed an opinion that perhaps because it's not their first fire dance. Since most of them repeat the ceremony year after year, for many years—they are able to quickly re-enter and re-access this particular state. The body and mind "remember" the state, and it probably can be achieved automatically and almost instantaneously, much as I experienced personally during the Tony Robbins seminar.

The coals are spread into a large glowing circle. They are gradually dying out, flickering and growing dim, declining and flickering again, as if they were struggling against dying, extinguishing, disappearing into nothingness. But, despite their struggle, they are still dimming, turning into ash, and finally only occasional red spots are glowing in the darkness. The temperature is still, I believe, no less than 200°-300°C—quite sufficient to get burned. I hear the music—the dancers are coming. The musicians with their instruments are in front, followed by a fire dancer holding a pot of incense. Beside him are two other dancers holding two big white candles, and finally other barefoot dancers come, some of them holding their icons.

The lights of the square are turned on, but still it's dark. I try to move closer to see their faces, although the police attempt to keep observers at a distance. Still, I am fortunate to get close enough to see that some of the dancers are clearly in an altered state, in ecstasy they look through people without a sign of recognition in their eyes, as if not seeing anyone or anything. With other dancers, I could definitely maintain an eye contact—they seemed to be looking inside but still were able to see me and other people around them. From 25-30 dancers, roughly about two thirds appeared to be in a state of ecstasy and one third did not. I noticed an old woman who was standing on the embers for at least three seconds, during which time she bent down and put her hands on the ashes, as if playing with them. But most of the anastenarides were always in movement, dancing with small steps, on and off the ashes, off and on.

It is very interesting that the fire-dancers have a custom of entering the fire from the west and going towards the east, although no one could tell me why. Their answers were that we found it as it is and we follow it. I wondered if the reason is that we who come from the West need to learn the wisdom of the East, the wisdom of Indian yogis and Chinese qigong masters and acupuncture practitioners who are familiar with the "secret wisdom of the mind and body"—that very wisdom which permits anastenarides to dance unharmed on fire.

■

Athens, May 24, 1986

The next evening I was back to Athens and was sitting with Dr. Vittoria Manganas, discussing my observations in Langadas. She remembered that the previous Archianastenaris, Stamatis' father, used to stand on the coals for several seconds, take hot coals and ashes in his hands and put them on his face, as if he were washing it.

Makrakis cites an instance when a woman anastenarissa crossed the fire on her knees and sustained no burns.[10] Various researchers observed many dancers as they stooped on the edge of the fire, pounding the coals with their open palms and shouting: "*Stahti na yini! Stahti na yini!*" (May it turn to ashes! May it turn to ashes!) Fire dancers believe that by reducing the firewood to ashes all evil will be placed under control and that the successful firewalking will usher in a year with less illness, death, failure of the crops and other problems.[11]

Dr. Manganas also mentioned an experiment with anastenarides, conducted by a group from the Free University of Berlin together with Dr. Christos Xenakis from Greece, a neurologist who studied in West Germany. Since they believed that the release of endorphins might be responsible for blocking pain during the fire dance, they injected intravenously four anastenarides with Naloxone (an endorphin antagonist) 30 minutes before the fire dancing. However, not one of the dancers reported pain, burn or other noticeable effects.

Later, we finished our more serious conversation and were sitting in Dr. Manganas' apartment, listening to taped songs of the fire dancers. She tried to translate some of them to me. After struggling through Greek and Italian (Dr. Manganas is of Italian origin), I wrote down the beautiful English words:

I'll not be burned
And you'll not be burned,

But how can we illuminate the night
And drive away the darkness? ...

In my inner vision, I was still seeing a blazing fire in darkness,
and the song sounded to me like, "How can we illuminate the night
with faith and drive away the darkness of doubt and skepticism?"
We all are trying!

4. Where Scholarly and Mystical Teachings Intersect: Ancient Wisdom and Contemporary Psychology

Many enthusiasts view firewalking as an illustration of our
ability to create our own reality, i.e., that by merely changing in
mental attitude we can change our reality and make the "impossible" indeed possible. Daniel Gunther, a medical professional,
commented after his firewalk with Buddhist devotees in Brazil:

All of a sudden my sense of the possible, my entire
framework for how I view the world, changed, and it was
not when I walked over the coals, but *when I decided to do
it*—when I took my shoes off, rolled up my pants, and knew
that I was going to walk across.[12]

The idea that a change in our thoughts and views changes our
experience is by no means a new one. In various forms, although not
related to something as "drastic" as firewalking, it can be found in
literature and poetry, in writings of ancient and contemporary
mystics and in so-called "channeled books," which sometimes take
the concept to the extreme:[13]

Your experience in the world of physical matter flows
outward from the center of your inner psyche. Then you
perceive this experience. Exterior events, circumstances
and conditions are meant as a kind of living feedback.
Altering the state of the psyche automatically alters the
physical circumstances.[14]

Whatever I see reflects my thoughts. It is my thoughts that tell me where I am and what I am. The fact that I see a world in which there is suffering and loss and death shows me that I am seeing only the representation of my ... thoughts, and am not allowing my real thoughts to cast their beneficient light on what I see.[15]

I found, however, that in looking for the evidence that we all, consciously or unconsciously, create our own reality in our every-day life, we can easily uncover them without venturing into something as "esoteric" as firewalking. The fact that our unconscious beliefs and attitudes, at least to a degree, determine our perception of the world around us has been well established both in contemporary psychology and in our everyday life experience. Psychologist Lawrence LeShan summarizes this perspective as follows:

Whether reality is "friendly" or "unfriendly," "nice" or "not nice," "loving" or "hostile" seems to depend largely on us. We know this so well, it is said repeatedly in cliches: "When you are in love, everything is beautiful." "The pessimist sees the glass half-empty, the optimist sees it as half-full." "Beauty is in the eye of the beholder." "Keep your eye on the doughnut, not on the hole." We know that to one person the sea, or the desert or the mountains or the city, is beautiful and restful. To another person it is threatening, hostile, ugly, upsetting. One morning we arise and see the beauty in the snow. Another morning we see it as a troublesome mass of white, ugly material to be gotten through. To a lover, the loved one is beautiful. Another may strongly disagree.[16]

In other words, as the poet John Milton wrote, "The mind ... can make a heaven of hell, a hell of heaven."

One vivid example of scholarly demonstration of this concept can be found in my native Soviet Union or, more precisely, in Soviet Georgia, in research conducted by the Georgian psychologist and philosopher Dr. Dmitri Uznadze and his followers.

For a Soviet psychologist, the words "Uznadzean set theory" are associated with a number of experiments demonstrating that certain attitudes or "sets" determine a subject's perceptual acts. Let me describe one of these experiments known as the "Uznadze effect."[17] The subject is asked to focus his eyes on the screen of a tachistoscope and is told: "Two circles will be shown briefly. Each time you see the circles, I want you to tell me if they are equal in size or not. If you think they are unequal, tell me which circle appears larger to you." Then two unequal circles (20 and 28 millimeters in diameter) are shown several times. After these initial or "set" trials, two equal circles (24 mm) are flashed onto the screen. The effect usually obtained is the illusion that the circle shown at the former position of the 28 mm circle is "smaller," and the one that takes the place of the 20 mm circle is "larger."[18]

Uznadze explained this phenomenon as the result of a "set condition" formed during the initial trials: "As a result of the initial trials a special condition is created in the subject, a condition that cannot be explained as any state of consciousness."[19] The interaction of the critical stimulus, equal circles, with this set conditions causes the illusory effect, i.e., the mind of the subject is "set" to see unequal circles and thus perceives the equal ones as unequal.

Uznadze repeated the initial trial (with unequal circles) with the subject under hypnosis and then, with the subject awake, showed him the critical, equal objects. The effect was exactly the same as when the initial trials were conducted in an ordinary state: the illusory vision of equal objects perceived as unequal. His further "set" experiments with drawings and objects (i.e., equal/unequal balls) uncovered similar visual, weight, and size illusions. Uznadze concluded:

> Phenomena discovered in our experiments unambiguously show that in the psyche we have not only conscious but also nonconscious processes, which can be characterized as the domain of sets.[20]

Another example of how our inner attitudes determine our perceptions of the outer world can be found in conventional psychological tests commonly accepted in this country. The most popular among these projective tests are the Rorschach Inkblot Test and TAT, the Thematic Apperception Test.

The inkblot test, developed by Swiss psychologist Hermann

Rorschach in the 1920's, consists of a set of ten standardized inkblots. They vary in color, shading, form and complexity. Subjects are shown each blot and asked to describe what they see in it. Psychologists found that one subject may perceive one of the blots as "flowers blooming in a field" while another subject may perceive the same blot as "blood dripping from a dagger."[21]

The TAT consists of 20 sketches depicting various scenes and life situations. The term "apperception" means "readiness to perceive"; the word "thematic" refers to the existence of themes or recurring plots. The subject is shown each sketch and is asked to make up a story about the people in it. Again, one can see an assailant with a gun in the picture while another perceives there a lover with flowers.

In this connection, another question arises: Is everyone of us alone in our perception of the external world or do we transmit our perception to other people and to other living beings? Results of some ESP tests suggest that we may "project" our perceptions and ideas onto others.[22] A Soviet study showed that even plants are sensitive to our projected thoughts. The researchers in Moscow found that it was possible to stimulate the growth of plants by transmitting the emotional signal "sun and water," and to retard growth with the signal "dry wind and salty soil."[23] Thus, we can communicate to each other what we, consciously or unconsciously, choose to project to the world: our limiting or releasing beliefs, our fears or fearlessness, our differences or our ultimate unity.

Contemporary experiments in psychokinesis also support the popular notion of the mind-over-matter power. While in the Soviet Union, I met several times with Nina Kulagina from Leningrad who could move objects without touching them. The objects included a compass needle, matches, cigarettes, empty matchboxes, and other wooden, metal and plastic objects. These apparent psychokinetic (PK) abilities of Kulagina attracted attention of numerous Soviet and Western researchers and were tested at Moscow University, the Physical Institute, and the Research Institute of Radio Engineering and Electronics of the USSR Academy of Sciences.[24]

Perhaps my analogies may seem simplistic but I intentionally want them to be uncomplicated and vivid. I have always been fascinated by encountering instances when ancient beliefs of shamans and mystics are corroborated by modern scientific findings.

Today we see that in some areas they do seem to blend together, demonstrating to us that it is indeed in our power to create our own reality. Is this power capable of protecting us from fire?

5. Beyond Firewalking

After several years of being "inside" firewalking, studying and teaching, I can say that, like Tolly Burkan, I am still in awe of it. I am fascinated with the power of this metaphor for assisting individuals in their psychological and spiritual growth. I am also fascinated with this magnificent demonstration of the power of *faith* to change our reality and to create another reality in which even mighty fire cannot harm us. I agree with Greek fire dancer Stamatis Liuros that to walk on fire, "the only thing you must have is *faith*— that's about it, nothing else, *nothing else*, works."[25] I agree with Robert Stuart Clifton, Abbot of Poh Ern Ssu Buddhist monastery in Singapore, who firewalked in the vicinity of Bangkok in 1955, that "if you have Faith, you can" walk on fire.[26] I agree with Hawaiian firewalkers that "faith and understanding are the essential qualifications."[27]

I believe that further research on firewalking is urgently needed, for it is here where we may find intriguing interconnections between our consciousness and the entire universe. On the other hand, if other than an "exotic" explanation is confirmed—say something simple, like an increase in the firewalker's perspiration rate providing protection (although I doubt that it is the case)—the meaning of the first step onto the blazing coals will not diminish in significance for those who dared to make it (it's known that one can be burned quite badly irrespective of the "mechanism" of protection). Neither would this knowledge reduce the power of firewalking as a metaphor for transforming fear into power (or into love) and as an indicator of the potential of the mind as healer. After all, even the perspiration rate varies greatly depending on the person's psychophysiological state and is not ordinarily under our voluntary control.

For many years only yoga practitioners could learn to voluntarily control their blood pressure and heart rate. Then, after biofeedback devices became an integral part of our lives, everyone could learn to do it within several hours, not years, as yogis did. However we do not discard biofeedback devices simply because their principle of operation is not a mystery for us, and this knowledge does not prevent the use of biofeedback for healing and self-regulation. With firewalking, it's still a miracle that our body (or better, mind/body) can adapt itself to such temperatures, whatever the "mechanism" is, and I can continue to teach "Overcoming Fear and Limiting Beliefs Through Firewalking" seminars without understanding the "mechanism." My purpose is a continuing exploration of what else we humans are capable of doing and achieving, especially in the area of healing.

I believe that not only a "perfect" firewalk, but also a minor burn or a blister could be beneficial for a person. Tolly Burkan once said: "People receive from a firewalk what they need. Some people need a lesson in humility more than a lesson in overcoming fear." Among many other considerations, one cannot exclude that some individuals may unconsciously "sabotage" success (this is known to be true not only for firewalking, but for other areas of life as well, e.g., sick people unconsciously resist becoming well and taking full responsibility in life). If they get burned during a firewalk, the surrounding world will remain as "simple" and "predictable" as it was before the firewalk, and not become a world in which the mind can stop fire from burning.

Buddhist monks in Brazil who practice firewalking believe that if one is suffering from an illness, one will have a pin burn on the foot on the acupuncture point that corresponds to the affected organ.[28] The fire supposedly burns the illness out through the acupuncture point. Psychologist and traveler Alberto Villoldo from California joined the Buddhist firewalkers in the outskirts of São Paulo and later described a healing effect of fire:

> I had a case of inflamed kidneys that had been bothering me for over a week. After crossing the fire, I found that I had a pin burn on my left foot that supposedly coincided with the kidney acupuncture point. Within three days my kidney condition had improved.[29]

I observed other instances when an individual blistered at the reflex zone of the foot reflecting a diseased organ. For example, a woman who had recently had a thyroid operation, found a painless blister at the corresponding reflex zone on the sole of her foot, as if she had an acupuncture or moxibustion treatment.

With great enthusiasm I repeat after Dr. Weil and his followers that apparently "the power that protects ... from burns can also cure disease,"[30] and when individuals awaken this power in themselves, spectacular healings may occur, on both somatic and psychological levels. Once I spoke with a man who was severely burned several years before, while rescuing his son from a room caught in flames. He has since been petrified of fire and often had nightmares that he was in flame again. After he came to one of the workshops and chose to firewalk, his fear of fire and nightmares completely disappeared. Others reported that they found strength for successful career change, for undertaking new ventures, re-establishing relationships and finding inner balance and harmony.

After hearing many of these informal testimonies, the authors decided to undertake a formal study of psychological effects of firewalking, the results of which constitute Part Two of the book. In this study, we were interested not in measuring the temperature of the coals and counting the number of steps taken by firewalkers, but rather in the effect this extraordinary event had on them. We wanted to know whether or not it changed their perceptions, attitudes, behavior, their views of the world and reality. We wanted to know what they experienced, whether their experiences had a transpersonal component and whether the firewalk had a lasting impact on their everyday lives.

As pointed out above, the perceived healing and growth seem to occur irrespective of what the scientific "mechanisms" of firewalking are. One might think that exotic "superconductivity" sounds very dramatic and an increase in the perspiration rate is completely "uninspiring." *NO!* I completely disagree: This *is* our potential. And its value for all of us, as humans, is largely unrelated to concrete "mechanisms," for the phenomenon undoubtedly has several levels. If we find that it can be explained at a relatively simple level, it does not mean that there are no other, deeper and more subtle, levels of its manifestation. The prevailing attitude of those who walked on fire is:

I finally discovered a new way of being: as a human, I possessed limitless possibilities which I had actually finally touched upon. I realize also that all human beings have this potential.[31]

We can also talk about healing in a much broader sense. As we already mentioned, it has long been known that Greek fire dancers *"consider themselves healers of all the community."*[32] Similar beliefs and attitudes are widespread in other parts of the world where firewalking and fire dancing are practiced as a ritual. Transcendental Meditation (TM) advocates claim that the practice of TM by many individuals creates an inexplicable effect of the "social field" which results in reduced accidents, illness, unemployment, and crime (as measured by statistical social indicators) in their communities.[33] I am far from endorsing their claims, but, since I have become more familiar with firewalking, my thoughts keep returning to the possibility that firewalking has equal potential to play this role. After all, many ancient legends and rituals have already been found to be based on facts, rather than on people's imagination. Why not another one? ...

I also feel that to be able to receive and understand our inner guidance, to listen to our inner voice, inner Guide, inner Teacher, Master within is the most important stage in our spiritual development. This is my lesson from the firewalk where the most important moment is to look inside, to ask and to feel whether it is all right for me to walk. If the answer is positive, then what is left is to go through the barrier of fear, let go of my resistance and to move forward, over the coals. The inner wisdom of the mind and body will do the rest— everything that is necessary to protect us from fire. As Buddhist priest Robert Stuart Clifton wrote after his firewalk, "The truest answers are within yourself."[34]

My introduction to firewalking taught me another very important lesson that I keep repeating over and over again in these pages: We do create our own reality, not only while walking over glowing embers, but also in our everyday life—today and tomorrow, in sun and in rain, in spring and in the autumn of our lives.

This adventure also taught me that fear is the major obstacle for growth, and now I see firewalking is a powerful instrument, a metaphor for overcoming fear and our limiting beliefs. Learning and teaching firewalking was the greatest challenge I had encountered in my life. Those who knew me had no doubts that for me, to rephrase Archimedes' famous maxim, the motto, "give me a challenge, and I will move the earth!" was the most important force leading me further in my search for meaning, growth and understanding. Perhaps this is one more reason why I was so attracted to firewalking.

In my observation, most of the participants of firewalking seminars seem to understand that firewalking is by no means the ultimate goal, but just the beginning—the gates or door to better understanding ourselves, our consciousness, and the universe. As my fellow firewalking instructor Michael Sky commented, having learned our lessons from firewalking, "we can transform any fear into positive evolutionary energy, we can transform any crisis into an opportunity for growth, and we can turn any confrontation into a cause for celebration."[35]

■

Let me conclude this chapter on a personal note. The afternoon after I finished a major part of this manuscript, I meditated on the theme of fire and, while in meditation, had an unexpectedly beautiful image: I saw myself as a beacon, as a guiding light that could provide light for everyone who needed it and could lead everyone along the path of spiritual understanding, so that they themselves would become pure light, the light of transformation and unity. By a meaningful coincidence, I received a letter from my friend and colleague in Moscow, Barbara Ivanova, that contained her "psychographic" (i.e., written through automatic writing) poem describing a similar image. I was deeply touched and inspired by her beautiful poem in Russian, and as I was pondering the mystery of how this symbolic image transcended the space between Moscow and California, rhymed lines appeared in my mind, and in a few minutes I had a poem in English on the same subject. It blends together my fascination with firewalking, the symbolism of light and fire and my own spiritual search:

Firewalking

Light a candle in me,
   my invisible teacher,
Turn me into a living flame,
Make me a guiding light,
Illuminating the Path for others.

From a poem by my dear friend, Barbara Ivanova,
written in Moscow in her native Russian.

We light the Path
for those with a spark,
for all who ask
for guidance to embark
on that eternal journey
that we are led to race
along the path that's thorny—
and problems we embrace!
I am a living flame
that will rekindle your light
which you are to reclaim
by your God-given right!

PART TWO

An Investigation of the Changes Perceived by Individuals After Their Firewalking Experience

Nothing is permanent but change.

Heraclitus, quoted in Diogenes Laërtius (fl. 200 A.D.),
Lives of Eminent Philosophers

Chapter 5
Present Study: Methodology

They know enough
who know how to learn.
Henry Brooks Adams, *The Education of Henry Adams* (1907)

1. Firewalking and Psychological Change

Firewalking, a widespread phenomenon,[1] may demonstrate a link between physiological and psychological processes, and provides an opportunity to observe the effects of one's beliefs on one's bodily interaction with the physical world. While some attempts have been made to study physical and psychophysiological aspects of firewalking,[2] there is little research on the psychological concomitants of the phenomenon.

Across America, contemporary firewalking workshops inspire individuals to cross the coals as a means to overcome fears, increase self confidence, and develop personal power. These claims remain largely unvalidated due to the lack of research on the psychological impact of firewalking. The study by Blake focusing on the personality correlates of successful firewalking, merely emphasizes the need for further investigation into the possible short- and long-term effects of firewalking workshops and ceremonies.[3]

What happens to the individuals who walk across hot coals? What meaning does it have for them? Does it affect their lives? If so, how? In approaching questions such as these, we are entering into the relatively undeveloped and empirically uncharted territory of qualitative human experience. Hence, as Barker notes, we must reconcile ourselves to conducting "exploratory" research.[4] Such research emphasizes discovery rather than quantitative analysis, with the intention of opening our eyes and minds to lived experience.[5]

The present study explores the qualitative aspects of the human experience of firewalking, while seeking in an encompassing way to investigate the effects of firewalking on the individual who has accomplished a seemingly impossible feat. The purpose of this research is to investigate the nature of the experience and to describe the individual's assimilation of their firewalk experience and the perceived impact on their lives.

By obtaining in-depth descriptions of the after-effects of firewalking, we can move to an increased understanding of this area of human experience. With particular attention to the shifts which may occur in the lives of individuals following a profound and heretofore "impossible" action, the present study provides a window into the broader reaches of the human psyche.

Another issue which has long been debated in connection with firewalking is whether firewalkers enter an altered state of consciousness and, if so, what the specific characteristics are of such a state.

The contention that firewalkers and fire-handlers are in "trance" or, more precisely, in an altered state of consciousness, has been frequently expressed in the literature.[6] An altered state of consciousness (ASC) can be defined as any mental state induced by various physiological, psychological, or pharmacological maneuvers or agents, which can be recognized subjectively by the individual himself (or by an objective observer of the individual) as representing a sufficient deviation, a *qualitative* shift in subjective experience, psychological functioning or behavior from certain general norms for that individual during alert, waking consciousness.[7] Major reported characteristics of ASCs are alterations in thinking, disturbed time sense, loss of control (or gaining power through relinquishing conscious control), change in emotional expression,

What Meaning, If Any, Has Firewalking Had in Your Life?

Eighty percent of the questionnaire respondents offered specific answers as to the meaning of firewalking in their lives, with only 20%, four participants, finding the question "not applicable" or meaningless. Confidence, acceptance, and the possibility of "creating my own reality" were the topics most commonly mentioned. The firewalking experience was "assuring" and "exciting" for many or, as one woman wrote, "I have done something very special." Other comments ranged as follows:

My attitude toward apparent "limitations" has changed greatly.

It was a great example, self experienced, that mind over matter is a fact.

It reminds me that I can do unexpected things.

[Firewalking] reminds me that I can continue taking positive risks to create the reality I want.

It helped me accept the existence of other realities on levels deeper and more meaningful than the intellectual.

A metaphor for all the things in life that look difficult or impossible that are possible if you pursue them congruently.

I am more confident about myself and my inherent abilities.

Four subjects, 20%, found no meaning in the fire-walking experience, commenting, "I don't feel differently, it had no particular meaning," and simply, "Once a skeptic, always a skeptic." Finally, one woman summarizes her experience this way, "It just seems to me that I walked on fire nine times, nothing more, I regret to say. I wish I had a breakthrough of some kind."

2. The Intensive Interview

The Participants

Twenty individuals were interviewed by telephone or in person, including 8 men and 12 women. Their ages ranged from 17 to 66, with most being between 30 and 40. Forty percent of the respondents attended the workshop out of curiosity, while 30% attended in hopes of personal growth. Friends or relatives urged 25% to attend, while just one participant attended with the intention of overcoming fear.

For participants over the age of 20, 82% had completed college or beyond with 47% holding a master's or doctorate degree. The distribution of the age and educational levels of the interview respondents can be found in Tables 10 and 11.

Table 10
Age of Interview Respondents

Age	Number	Percentage
11 - 20	3	15
21 - 30	0	0
31 - 40	5	25
41 - 50	8	40
51 - 60	2	10
Over 61	2	10
Total	20	100

Table 11
Education Level of the Respondents
over 20 Years of Age

Category	Number	Percentage
Completed High School	3	17.6
Completed College	6	35.3
Master's Degree	6	35.3
Doctorate Degree	2	11.8
Total	17	100

■

Personal Experience Prior to Firewalking

Again, to gain information as to the profile of firewalking participants, the interviewees were asked to rank their experiences in a number of areas on a one to five scale (1—no experience, 2—a little, 3—some, 4—much, 5—a great deal of experience).

Meditation and Personal Growth Workshops: Respondents were asked to consider their personal experience in the realm of meditation, specifically the degree to which they regularly practiced meditation. In addition, they were asked to rate their experience and attendence at personal growth workshops. Fully 80% of the respondents reported that they had some experience to a great deal of experience with meditation, and 75% had attended some to numerous personal growth workshops. In both cases, only 10% of the sample reported no experience with either meditation or workshops. The data collected from this aspect of the questionnaire can be found in Tables 12 and 13.

Study and Experiences in the Spiritual Traditions: Interviewees were asked to rank the degree to which they believed they had studied the spiritual traditions, including study within the context of an orthodox religious system. In addition, they were asked to consider their personal mystical experiences. In both regards, 62%

Table 12
Meditation Experience of the Respondents

Category	Number	Percentage
A great deal of experience	7	35
Much experience	3	15
Some experience	6	30
A little experience	2	10
No experience	2	10
Total	20	100

Table 13
Personal Growth Workshops Attended
by the Respondents

Category	Number	Percentage
A great deal of experience	10	50
Much experience	3	15
Some experience	2	10
A little experience	3	15
No experience	2	10
Total	20	100

of the sample reported some experience to a great deal of experience with spiritual study and mystical experiences. However, whereas 26% reported no experience with mystical experiences, only 10% reported a total lack of study in the spiritual traditions. The results of this aspect of the intensive interview can be found in Tables 14 and 15.

Table 14
Spiritual Study of the Respondents

Category	Number	Percentage
A great deal of experience	7	35
Much experience	4	20
Some experience	2	10
A little experience	5	25
No experience	2	10
Total	20	100

Table 15
Mystical Experiences of the Respondents

Category	Number	Percentage
A great deal of experience	5	25
Much experience	6	30
Some experience	1	5
A little experience	3	15
No experience	5	25
Total	20	100

Mind-Altering Drugs: In the area of mind-altering drug experience, an overwhelming 50% said they had "no experience" with drugs. Two participants, 10% of the sample, acknowledged having a great deal of experience with drugs, and only one individual had "much" experience. The results of this inquiry can be found on Table 16.

Table 16
Mind-Altering Drug Experiences
of the Respondents

Category	Number	Percentage
A great deal of experience	2	10
Much experience	1	5
Some experience	5	25
A little experience	3	15
No experience	10	50
Total	20	100

Thus, the firewalkers who were interviewed, excluding those under 20 years of age, were well educated men and women of middle age. Most likely they have had experience with meditation and have taken several personal growth workshops. In addition, they have studied religion and had experiences they consider to be "mystical." They have not had experiences with mind-altering substances.

■

Questions Directed to the Seminar Experience

The Firewalking Workshop: Despite the fact that the interviewees are an experienced group of participants who have taken many personal growth workshops and have a breadth of experience, most found the workshop to be valuable, with 75% appreciating the workshop and firewalking instructor.

Attitudes Toward the Group: Participants reported an evolving feeling of the group's connectedness during their experience in that prior to the firewalk, 70% felt no sense of the group or did not have a positive attitude toward their colleagues. After the firewalk, however, the figures reversed, and 50% felt highly connected and bonded to the group.

Two interviewees mentioned their belief that the group was

directly responsible for enabling them to firewalk. In addition, 2 participants mentioned, "I didn't like the group, but I needed them to walk on fire!" and "At first I thought the group was like a scene from [Charles] Manson...but afterwards I felt bonded to them. It was a peak experience!"

Crossing the Fire: The large majority of firewalkers, 55%, reported "no change" in their feet after firewalking. Twenty-five percent found redness on their feet, and 20% found hot spots or blisters.

Of the 5 interviewees who were blistered, most had stories which they felt explained their injury. Three firewalkers, when walking across the coals were initally surprised to find the coals "cool." They reported that as soon as they broke their concentration to realize "It's cool!" or a similar thought, they immediately felt the heat and were blistered in that moment. Others found the blisters minor and noticed they disappeared in a few minutes or in a few hours.

Two cases emerge as unique. In one instance, a woman who was performing her second firewalk decided to stop in the middle of the fire pit to pick up coals in her hands. Her hands were not burned while carrying the coals, but she found a hot spot on her feet. In another case, a woman crossed the coals to find three small blisters which caused no pain and "immediately" disappeared. But three weeks after the firewalk,

> The blisters reappeared in exactly the same places! I was undergoing a time of intense spiritual change, and I believe it was a sign of reinforcement for the changes I was experiencing.

Approaching the fire pit, 85% of the subjects felt the heat of the coals, some quite intensely, while only 15% did not feel its heat. In one instance a woman who found no change in her feet after walking recalled her experience prior to the walk:

> The coals were intensely hot! I was certain I wouldn't walk. I had a gold bracelet on and when I was standing near the fire, it got so hot that I took my bracelet off so it wouldn't *melt*!

This same woman found the same coals to be cool when she crossed them minutes later.

When responding to the open-ended question, "How did the coals feel?" the common descriptor was "crunchy," with 55% selecting this word to describe their experience, and 20% finding them "crunchy and warm." Twenty percent of the firewalkers thought the coals "hot" while the same number found them "warm." A surprising 20% found the coals to be cool, and as mentioned, two participants found the coals to be cool initially, but as soon as they stopped to notice this, the coals felt hot.

■

Thoughts and Feelings

Before the Firewalk: Prior to actually crossing the coals, the dominant mental and emotional state was fear. Seventy-five percent reported that they were feeling "scared," "fearful," "panic," or "desperate" prior to the firewalk.

None of the interviewees reported experiencing feelings of doubt prior to walking, and 20% felt calm, confident, or a sense of inner peace. One participant felt a sense of adventure and discovery. Noteworthy are three individuals, one who felt "powerful" prior to crossing the coals and another who felt "drawn to the coals." Finally, one man reported that, "I saw Jesus floating above the far end of the fire pit, drawing me with His love across the coals."

During the Experience of Firewalking: Fifteen percent of the interviewees could not recall a specific thought or feeling while on the coals. The same number felt they were "spaced out" or in a trance during the firewalk. Another 10% felt a protective "glow" around their body while walking. One woman thought in the middle of the firewalk, "My skirt is on fire!" and in that moment felt the sting of the fire and experienced a burn.

Five percent of the participants had unusual reactions while crossing the coals, including two individuals who felt intensely close to God: one who saw Jesus across the coals, and another who felt she was healed from her spiritual crisis after a time of being "out with God." Another individual simply told herself to "Keep walk-ing!" Of the 30% who could not remember what they were thinking or feeling during the walk, one mentioned her pleasure that the migraine headache she had been experiencing subsided during the firewalk.

After the Experience of Firewalking: The moments immediately following the walk across the fire pit were described by many interviewees as euphoric. Fifty-five percent expressed feelings of "ecstasy," "complete exhilaration," or "a peak experience." Another 15% expressed feeling "pleased" or "happy." Feelings of "relief" were reported by 10% of the subjects, and 10% expressed feelings of confidence and accomplishment. Three individuals, or 15%, expressed a sense of skepticism—"Did I really do that?" or anti-climax, "I wasn't as high as I thought I'd be." Finally, one simply felt "close to God."

■

Summary of the Firewalk Experience

Three-quarters of the participants interviewed appreciated both the workshop and the group, noticing a moderate difference in the level of connectedness with the group after they have firewalked. They had a 50/50 chance of having hot spots, slight burns, or blisters. Although 20% of the firewalkers felt calm and confident prior to crossing the coals, 75% felt fear. Seventy-five percent also were surprised at the crunchy quality of the coals. More than half were ecstatic after firewalking, 15% were pleased, 10% felt confident, and another 15% were skeptical regarding their accomplishment.

3. Since the Firewalk...

Completing the background portrait of the interviewee, we can explore the changes, if any, that individuals have perceived in themselves since their firewalk. Has their accomplishment of an "impossible" feat touched their lives? Are they thinking or behaving any differently? The final 13 questions which constitute the Interview Guide delve into these areas, ranging from whether or not the firewalk experience crosses their mind, to their theories about firewalking, to the changes they might perceive in their daily lives.

Code names have been given to certain subjects in order to more easily track their attitudes and beliefs and to create a character portrait which will continue to serve as we enter the discussion phase of the research.

■

Do You Think About Your Firewalking Experience at All?

Among the interviewees, firewalking is an experience which, once accomplished, is thought about a good deal. Fully 85% think about their firewalk occasionally, often, or very often. Just one respondent did not think about his experience at all, and an additional two, 10%, think about it rarely.

Of those who thought a great deal about their experience, several were reminded of it in their daily lives, such as a parapsychology teacher who speaks to her classes about it, and Polly, a woman whose life has changed dramatically since the firewalk. As with the questionnaire respondents, several individuals mentioned that they think of firewalking "occasionally," when feeling low or in times of flux, when courage is needed for a change.

Many subjects who have walked on fire keep photographs of themselves around the house, to look at when they "need a boost." Most of the firewalking instructors also have the participants write out a card which says somethiing to the effect of, "I walked on fire. I can do anything I choose." Like the photographs, and many times combined with them, the subjects often or occasionally read or recall this statement and are empowered to move forward in their lives.

■

Have You Noticed Any Differences in Your Relationships?

Among the population of interviewees, 25% believed their relationships were the same, and had undergone no changes, compared with 55% who felt a moderate to significant change or a breakthrough. Twenty percent of the subjects had found some minor changes in their relationships. Fifteen percent of the subjects who acknowledged moderate or some positive change in their relationships also mentioned that they could not necessarily relate the changes directly to the firewalk.

Eight individuals, 40% of the subjects, felt they had a significant change or a breakthrough in their relationships after firewalking. One woman said simply, "There has been a significant change in my relationships. I *have* one now."

One respondent, whom we will code name "Polly" for this discussion, when asked about changes in her relationships exclaimed, "I've now got a GOOD one! That's a *sigNIficant* change!" She has found herself more accepting, more trusting, and less bothered by "the small things." She continues, "...I used to feel persecuted in my relationships, as though I was always the victim. Now I realize that *I'm* responsible for my own feelings..."

Another noteworthy case is Naomi, who reported:

I was astonished that my first thought after I finished the firewalk was, "If I can do THIS, I can stand up to my mother!" It blew my mind. But when she talked to me later she said, "Don't you *dare* firewalk!" But I had already DONE it! It felt great to stand up to her...

Of those who felt moderate or significant changes, acceptance and honesty are key words used to describe those changes. As one man commented, "I am less rigid. I now look less at what should be and more at what is. And I can accept what is." Another commented, "I am much more honest. I can now acknowledge and maintain good relationships."

On a particularly upbeat note, one woman has certainly seen a breakthrough in her relationships. She laughed, "Oh, there's *defi-*

nitely been a breakthrough! I met a fabulous guy at the workshop and we're having a great time together!"

■

Have You Been More or Less Fearful Since Your Firewalk?

Among the interviewees, an overwhelming 80% noted that they had experienced a breakthrough or moderate to significant change in the degree of their fears since firewalking.

Twenty five percent of the interviewees believed they had a "breakthrough" in their realtionships and were "much less" fearful since firewalking. Forty-five percent, nearly half of the respondents, have been "somewhat less" fearful.

Of those who have been much less fearful, they noted, "I take more risks," "I dismiss fear more readily," and "I attempt more and give it my best, even under stress." One man wrote, "I have somewhat less fear. Now I think it's all right for me to use my courage to try things I would not have done before the firewalk."

A point of note is well stated by one subject who wrote, "There has been no change in my fears since firewalking. I've always been fearless!" Several individuals who noticed no change in their fears revealed similar attitudes: "I've always been a little crazy," or, "I've always been an adventurer." Thus, the brave individual who firewalks in the first place may be more courageous than the norm, and hence will note scant change in the degree of his or her fearlessness.

Finally, the youngest firewalker in this study is Tommy, a seven-year-old boy who walked twice across the fire. He is now "much less" fearful and more confident. "How can you tell you have less fears?" he was asked. "Because there was a 20-foot-high cliff at the lake, and I *jumped* off it!!"

■

Do You Deal With Your Fears Differently Since Firewalking?

Half of the interviewees have seen a breakthrough or a significant difference in the way they deal with their fears since firewalking. Including those that have seen a "moderate" or "some" difference in their behavior, the figure jumps to 70%. Thirty percent felt they dealt with their fears no differently than they had prior to firewalking.

Like the questionnaire participants, most interviewees found that they deal with their fears "more directly," or simply "set them aside." Two individuals who commented about their breakthroughs said, "They just go away!" and "I move right through my fears now. Nothing scares me."

A new pattern of confronting fears directly was also noted among those who found moderate or significant change in the way they dealt with fear. As one subject said, "I stare at my fears instead of sticking them under the bed. I can see them clearly now." One man commented, "At the age of 37, I overcame my fear of water and learned to swim. I even swim in the ocean!"

Of those who noticed no change in dealing with their fears, 30% of the sample population, one woman, who had found "somewhat less" fear in her life since firewalking commented, "I don't deal differently with my fears. I've always been a fearful person."

We can here return to Polly, a woman who has seen numerous breakthroughs in her life since firewalking. She finds now, however, that she is "more" fearful since firewalking. She told this interviewer,

I'm much different in dealing with my fears. Now I won't DO scary things that might harm me. I used to have no fear of death because I didn't care. Now, my life is so great, I won't take unnecessary physical risks because I don't *want* to die!

■

Have You Noticed Any Differences in Your Capacity to Take Risks?

Unlike the questionnaire respondents, the numbers of interviewees who found a greater capacity for risk taking remained well above half. Sixty percent of the respondents believe they are taking moderately to significantly more risks since firewalking. "Some" change was noted by 15% of the sample, while 25% felt they had no change.

Polly, whom we saw earlier now cares enough about herself not to want to die, commented, "I can take many more risks now, as long as they're not life threatening. I'm freer about jumping in and trying new things." Another noted, "There has been a significant change. I'm *now* a risk-taker!"

■

Do You Have Any Different Ideas About God or Reality?

Half of the firewalkers interviewed believed their ideas about God and the nature of reality had shifted. For many, their belief system was substantiated. As one subject commented, "Firewalking reinforced my current picture of reality. And this is NOT the picture I was taught in school!" Another said, "There's been no change. I've always believed that we are the God/Creator of our own lives." And another, "I've always had far reaching ideas about the universe." Finally, one woman mentioned, "There has been no difference. Firewalking just confirmed that there are things I don't understand."

One contradictory case is a woman who commented, "There has been no change. Only that the limits are not where I thought they were!"

Several participants have found a closer connection to their spiritual selves since firewalking. One woman said, "I have made peace with the fire gods—and myself!" Another mentioned, "I feel God's presence in my life more."

Thus, the firewalk experience serves to reinforce belief systems

172

or expand them, allowing for a more "flexible" universe. Or, as one woman commented, "Doesn't *everyone's* idea of God change *daily?*"

■

Are You Doing Anything Differently in Your Daily Life?

As we asked the interviewees to begin examining specific behaviors, we find that only three, 15%, saw no changes in their daily life after firewalking, while 85% percent of the respondents have noticed changes in their day-to-day existences. Affirmation cards or recalling the experience reminds the firewalkers, "When I think I can't, I return to firewalking and I know I CAN!" Again, life seems easier to deal with:

"I question things more and look for what IS possible instead of what isn't!"

"I'm not so worried about peripheral things and taking on the burdens of the world."

"I'm easier about the unknown, more accepting."

"Everything is substantially easier to deal with."

"I don't sit around wishing things were different. I'm *making* them different now!"

"I'm not waiting for the skies to open. I'm doing things whole hog or I don't do them at all. I'm a 100% person now. All the way."

Polly, for whom firewalking was generally a breakthrough experience, reported, "I'm doing lots of things differently. I don't sit around depressed anymore. I'm active. I have much more energy."

Tommy, following his firewalk, went to school and spoke with his teacher and friends about it. He said,

They didn't believe me. My teacher didn't believe that I'd

done it and the other kids laughed at me. So Mom sent in an article from the paper that said we *did* it. But, now I don't care about what they think as much. I know they can be wrong.

If it is easier for firewalkers to cope with life, it is because they find themselves to be more accepting of what they cannot change, and more in control of what they can change. As one woman commented, "I see I make limits for myself. Now I know there ARE no limits!"

■

Are There Any Specific Examples of the Changes You Perceive?

Following the previous question in pursuit of specific examples, 85% of the participants provided instances of what they perceived to be a behaviorial change or adaptation, with merely three interviewees, 15%, offering no specifics as to their behavioral shifts. Forty percent felt more confidence in their lives, reflected in variety of behaviors. Their comments are as follows: "I got into group therapy!" or, "I set up a seminar and people *paid* to come to it."

One woman explained what was a dramatic shift for her: "I was a pyrophobic. I didn't light a match until I was 19. Now, I even go camping!" When asked for specific examples of her behavior changes, another woman commented,

Well, now I'm doing lots of things that used to scare me, like jumping out of airplanes and scuba diving. Oh, and I also quit my old job and started my own business!

Other subjects use their affirmation card and the techniques they learned in the workshop to inspire confidence. One woman, 60 years of age, commented,

I was on a tour of China and Tibet and had to walk up hundreds of stairs to see the temples and shrines. One voice inside me would say, "It's too high, I can't breathe. I'm too old." But another voice would say, "You walked on fire, you can do *this*." And I did it!

Two other areas in which specific changes were noticed were in the realms of actual physical changes and in the subject's experience of time. Two individuals mentioned that they have been eating differently and exercising more. Polly noted that she was drinking less alcohol, which she used as "a tranquil escape."

The same number of subjects noticed a difference in their relationship to time, reporting, "My time sense has changed. I'm not driven by time." "I waste less time and make more money."

Finally, the most dramatic case of a behavioral change comes from Mark, a 35-year-old man who firewalked in a New Jersey workshop. He related the following story:

Six months after the firewalk, in the middle of the night I was awakened by fire engines coming down the street. But they didn't go past our street, they *stopped*! I looked out my window and saw people running down the street, and then I saw my mother's house on fire! I ran down the street with my knees shaking. It was a huge fire, with smoke billowing down the street and it was hard to see anything.

As I ran down the street, barefoot, I "geared up" for a firewalk! I began to pace my breathing and quiet my mind, preparing to walk into the burning house to rescue my mother.

As I got through the smoke, I saw it wasn't my mother's house, but her next door neighbor's. She is a big, fat woman, and I'm only 120 pounds, so I knew I couldn't lift her, but I was ready to try. Then the firemen said I couldn't go in anyway.

The firewalk is a controlled crisis, and I have definitely learned how to deal differently with a crisis!

■

How Do You Think You Were Able to Firewalk?

To evaluate the data regarding the reasons the participants have as to why they were able to firewalk, we can again apply the hypothetical categories established in Chapter III.

1. Firewalking is Explained by the Laws of Physics and Known Properties of Human Physiology

As in the questionnaire, the interviewees deny the purely physical explanations of firewalking which contend that the stones do not convey heat sufficient for burns. In every case, interviewees noted that some firewalkers at the seminar were burned and others were not, and there appears to be no correlation between whether burns were suffered by the first to walk or the last. That is, one respondent walked unharmed across the coals the first time, but was burned a second time, as she walked near the end of the workshop when theoretically the coals had cooled.

Merely one interviewee ascribed specifically to this hypothesis, postulating that firewalking can be explained within the framework of classical physics. He proposed, "I think it was the cool temperature and the wet grass. It was *not* paranormal. I think skin doesn't burn easily." The participant was surprised to learn after the interview that in fact skin scorches at a lower temperature than the cotton fabric he was wearing.

2. Firewalking Can Be Explained With the Framework of Deception

None of the firewalkers in this study believed they were deceived or tricked, and none of the interviewees mentioned this as a possibility.

3. Firewalking Can Be Explained by Psychophysiological Changes Induced in an Altered State of Consciousness

The notion of a trance or hypnotically induced altered state of consciousness was mentioned by three interviewees as a possible reason why they were able to firewalk. They mentioned this in the context of the group energy, with comments such as: "It was the group and chutzpah!" and "It was the group energy combined with my personal energy. I couldn't do it alone." Another wrote, "It was the group that called in the extra energy. When I am doing massage, my hands can make someone else feel hot all over. It's group energy."

4. Firewalking Can Be Explained by the Power of Belief

Three of the interviewees ascribed some degree of personal power to forces greater than oneself, be they the physical forces of the universe or the power of God to account for their firewalk. Naomi, for example suggested, "It doesn't make sense. Only that I surrendered to a higher power, or God or something, and I did it."

Another subject, vacilating in her theoretical approach to the phenomenon, commented, "I have no idea. I think it has to do with our religious or spiritual beliefs. It was my belief system of the moment...." Farther out on the spiritual spectrum, but evincing strong conviction was another subject, who reported,

"Fire is the friendliest of all the elements. It is the easiest to work with. In cultures all around the world, fire is the traditional way that God visits us. It's God's way of saying, 'You can do things you think you can't do!' "

Yet, the vast majority of the respondents in this study did not turn their power over to a higher source, but choose to hypothesize that mind over matter explains the phenomenon.

5. Firewalking Can Be Explained by "Mind over Matter"

Again, 50% of the participants believe that their accomplishment is due to the control of their mind over the material world. Their descriptions are as follows:

"It's focused consciousness, like in childbirth. If you pay attention strictly to one thing, you don't feel other things."

"If we control it, we can use and flow with our mind."

"The mind can totally control our reality. I'm creating it all the time!"

"The power of my mind, the energy, the focus."

177

Agreeing with this hypothesis, Polly reported,

It was my mind over matter. Some of it was due to the hypnosis in the seminar, telling us that the coals were cool moss. I did as I was told, and repeated six times, "As I take the first step, my body will do whatever it needs to do to protect itself." But the coals were *hot*. It wasn't science fiction! I did it with the power of my mind and my concentration.

Finally, an apt "mind over matter" hypothesis was proposed by Tommy, our youngest subject, in a marvelous conversation with the interviewer which went as follows:

"I *know* it was my mind, because I meditated before I did it!"

"What do you mean, 'meditated,' Tommy?"

"I mean concentrated. Like with the seeds."

"Seeds?"

"Yeah. We meditated on some seeds before we firewalked so we could see how good we can concentrate."

"What did you do?"

"We got some seeds and put them in water and then we concentrated on them to make them grow."

"Did you make yours grow?"

"Yeah, but a lot of people couldn't."

"So you concentrated like that when you were walking on the coals?"

"Yeah. I meditated real hard, then the first time I ran. The second time I walked."

"How do you think your meditating helped you walk?"

"I don't know…"

6. Firewalking Can Not Be Explained … By Me.

Like Tommy, five other subjects, 25% of the sample population, could not explain firewalking nor offer a theory as to its existence. One woman wrote, "It doesn't make sense ... only that I surrendered...."

Still others were content not to know, in fact, to feel comfortable in not knowing, as did Mark, who had prepared to firewalk in order to save his mother from her burning home:

> I don't know. And I've enjoyed not knowing ... not having to worry that I don't understand. Or that someone else knows and I don't. It doesn't bother me at all. For me, *that's* an accomplishment!

Another woman has confused the issue yet further:

> I'm still curious about the property of coals when they are pressed, whether they lose heat or not, but I still have no answers. Shortly after the firewalk, I was sitting by the fire, thinking about it. I reached into the fire and picked up a burning log. My hands weren't burned, but all the hair on my arm was burned off! But now, [one year later] I *do* get burned when I touch hot coals. I'm confused about it.

Before moving into the more direct questions as to whether the subjects actually felt changed by the experience of firewalking, we can summarize this point of view most adeptly with the words of Dr. Willis Harman in his interview as part of this research:

"Firewalking? It is a Great Mystery...."

■

Do You Feel Changed in Any Way by Your Firewalking Experience?

Looking to the deeper levels of personal awareness and experience, interviewees were asked to look within to see if they felt changed in any way by their experience. An overwhelming majority, 90% of the sample, replied that they felt they had a breakthrough or were moderately to significantly changed. Of the three who felt it was a breakthrough, one elaborated, "It was a breakthrough to 'total knowing.' "

The five participants, 25% of the interviewees, who felt "significantly" changed by the experience included Polly, who wrote, "I have room to grow. "I feel a general positiveness. Before, each stage of growth was depressing. Now, they're all wonderful!" Half of the interviewees felt "moderately" changed, evincing a general increase in their level of confidence and self-assurance, commenting, "I take more chances," and "I question the limits of new circumstances." One hearty soul said, "It was another step, but not monumental. What's next?"

This later point of view is shared by the several interviewees, who felt they had changed little or not at all. "It's a step on a series of investigations," and, "Firewalking was a step along the way," they mentioned, but changes cannot be attributed to that one experience. "I had already skydived, rock climbed and done rappelling and river rafting, so it wasn't that big of a deal." Of interest is Naomi, who felt "changed" for a while. She continued,

It was a quick fix for me. For a while it was a breakthrough. But then I felt like I got egotistical and self-righteous about it, and thought 'I can do *anything*.' That's not a good fire to fan. Now I'm learning humility and things are different. I have to discount it because I'm afraid of the egotism.

(Although we will pursue this circumstance in more depth in the subsequent chapter, it is worthy of mention at this point that Naomi felt she had a series of breakthrough changes immediately following her firewalk. Her business improved and she had more clients, she had the experience of "standing up" to her domineering mother, she felt more self-confident, and she felt God's presence in her life more. When we interviewed her, she was at a point of discounting her firewalking experience of three years prior. Now, as she attempts to learn "humility" and avoid what she perceived as "egotism," her business is poor and she's "broke.")

In a similar instance, a 50-year-old woman felt she had not changed, yet when asked about the meaning the experience held for her she exclaimed, "It was great for my self-esteem. Everyone should do it! It's a WOW! A big moment!"

Mark offered a more philosophical viewpoint about the nature of his changes, remarking,

> Change is a funny word. I'm still insecure, and I'm always working on myself. But when I need to "know" something about myself in a clear, positive and streamlined way, I remember firewalking. In those moments, we change. My feet, my legs, my hair changed in order for me to firewalk. Now, I remember I *can* change. But I'm not "changed."

In the dimension of changes, an encompassing viewpoint is expressed by a 19-year-old girl, who was just 14 when she walked:

> Have I changed? I'm changing all the time. I'm supposed to change—I'm a KID!

■

Do You Feel Differently About Yourself?

Among the interviewees, the overwhelming majority, 85%, feel they had a breakthrough or now hold moderately to significantly different opinions of themselves. Both of the individuals who felt they had a breakthrough also felt they had changed to the degree of a breakthrough in the previous question. One writes, "Before I firewalked, I thought, 'I'm so screwed up, no one likes me.' Now, I like *myself*!"

Mark also felt his firewalk had been a breakthrough. In the interview, Mark explained that he had a particularly traumatic life experience—a severe case of mistaken identity—just prior to the firewalk which left him feeling despondent, uncertain, and paranoid. For him, the firewalk was truly a breakthrough, in which he reports, "I had a positive self-affirmation in my entire body—every *cell* of it." After trying times, Mark found his self confidence and positively reinforced self opinion changed him "dramatically."

For the 70% of the firewalkers who felt moderately to significantly different about themselves, the major changes were in the areas of confidence and self-assurance, as reflected in the following statements:

"I can now allow for more change."

"I am much more clear."

"It was motivational. I feel I can do anything."

"I'm more confident and I like myself better. I have a clearer knowledge of my own personality.

"I changed moderately, I guess, when I allow myself to see my progress.

"I'm more confident about myself and my inherent abilities."

Polly also felt she had changed significantly, commenting, "I've gone from negative to positive—from half empty to half full."

Looking finally at those few individuals who do not feel differently about themselves, we see several contradictions. The three individuals who did not feel differently about themselves *all* felt that their lives had changed moderately or significantly for the better in the previous inquiry. One woman, for example, who reported that she felt "significantly" changed by the firewalking, with improved interpersonal relationships and a reaffirmed faith in God, also said she felt no different about herself.

Thus, we find with few exceptions that firewalking is truly an experience of change, with 85% the successful firewalkers feeling moderate or significant changes in their attitudes, beliefs, and behaviors as well as their views of themselves.

■

What Meaning, 7f Any, Has Firewalking Had in Your Life?

Fully 80% of the interviewees believed that firewalking had been a meaningful and impactful experience in their lives. Merely four interviewees assigned little or no meaning to the event, and replied with comments such as, "It was a fun thing to do and it probably empowered me, but it was also 'just another workshop.' " and "I was impressed but not surprised."

The large majority of interviewees who responded to this question, however, indicated that firewalking gave them enhanced confidence, and that is was an experience they would recommend to others. As one woman related, "I chuckle to myself when I say I 'can't' do something. Then I go ahead and do it." "It's a strong, uplifting experience," "Everyone should do it," and "It's a great time," were common remarks among the respondents. Others said simply, "It was a good feeling," or "I'm glad I did it!" One woman related,

I'm glad I had a blister to validate my experience! Firewalking gave me the freedom to experience and express my feelings. I know now that I can always trust my inner guidance. I learned to *trust* my inner guidance...and I loved singing with the group!

Several individuals felt the primary meaning involved the impact that firewalking had in terms of the information they received about the possibility of "creating their own reality." In other words, this subject population translated their "mind over matter" theories into their lives. One subject related, "It is the most impressive demonstration of the power of the mind I have ever seen." Another commented, "It is dramatic proof we are creating our own reality."

Drama was a common theme. In an extended interview, one subject effused,

It's so dramatic. I wanted to scream in the streets, "It's *great* to be alive!!" It's the most dramatic thing that's ever happened in my life. Everyone should do it.

As anticipated, the drama was shortlived for several subjects who reported that the confidence or impact they felt initially had dwindled over the year or two or three since they had firewalked. It was intended in the parameters of this investigation, however, to examine precisely this phenomenon, and avoid the first flush of emotions which follow such an experience. Ten percent of the sample population specifically noted that this was the case, with comments such as,

> It was a significant event and I have much respect for it. It was enjoyable, but it doesn't impact your life except when you run across difficult things. I was more excited about it immediately afterwards.

> I felt WOW at the time. But later, I asked myself, "Is it really so amazing?" You forget it's phenomenal. But everyone should do it. The big moment is getting across the threshold.

For another 10% the experience was even less phenomenal:

> "It was a fun thing to do and it probably empowered me, but it was just another workshop."

> "I don't know if I'd do it again. It would depend 99% on myself and knowing of the support of the others."

Another disenchanted firewalker was Naomi, who saw a noticeable improvement in her life immediately after firewalking, but now, three years later, broke and unhappy, she said,

> I want to discount it because I don't think one great experience should change your life. But it *did* change my life for a time....

Prior to exploring the convergences and divergences revealed by the dual methodologies, we can conclude our analysis of the interview results by allowing three of the "people" we have met through the interviews to speak for themselves about the meaning firewalking has had in their lives. First, Tommy:

> It was important to me. At first I felt real powerful, even though the kids didn't believe me. I know it will make a difference in my life. I think of it everytime I see fire.

And Polly:

I feel it encouraged my growth for the rest of my life. Afterwards, I drove home listening to *Switched on Bach* and was wide awake for 42 hours, high as a kite. Now, whenever I need a boost, I just listen to that music and it takes me back to that powerful time. I fall back to it often.

And finally, Mark:

It was a beautiful experience. In those profound moments, we are truly transformed. For me, it was a landmark I can return to for a sense of power and clarity in myself. I will always know that I can again change and optimize myself.

In concluding this section, we offer a final thought which embraces many of the interviewees and this researcher as well. A young college student, who walked three years ago at the age of 16, thoughtfully remarked,

Firewalking was a peak experience—and a natural high. I know that fire has in many cultures been the traditional way to get to a spiritual state. It tells me that there are still mysteries out there that we don't understand. But…I don't know…I'd like to see Water Walking!

4. Firewalking and Peak Performance

As mentioned previously, the literature of firewalking alludes to the fact that firewalking may be related to peak performance, or "behavior that exceeds one's predictable level of functioning, [and] represents superior use of human potential."[3] By applying Garfield and Bennett's linguistic descriptors for peak performance[4] as enumerated in Table 1 above, light is shed on this area of personal experience.

Garfield and Bennet offer 12 descriptors, including intense concentration, a sense of power, without conscious thought, an insulated state, surrender, focus, and ecstasy, among others. The results of the present study demonstrate that some of the indicators for an altered state were perceived by the firewalkers, though not necessarily described as such.

Examining the data, we find that 85% of the respondents of both groups used at least one of the linguistic descriptors at some point in their questionnaire or interview. Only two descriptors were not used in the present data: "automatic pilot" and "nonattachment." Every other descriptor was utilized verbatim by the respondents to describe their experience of firewalking.

As seen in the previous analysis of results, nearly half of the firewalkers felt joy and ecstacy after firewalking. Nine subjects, 22.5%, mentioned "surrendering" to the experience and 30% reported intense focus or concentration. During the walk, 52.5% reported that time was "not normal," adding in most cases that it seemed to slow down. Nearly 30% walked on fire without holding a conscious thought. Finally, 27.5% were "consumed by the momentum of the event" and did not remember holding a conscious thought, and 20% reported that they were in a trance or expanded state which included a "white glow," perhaps the "insulated state" described by Garfield and Bennett.[5] The findings derived from the data are found in Table 17.

Thus, it would appear that firewalking may be a "peak performance" which culminates in "an intense and highly valued moment."[6]

Table 17
Linguistic Descriptors for Peak Performance
Applied to the Firewalking Samples

Description	Questionnaire		Interview		Both	
	N	%	N	%	N	%
automatic pilot	0	0	0	0	0	0
intense concentration	3	15	4	20	7	17.5
sense of power	2	10	1	5	3	7.5
consumed by the event	4	20	7	35	11	27.5
no conscious thought	4	20	7	35	11	27.5
insulated state	5	25	3	15	8	20
nonattachment	0	0	0	0	0	0
surrender to the action	4	20	5	25	9	22.5
alteration of time	9	45	12	60	21	52.5
focus	2	10	3	15	5	12.5
new source of power	2	10	2	10	4	10
joy and ecstasy	7	35	10	50	17	42.5

Chapter 7
What Have We Learned?
Discussion

The Universe is change;
our life is what our thoughts make it.
Marcus Aurelius Antonius (121-180 A.D.), *Meditations*, IV, 3

1. Our Assumptions

Investigations by cognitive and social psychologists indicate that one's state of expectation, frame of reference, mental set, or conceptual scheme will influence what one "sees," and therefore affect the objectivity of any particular research.[1]

One attempt to deal with the problem of objectivity and interviewer bias has been made by Valle and King, who recommend the use of "bracketing" to control bias.[2] By bracketing our preconceptions and presuppositions—identifying and making them as clear as possible—we can suspend these notions, or at least make the reader clear about them. It is hoped that we can transcend some degree of personal bias by making these assumptions emerge at the level of reflective awareness.

We would here apply two primary brackets around the research: (1) the interviewer's frame of reference that transformational experiences have an impact on the experience, and (2) that the experience of breaking through what was heretofore perceived to be a limitation would enable individuals to think of breaking through other perceived limitations on a larger scale.

To elaborate, our history in transformational experiences, particularly two years of utilizing the ropes course with business-people conducted by Joan Steffy, has demonstrated that a short-term positive effect occurs regularly. Thus, this frame of reference leads us to a mental set in which we "expect" some change in the firewalker. Coupled with this, however, was a genuine curiosity as to the long-term effect of such a dramatic experience. This latter point, together with a foreknowledge of the first bias, led us to exclude recent firewalkers from this research.

Secondly, these researchers' conceptual scheme contains another potential bias. It is our fond hope that if individuals begin to break through limitations they have been taught in school and at home, such as "Fire will always burn you," we can break through limitations taught societally. That is to say, to reconsider such notions as competition at all levels, national security over natural security, war as a means to economic advantage, and so on.

The reader will do well to take these presuppositions into account, to bracket the biases as they occur in this discussion, and to arrive at his or her own conclusions.

■

The Meaning and Impact of Firewalking

For this investigation into the impact of firewalking, some primary questions arise in the months following such a profound experience: Do we change because we have done it? Can the experience be translated to other areas of life? Is it translated? Who translates it and uses it? How do they translate it? Does it work in day-to-day life? How do they know it works?

In the preceding chapter, we found the results indicated that people are impacted by firewalking; that three months to three years after firewalking, two-thirds of the individuals perceive they have changed. Most feel differently about themselves because they accomplished the "impossible." Most can give specific examples as to how they perceive they feel and behave differently. Thus, we see that the experience can be and is translated into the general life experience of the majority of subjects.

Yet, which people gain the most from the experience? Which gain the least? For whom does the experience not translate into their lives? Why doesn't it? What are the differences between those who see changes in themselves after the experience and those who do not? At this point, we range out of pure data analysis and into a more interpretative mode of understanding.

Here, the model of Sellitz is useful to aid the discussion. Included in the model are: (1) intuitively grouping cases that seem to belong together; (2) studying contrasting groups to determine differences between the two; and (3) noting matters which seem contrary or surprising to common sense and searching for possible explanations for the discrepancies.3 This, then, is the model with which we will concern ourselves in the course of this discussion.

The Sellitz model will be applied by first grouping the cases intuitively together, and then examining the contrast groups for each. We have three such intuitions: (1) that most people will benefit; (2) that people with little experience in meditation, personal growth and the like will benefit more dramatically from the firewalk; and (3) that people who have had more experience in personal growth, meditation, and spiritual study will have less impact from the firewalk.

Finally, we will seek out those matters which seem surprising and contrary to common sense and search for possible explanations for the discrepancies.

Without attempting to present a numerical data analysis, we can facilitate this complex discussion by applying a numerical scale to evaluate two areas of the firewalk experience: (A) the subject's ratings of their experience in meditation, workshops, mystical experiences, spiritual study, and mind altering drugs prior to firewalking; and (B) the degree of change associated with fears, relationships, and the capacity to take risks, as well as the subject's personal estimation as to whether they believe they have changed and if they feel differently about themselves. The following scales have been applied:

5—(A) a great deal of experience or (B) a breakthrough
4—(A) much experience or (B) significant change
3—(A) some experience or (B) moderate change
2—(A) a little experience or (B) some change
1—(A) no experience or (B) no change

Thus we can enhance this more reflective, qualitative, and intuitive discussion concerning the impact of the firewalking experience.

2. Intuitive Groupings: Experience and Impact

As researchers who have been interested in the phenomenon of transformational change for over a decade, our intuitive prediliction was to believe that: (1) most people will feel they have benefitted from the experience; (2) people who have had little experience in transformational work such as the firewalk will have a greater impact from the experience; and (3) that those who have had a great deal of experience in personal growth and transformation will find the firewalk to be generally less remarkable.

In line with the Sellitz model, these intuitive groups will be examined along with those response groups which are in contrast to the predicted groupings, and those which seem contrary to our "common sense."

■

Intuition One: Most People Will Benefit

In fact, 65% of the sample population felt they had benefitted from the firewalk experience to at least a moderate degree, and that it had a positive impact in their lives. By applying the same numerical scale to categories (A) and (B), we find that in comparing the level of relative personal experience to the degree of change,

two-thirds found a benefit equal to or greater than their experience. That is, of those with moderate experience, a mean of 2.9, 65% found firewalking to be a moderate to breakthrough experience, a mean of 3.5. Only 35% of the subjects had less benefit from changes than their experience warranted.

The contrast group to this first intuition is scant, consisting of individuals such as Laura, whom we have followed throughout the data analysis.

■

Intuition Two: Less Experience Means More Benefit

In 28% of the 25 subjects who experienced benefit, the level of previous experience was significantly below the level of the reward. Simply stated, seven individuals with scant experience in the field of transformation benefitted to the level of a breakthrough or significant change, thus validating the second intuitional premise.

To gain further insight into this phenomenon, we can look more closely at these individuals. Primarily in their thirties and forties, these four men and three women had a slight amount of experience in personal growth experiences, half had never experienced a mind-altering drug, and only one was a regular meditator, with the rest having had no experience or merely an introduction to meditation. More than half did not like the group experience or the workshop, and two were burned.

Yet each subject felt in some way that firewalking had been a breakthrough for them. Fully half perceived they had a break-through in the degree of their fears in that they experienced "much less" fear since firewalking. One had a breakthrough in dealing with his fears, commenting, "They just go away!" Three subjects found a breakthrough in their capacity to take risks, and two individuals, 25% of this sample, perceived breakthroughs in their relationships with others.

Finally, five subjects in this category, or 62.5%, felt they had a breakthrough or significant change in their life after firewalking. "I'm more comfortable and confident with myself and others," "I look for the positive in each adversity," and "I take more chances" reflect the type of changes they feel. In addition, six subjects, 75% of the sample, felt a breakthrough or significantly different about themselves. Their feelings are encompassed in the words of one man who said simply, "I like myself better."

■

Specific Cases

A 60 year old man with a high school education appreciated both the workshop and the group. He has had scant experience with meditation or drugs, but has done a moderate degree of study and several workshops. His firewalk was a breakthrough for him in terms of his life changing and his confidence soaring. Prior to his walk, he was in a state of "abject terror," and afterwards, ecstatic. "The elation was so great," he writes, "like being with a girlfriend on a front porch swing. It only takes 15 minutes for the whole night to pass."

Three subjects in this grouping found that they grew to appreciate the group, and also valued the workshop. All of these respondents reported breakthrough changes in their lives as well as an enhanced self image. Two had breakthroughs in the level of their fears, and all were able to take significantly more risk.

Another three subjects who had scant experience in meditation or the esoterics prior to firewalking found they liked neither the group nor the workshop. All had done a few workshops, but had had no mystical or spiritual experiences. All felt they had breakthroughs in their level of fear and capacity to take risks, and significant differences in their attitudes toward themselves.

One of these subjects is Polly, whom we have followed in her depressed states prior to firewalking through to her truimphs which are recalled when she turns on *Switched on Bach*. Polly was undergoing a time of intense pain and trial in her life, with her husband finding a younger woman and her children leaving the house. Today, her life is successful: a new career, a satisfying relationship, and challenges to keep her moving forward. She attributes much of her success to the lessons she learned from firewalking.

Thus, we find that 17.5% of the entire population can be grouped among those who had slight experience with the esoterics or transformational belief systems, but were significantly impacted by the experience of firewalking.

■

Contrast Group One: Little Experience Begets Little Benefit

In contrast to Intuitive Group Two, in which those with scant experience in the esoterics significantly benefitted from the firewalk experience, this group with little experience gained little or nothing from firewalking.

Five subjects, or 12.5% of the sample population, fall into this category. They are three men and two women, all of whom came to the firewalk out of curiosity, and two of whom were slightly burned. Two of the subjects, a man and a woman are over 50 years of age. Three of the five subjects, when asked to theorize about firewalking said, "I don't know."

Two similar cases are men who both have Master of Arts degrees, and did not value the workshop nor enjoy the group experience. Neither had ever tried drugs nor spent much time in workshops or studying spiritual traditions. One, however, does "believe in God" sufficiently to have said a prayer just prior to firewalking. Basically, neither has seen any change in their lives or their behavior since the firewalk, aside from one having noticed "somewhat less" fears in his life. Of interest, neither man had a theory as to how firewalking transpires. One wrote, "Firewalking had no particular meaning for me." The other explained,

I suppose it's nice to say I firewalked, but I rarely tell anybody. It's not something one can slip into a conversation without getting strange looks. Still...it was fun.

Another young man who firewalked while still in high school had done some study of the spiritual traditions, but had no experience in other areas. He was not burned, and did not have a theory as to how firewalking occurs. He wrote:

193

It was an interesting experience and I'm glad I was able to participate. However, it has had very little impact on my life besides reaffirming my belief that there are still things science cannot account for. The value of the firewalking experience for me was as proof of potential, not of God.

Two women are also included in this sample group. One woman attended in order "to impress" a man in whom she was interested. Although the coals felt cool, dry, and crunchy, she did suffer several blisters. About the workshop, she writes, "I walked on fire when it was over. Whether the workshop training had any bearing on that, I don't know." The group "made no difference." Immediately after the workshop, she reports, "I was most impressed with seeing soot on people's feet. I didn't wash my feet for days!" But now, four years later, she writes, "I don't feel differently and it had no meaning. Once a skeptic, always a skeptic."

Finally, one of our in-depth personalities, Laura, belongs in this category. Fifty-eight years of age, Laura has firewalked nine times. She believes the seven workshops were valuable for her, and found the groups "all right" although very mixed. Laura was not burned, and afterward, she "cried because I was so happy I did it!" Now, despite the fact that she keeps a photograph of herself in her kitchen, she is "still the same old horrid person," has "poor" relationships, and is "trying to loose weight. [I] haven't lost an ounce in five years." Laura concludes, "It just seems to me that I walked on fire nine times. Nothing more, I regret to say. I wish I had had a breakthrough of some kind."

Thus, within the sample population of firewalkers, of those who have an esoteric experience level below "moderate," that is, just a slight experience or a mean score of 2.6 or below, 27% find the experience to be without significant or even moderate impact.

■

A Closer Look at Group Two

Although the majority of individuals from the sample population fall into the large middle category of people who benefitted from firewalking and felt a positive impact in their lives as a result of the experience, at either end of the veritable bell curve are two groups in contrast.

What is different about these subjects? All have scant experience in the esoterics, but some gained a great deal from firewalking while others gained little or nothing. What factors can we isolate about these groups? Their ages are virtually identical, with the mean age for those who benefitted being 42, or 38 for those who did not. In both cases, there are slightly more men at these extremes.

The group which perceived no impact on their lives from firewalking was significantly better educated than those who changed. That is, the mean educational level for the "non-changers" was a Master of Arts degree, while the mean level for those impacted by firewalking was *less* than a Bachelor of Arts degree. This, then, is the first meaningful insight as to the reasons for the contrasts between the groups.

Secondly, we find that the reasons for attending the firewalk seminar varied significantly. All of those who did not benefit came initially out of curiosity, while only one of those who experienced positive change came solely out of curiosity. The others came for personal growth or because a friend had urged them to attend. Thus, those that came with the intention of growing, did.

Looking to the intuitive factors which are drawn from innuendos within the questionnaire and the interviewer's field notes, we can offer additional insights into the differences between these groups. In the case of those who benefitted from firewalking, for example, we generally find a freer expression of emotions. That is, all but one subject in this group expressed a dramatic emotion before, during or after the firewalk. "Abject terror," "panic," and "desperation," experienced prior to firewalking were coupled with "ecstasy," "utter exhilaration" or tears of joy after the walk.

Those well educated individuals who perceived scant impact from firewalking, on the other hand, expressed "calm," "doubt," or "concentration" before the walk, and "relief," "bravery," or "skepticism" following their accomplishment. Thus, the ability to contact and express one's emotions may have an influence on the degree of impact which results from a profound personal experience.

Examining the theoretical approach of the two groups, we find that the group that benefitted was more willing to venture a theory of "mind over matter" or "belief," that is, a theory which is outside of the frame of known scientific laws. Of those that did not change, only one suggested the power of her mind. Three did not know and one ventured, "Leidenfrost. If not that, I don't know."

Viewed from this angle, it would appear that those who benefitted from firewalking are more willing to "play outside of the dots," so to speak, and explore unconventional ways of thinking. Similarly, they may be more willing to be wrong and risk ridicule rather than to stay in the middle without a risk by saying, "I don't know."

Thus, we might conclude that those that benefit from firewalking, even though they have had scant previous experience with unusual phenomena, are those with less formal education—which certainly tends to stifle creative thinking in favor of the traditional academic methods. They are an unconventional group, interested in personal growth, in touch with their emotions and willing to play outside of the known rules. They are probably individuals who are more fun to know than their contrasting counterparts!

■

Intuition Three: More Experience Means Less Impact

Six individuals, or 15% of the entire sample population, exemplified the intuitive idea that those who have had a great deal of experience in the esoterics will not find firewalking to be a particularly remarkable or impactful experience. Half of the subjects in this group felt the firewalk had resulted in "no change" in any area of their lives, while the other half felt they simply could not attribute their changes to firewalking.

Two of these subjects are well educated men—one with a Ph.D.—in their thirties, who rank themselves as having a great deal of experience in meditation and extensive study in the spiritual traditions. Both have had fewer mystical or spiritual experiences than the degree to which they have studied and neither man found the group nor the workshop valuable, with one noting that the group was "a bit 'New Age blissed out.' "

Both men perceived they had not changed at all, except for one noticing a minor increase in his capacity to take risks. Both men answered the questionnaire with terse, one word answers, with one concluding that the experience was "fun," while the other wrote, "It was a nice experience. I'm not sold on it. I feel 'one event' conversions are of limited value."

A 43-year-old man with a great deal of experience in meditation, and more mystical experiences than study went to the firewalk to overcome his fear of coals. Regrettably, he found no change in any area of his life, including the degree of his fears or his way of dealing with them. Worthy of note is that this man is a river rafter, mountain climber, and skydiver who has already undertaken to lay many of his fears to rest with such sports. It would seem that firewalking did not live up to his expectations, although he concluded, "It's an exciting, resourceful experience, which I've done five times!" This final comment, pointing to the question of why an individual would pursue an activity which holds no perceived benefit is an issue we will consider later in the book.

Another man in his thirties, with a high school education, attended the workshop as a growth experience, and then attended a second time. He found neither workshop helpful, however, and was "not concerned" with the group. He has studied the spiritual traditions extensively and had many mystical experiences. He has also attended many workshops and had a moderate degree of experience with meditation. "Years ago" he experimented extensively with mind-altering drugs. He believes himself to be "an adventurer in many respects, always looking for new challenges."

This subject thinks about his firewalk experience "often," mentioning, "How can you forget such a thing?" Yet, he finds no impact from his firewalks, aside from a temporary degree of healing, about which he writes,

> I have sarcoid of the lungs and have lost 80% of my lung function. I always breathed easy for a while directly after each walk, but there was no real, lasting healing.

Finally, two men who are friends attended the same firewalking workshop. They have worked with a local institute which studies the limits of our human frontiers, particularly in the realm of parapsychology. Both have extensive experience in meditation, study in the spiritual traditions, workshops, and mystical experiences. For both of them, the firewalk was simply a confirmation of the expanded reality they "already knew existed" and "just another step along the way."

Thus, we see that nearly one-fifth of the population with much esoteric experience finds the firewalk falls short of a breakthrough learning. But must we be jaded in this regard? Are powerful experiences only for the uninitiated? Do any of those individuals with a great deal of experience and self awareness find the firewalk a meaningful experience? Again, we find that there are a number of individuals who contrast with these subjects.

■

Contrast Group Three: Much Experience Means Great Benefit

Four subjects, or 10% of the sample, contrast this previous group. That is, they have had a significant degree of experience in transformational studies, meditation and the like, and also gained a great deal from the experience of firewalking.

Included are three men and one woman with a mean age of 40. Two have Bachelor of Arts degrees and two have Master's degrees. Two of the men attended the workshop for the purpose of personal growth, while one attended "on a whim," and the woman attended because she is a "workshop junkie—I had to do it."

Among this group of subjects who contrast the "norm" is Mark, another previous in-depth study. Mark has had a great deal of experience in altered states, meditation, and esoteric studies, and felt that firewalking would be "a good way to enter the altered state." He thinks of himself as "Buck Rogers or Tom Sawyer, always looking for something new, novel, and exciting."

Mark found firewalking to be a breakthrough experience in many aspects: his capacity to take risks, the way he deals with his fears, the way he feels about himself and the degree to which his life has changed. It will be recalled that Mark was prepared to firewalk when he thought his mother's house was on fire. For Mark, firewalking was a "landmark."

The two other men in this group, both in their forties with

extensive transformational study and experience, found the workshop helpful and enjoyed the group. One wrote, "The group seemed to be one, big, happy family—before, during and after." The other wrote, "My feeling about the group became one of admiration during and after the walk." Both also theorized that their accomplishment was due to "mind over matter."

In terms of changes, one found significant differences in his way of dealing with fear, and the level of his fears. He also felt significantly changed and different about himself. He noted that, "reality has taken on a much more flexible meaning," and concludes, "My attitude toward "apparent limitations" has changed greatly. Is there anything I can't do?"

The other individual found significant differences in his feelings aboout himself, in his relationships, in his capacity for risk-taking, and in the degree to which his life has changed for the better. He writes, "My time urgency has diminished, my expectation of others has vanished, and I am moving more directly at my chosen outcomes." He concludes,

> The firewalk is a very remarkable way to get the attention of people to prove that 'as a man thinketh, so is he,' and so he can do.

Finally, the woman in this section of the study must be considered separately, for she is Naomi, whom we met earlier in this chapter. She is a 41-year-old woman with extensive experience in the esoterics. She appreciated the workshop, but had an unusual attitude toward the group: "They were all into themselves. There was not a bond and they were not important to me. But if there were no group, I wouldn't have walked."

Naomi, it will be recalled, had a series of breakthrough experiences immediately following the workshop, three years previous. She felt confident, her business and finances improved, and she stood up to her domineering mother. It "blew her mind." She felt, and proved to herself, "I can do anything." In the intervening years, however, she has come to feel that this attitude of "self-righteousness and egotism" was inappropriate. Instead, she has in the last 18 months strived to learn "humility." She commented, "I don't recommend firewalking now because my ego soared." So did her business, and her life.

Prior to the interview, Naomi had not made the connection between her perceived "egotistic" attitude and the successes she was experiencing in her life. At the conclusion of the interview, she commented,

> I hadn't thought of it at all this way before. I just thought it was bad to feel like I can do *anything*— really egotistical and all that. Now I don't feel that way and I'm broke. I need to reconsider firewalking and the way I felt after it. I guess it was pretty good after all....

Naomi has again benefitted from her firewalk experience, through a stranger simply asking her questions. Like those other individuals in this contrasting group, she can allow and acknowledge the impact and the positive change it held for her.

■

A Closer Look at Group Three

Is there hope, then, that individuals who have pursued extensive investigations in the realm of transformation can still have transformational experiences? Yes, although the character traits which differentiate those that have continued profound experiences and those that do not are, again, important.

The educational level of this contrast grouping is virtually identical, as well as the theoretical approach. By and large, those that have pursued unconventional, esoteric study and experience acknowledge and hypothesize that the the power of the mind is greater than the physical world. None of the subjects with significant previous esoteric experience ascribed firewalking to known properties of the physical world, Leidenfrost, or the wet grass.

Again, we do find a difference in the emotional realm. Those that perceived less impact in their lives were more likely to have felt "relief," or "well being" following their firewalk, while those who felt they benefitted from the firewalk experienced "ecstasy," "total elation," or tears of joy. Mark "almost cried."

The contrasts between these groups seem less dramatic than those who had scant experience in the esoterics prior to their firewalk. Between both sets of contrast groups, whereas educational level and theoretical approach are not differentiated, the factor of emotional development is the common thread. That is, the majority of those who benefitted from firewalking were those who experienced an emotional abyss prior to firewalking and a peak of exhilaration following their walk. Hence, these appear to be individuals who are in touch with and express their emotions more freely than their contrasting counterparts.

■

Illogical Groupings: Matters in Contrast to "Common Sense"

The final areas for exploration in this investigation are those "matters which seem contrary or surprising to common sense."[3] Two areas stand out as posing this sort of contrast. For one, those subjects who find no value or scant worth in their experience of firewalking, yet pursue it or recommend it to others. Second are those subjects who find many areas of behavioral differences but think they have not "changed" as a result of firewalking.

"Firewalking Didn't Help Me, But Everyone Should Do It!"

There were four subjects who fell into this group of what is surprising for this researcher and contrary to common sense. Common sense dictates that when something is good for us, or has been valuable in our experience, we may do it again or recommend it to others. When something has been bad—a restaurant, a movie, a worskhop—we do not suggest that others eat there, see it, or participate. Similarly, we don't go back to the restaurant or the movie again, or pay additional money for a workshop which was of no benefit.

Yet 10% of the total subject population appear to be doing precisely the opposite. They feel no differently about themselves, and have perceived scant or no change in their lives, but they attend firewalking workshops repeatedly and recommend to others this experience which did not serve them.

To look at these cases more specifically, we must in this case refer only to the questionaire, since none of these subjects were in face-to-face dialogues with the researcher. Thus, no field notes were taken, nor intuitive impressions recorded.

Subject A, whom we will name Albert, went to the firewalking seminar to overcome his fears. He has a Bachelor's degree and is in his forties. He was not burned, and was generally unemotional about his firewalk, feeling "excited" before the walk, "tranced out" during it, and "happy" when it was done. Since his firewalk, he feels no change in himself and does not perceive himself differently. He has noticed no differences in his relationships, the level of his fears, the way he deals with his fears, or his capacity to take risks. Yet Albert concludes his questionnaire by saying, "It is an exciting, resourceful experience which I have done five times!" Given that Albert is firewalking with Tony Robbins, the most expensive of the instructors, it is most curious that he repeats such a worthless experience.

Subject B, Bertha, went to the firewalk out of curiosity. She would not disclose her age, although she is a Ph.D. She was frightened prior to walking because that morning she had a "vision" of herself lying in bed, burned. She did suffer a slight burn, which went away immediately. Since her firewalk, she has also seen no changes in herself in any regard. She commented, "I'm not into personal growth. I didn't expect a change, I was thinking scientifically. Later I wondered if it was even amazing at all." She concluded our interview, however, by saying emphatically, "Everyone should do it!"

Subject C, Charlie, attended the firewalk to further his personal growth. He has completed high school and is in his late thirties, having walked the first time in his young thirties. Charlie was "excited" before his walk, "spaced out" during it, and "very happy" afterwards. Charlie feels "some" change in his life and the way he feels about himself, but no changes in any other respects. Charlie has firewalked three times.

Finally, Subject D is Laura, our "maximum cross-ee," who has walked the coals nine times. At one workshop, she walked four times. She keeps a photograph of herself walking on coals in her kitchen, but has seen no change in her life. After nine crossings, she is "still the same old horrid person." Why did she walk nine times? What is in the character make-up of these individuals that they pursue an activity with dubious results? Is it so mundane as to be simply masochistic behavior? For this researcher, common sense dictates that these subjects have low self-esteem, perhaps they do not feel worthy of valuable experiences. Perhaps they are sufficiently hampered as to be afraid or unwilling to admit to change. Three of the four attribute their success to the power of their mind, but have not gone on to empower their minds sufficiently to change their lives beyond the firewall. Yet, perhaps they are simply "thrill seekers," going for those brief moments of ecstasy they felt immediately after walking on fire.

"I'm Doing Lots of Things Differently, But I Haven't Changed"

This is the second group of subjects which were noticeably against the grain of common sense and offered surprising responses. Common sense tells us that when we start doing things differently in our lives, or notice that things around us and the way we perceive them are different, we have probably changed, at least to some degree.

Yet, three individuals who saw numerous differences about themselves and their daily behaviors did not believe that they had "changed" in any way. In this circumstance, however, all of the noteworthy and surprising subjects were personally interviewed, so the researchers' field notes become valuable.

Subject E, Emily, is in her early thirties and holds a Master of Arts degree. She attended the firewalk with a friend, twice, for the purpose of building her courage and self-esteem. She was emotionally expressive about the experience, feeling the range from "desperation" to "very exhilarated." Emily has seen significant differences in her relationships, perceiving that she is less rigid, "looking more at what is rather than what I think should be." She also deals with her fears in a significantly different manner. In her daily life she "questions things more," and had what she feels to have been a dramatic "reaffirmation" of her faith in God. Does she feel differently about herself in light of these changes? "No."

Subject F, Farquar, is a college student who walked when he

was 16, having been taken by his mother to the seminar. Today, he approaches his fears differently, and does not reject things so easily, It was a "meaningful" experience, after which he felt "very high and successful." Firewalking left "more open doors" in his life, including the intensely "peaceful" feeling he had when he was crossing the coals. Does Farquar perceive changes in his life or feel differently about himself? "No."

Finally, Subject G, Gertrude, is a woman in her mid-thirties who attended the workshop with her mother, and was curious about the phenomenon. She particularly enjoyed the rituals which surrounded the workshop in regards to the fire, but felt little emotion about the walk: she was determined, then "blank," and "pleased" after she had walked. Firewalking was "motivational" for Gertrude, and has been especially important in recent months when she has changed jobs and is doing particularly challenging work. She often looks at her affirmative signature card, "I walked on fire, I can do anything," when she "needs a boost." Does Gertrude perceive any changes or feel differently about herself? "No."

What can we learn from the field notes in these surprising cases? One interesting commonality is that all of these subjects held no theories as to how firewalking occurs. Emily was "still curious," and Farquar said, "There are still mysteries we don't understand." Gertrude commented, "I have respect for it, even if it doesn't make sense."

This final comment also ties together some aspects of the field notes. Gertrude had respect for "it"—fire/firewalking—but did not have respect for the people who did it, most notably herself. Similarly in all cases we noted something to the effect of "poor self perception" on these subjects. All of them were able to see that things around them had changed but needed the stability of the "same person" at home. This need for stability in the personality structure was noticed, which indicates some insecurity in the capacity for change. On a purely intuitive level, this researcher completed each of these interviews with some sadness, feeling as though these individuals were seeking some form of completion or satisfaction, and then denying its realization in themselves.

3. The Spiritual Dimension

Over half of the interviewees and 25% of the questionnaire respondents reported a change in the spiritual dimension, in the realm of their ideas about God and the nature of reality. For many of them, the change was profound. Participants reported feeling God's presence in their lives, direct communication with Jesus, and deep healing with the Creator, as well as the realization that God is within each being rather than "up there." This sense of spiritual connectedness is much like the reports of firewalkers around the world,[4] as well as the spirit which calls the Anastenarides into the fire.[5]

Three other instances are worthy of note in this regard. One woman in the study who reported a new connectedness with God also stopped in the middle of the firewalk to pick up coals in her hands, with no effects or burning whatsoever. Like Coe,[6] who held coals in his hands, this individual was testing, and validating, her view of reality. After the firewalk, she sat beside a fire musing as to the hows and whys of her experience. She picked up a burning log in her hands, at which point her hands were not burned but all the hair on her arms was singed.

Another woman reported a feeling of being in contact with "supernatural" knowledge, much as the capacity of the Bulgarian Nestenaries to "utter prophecies."[7] In this case, she felt she had prior access to information which guided her to make what were later proven to be correct decisions in averting disaster on a summer holiday.

Finally, when asked how she thought she was able to firewalk, one participant replied, "Fire is the friendliest of all the elements. It is the easiest to work with." This respondent bears a striking, if less dramatic, resemblance to the Greek fire dancer who explained, "You feel love for the fire … You go into the fire freely."[8]

Of interest, two respondents reported being surrounded by a "glow" of protection. Such reports call to mind the "unidentified force" which protects the firewalkers in Kenn's study of firewalking in Hawaii.[9]

In conclusion, it should be noted that fully half of the firewalkers concur with LeShan[10] and Pearce[11] that it was the power of their mind mastering matter that enabled them to firewalk. Given the high level of education and previous experience of the participants, it would appear that the sample is taking a more sophisticated position than that of "belief" in a higher power.

4. Our Study and Future Research

Often the case with many research attempts, as many questions are raised as answered, and loopholes are uncovered which were not evident beforehand.

One pitfall of which we were aware beforehand was the lack of a concrete means to infer causality: Are the behavior or attitudinal changes perceived by the subject in fact caused by the firewalk? To a greater degree than expected, the participants themselves provided a corrective measurement, seen in their unwillingness to attribute changes solely to their firewalk.

In other areas, the questionnaire was particularly at fault, inasmuch as we now see that it was too involved and complex for most individuals to give other than terse, one word answers which lack the depth called for by research such as this. Done again, the questionnaire would be simpler and more to the point.

We would also surmise that many of the divergences in the research between the subject populations were a result of the ill-designed questionnaire, which asked for too much in too little space, and presented the questions in an illogical order.

The questions need to be arranged differently, both in the questionnaire and in the Interview Guide. We found that we were asking the deeper questions, which called for some degree of self-awareness, quite early in the inquiry, leaving the less profound investigations to the end. In the questionnaire, the questions, "Do you feel changed in any way?" and "Do you feel differently about yourself" were placed immediately after, "Do you think about your firewalking experience at all?" This is too early to ask these most profound questions, which ask for reflection and introspection. Rather, they should have been placed after the questions about fears, risk, and behavior, which encouraged precisely the preparatory introspection asked for in the first questions. A short way into the interview proccess, we noticed this reversal and adapted the Interview Guide accordingly.

It is our belief that this discrepancy would account for the divergence in the two sample populations, wherein the questionnaire respondents had a significantly lower rate of changes perceived in their daily lives or feeling differently about themselves than the interviewees.

This limitation of the study also points to its strength: the corroboration of two methods to arrive at a more wholistic data pool. The study was "corrected" mid-stream, as it were, to provide a greater depth of response and insight into the human experience. Similarly, another strength is found precisely in this attempt to move further into the qualitative aspects of the psychology of human experience, rather than being limited to empirical, quantitative measurements of fire temperatures and debates as to how firewalking can be accomplished.

The science of human beings—human science—cries for such research, to lead us into new dimensions of ourselves, and to point the way to a better world. Too long have we spent clocking mice running the proverbial maze.

We can certainly envision a variety of follow-up research to extend and elaborate this study. Questionnaires and interviews with friends and family who have been witness to the firewalker's behavior over a period of time before and after the event would objectify the findings from this investigation. Interviews with firewalking instructors would be of value, to augment the information gleaned from the participants.

Further study into the nature of perceived change is called for, with questions which pursue different avenues than those in this study; questions which move deeper into the behavior and psyche of the subject. Will you now try things that you wouldn't have before? Has your decision style changed? Has your strategy for learning changed? These are questions which, in retrospect, interest these researchers.

It could be also interesting to apply Kenneth Ring's "Omega" questionnaires to participants of firewalking workshops. Ring designed a battery of questionnaires to study the impact of a near-death experience (NDE). This battery of questionnaires consisted of the following: (1) Background Information Sheet which included standard biographical data (name, age, education, and occupation); (2) Life Changes Questionnaire designed to test the effect of the

NDE in terms of increase, decrease or no change in attitutes toward appreciation of life, concern for others, concern with impressing others, materialism, and quest for meaning; (3) Religious Beliefs Inventory to test growth away from narrower denominational beliefs toward a broader spiritual universalism; (4) Psychic Experience Inventory to explore changes in a variety of psychic abilities and beliefs; (5) Future Scenario Questionnaire to examine what sort of vision of the future the individuals have after their experience; (6) Behavior Rating Inventory filled out by acquaintances who knew the experiencers well enough to report on whether or not change had occurred in the respondent.[12]

Kenneth Ring found that NDE provides impetus toward spiritual growth in terms of: (1) increased positive and decreased negative values or attitudes toward self, others, and life in general; (2) increased beliefs in broader, more universal "spiritual truths" rather than narrower, denominationally-oriented religious doctrine; (3) increased psychic sensitivity.[13] A later study that applied the battery of questionnaires to individuals who had had a UFO experience yielded similar results.[14] It would be interesting to find out whether other transformational experiences (e.g., spiritual visions or other mystical phenomena) carry with them similar impetus for spiritual and psychological change and growth, and whether firewalking belongs to the same category.

Finally, investigation within the population of non-walkers will be valuable. Do they learn anything from their decision or simply come away feeling defeated and unsuccessful? Are there any tools they have learned which will serve them later in life, or will they just be repairing their damaged self-image? Have they learned to listen, for example, to their inner voice, even when it says "no"?

5. A Composite Firewalker

To conclude the discussion of the impact of firewalking prior to summarizing our conclusions in the next chapter, we rely on Polkinghorne,[15] who notes that the final evaluation for qualitative research is not a statistical compendium, but ideally a vivid, accurate, rich, and elegant description of the firewalking experience and the effect it has had on the human beings who have accomplished the feat.

In this case, vividness can be described as the quality which draws the readers in, creating a feeling of genuineness. Accuracy makes the writing believable and enables readers to see the phenomenon as their own. Richness is that quality which deepens the description through colorful use of language and conveys the sensual tones of the experience. Finally, elegance discloses the phenomenon through simple expressions that give it grace and poignancy.

In order to meet these criteria in a description of the firewalk experience, the qualitative thoughts and feelings of the subjects emerge as the greatest source of information. We here delve into the data, using the words of the walkers themselves to offer a description of firewalking. What better way to understand the essence of the phenomenon than to move inside the mind of a firewalker....

Here is Harriett, our composite firewalker, whom we meet as she is about to cross the coals:

■

Harriett: The Essence of Firewalking

"...Fear. Stark terror. Desperation. Exhilaration. I'm feeling it all. What if I fail? I would look ridiculous with bandaged feet, trying to go to work on Monday...'Uh, well... I tried to walk across a biiig barbeque...' My knees are shaking. But, boy, if I do it, it'll make a great story! I'm so excited!

I wonder when I'll hear my inner voice telling me it's time to walk. Will it? Will it tell me I won't be burned? It's *so* hot! I'm glad I don't have to do this if I don't want to... But I want to. At least, I think I want to...Other people have walked across the coals—if they can do it, I can, too. It's so hot. What am I *doing* here? It's scary ...

What *am* I doing here? I'm here because I've heard about firewalking and I'm curious about it. I've always been curious... Standing next to this fire, I wish I *wasn't* the curious type. It killed the cat! Yikes, that's the wrong thing to think! Just listen for my inner voice. Maybe this will help me grow. I hope it does! I want to learn more about myself and this reality we call "life." I can overcome my fears. And, besides, Joyce recommended it. She usually knows what she's talking about.

There goes Paul, our instructor, across. Hey, he is really walking on those hot coals. That's a pretty convincing feat. I CAN do this! Wow—there goes some of our group across. Look at those people who have crossed. Look how happy they are! Listen to the group. I thought they were all New Age space cadet stereotypes, but, geez, we're all in this together. They're really encouraging me to go! I'm so scared! I can do it. I WILL do it! Yes, It's time to walk! GO!"

Crunch, crunch...

"I can do it. I can do it. Stay focused on the other side. Stay focused. Wow! I'm doing it! The coals are pretty warm. They feel like hot sand. But crunchy. Like walking across a warm astro-turf door mat. But they're silky. It's like walking across breakfast cereal with talcum powder on it! I'm concentrating. Time seems really slow... It's taking so long to walk across this fire. Funny, the coals are hardly hot at all. OUCH! Yes they *are*! Yikes! I felt the fire on my foot when I stopped concentrating!"

Crunch, crunch ... squish ...

"YEEEOOOWWWIEE! I'm off! I *did it*! I walked on *fire*! I *did it*! What a relief!! Everybody's hugging me! I feel so supported. I love this group of people! We *did* it! I can do anything! I'm about to cry! I've never been so high! Should I walk across again? I can do it! Ohhh... I'm SO HAPPY!! I've never been so happy!

Gee, all I have is a little burn. It doesn't hurt at all. Paul says it's good to get a little reminder of what we can do! Heeeyyyy...I just love these people! I walked on fire, I can do *anything*!"

■

An analysis of the data reveals that for most, the firewalk experience is fear, focus, and exhilaration; terror, concentration, and ecstasy. Just the other side of the proverbial existential "leap of faith," or "step" of faith, lies the elation of success, the pride of overcoming personal fear and doubt, the power of transforming fear into adventure.

Conclusions

The authors began this book with experiential observations and ended it with a scholarly study. We wanted the reader to move along this path with us, to share our findings, our frustrations, and joys of small discoveries.

The purpose of the this study was to learn whether individuals who have firewalked perceive that they have changed, either through their behaviors, beliefs, attitudes, or their perceptions of themselves. Indeed, that question has been reliably answered: Yes. The majority of people believe they have changed after they firewalk, at least to some extent.

The data were obtained from 40 participants, 20 of whom responded to a questionnaire mailed randomly to individuals on the lists of five firewalking instructors. An additional 20 subjects were interviewed by telephone or in a face-to-face intensive interview. All participants were known to have walked on fire.

The results indicate that firewalkers tend to be well educated middle-aged men and women. Eighty percent had a college or graduate education, and more than half have attended personal growth workshops and studied their own or other religious traditions. Many are meditators and have had mystical experiences, although usually without the aid of mind-altering drugs.

Eighty percent of the participants found the firewalking workshops they attended to be valuable. Half of the individuals found "no change" on their feet after crossing the coals, while the other half noticed redness, burns, or blisters, although none were serious. Two-thirds of the firewalkers felt fear when they firewalked, and ecstasy afterwards.

Regarding the specific research questions addressed in the present study, the following conclusions can be drawn:

1. Seventy-five percent of the participants noticed a positive change in their lives which they attributed to firewalking.

2. The major areas of change reported are in the areas of self-confidence, personal power, and self-esteem. Two-thirds of the participants reported less fear of other events after firewalking. Sixty percent claimed to take more risks and to deal with their fears more positively, and half of the participants noticed beneficial changes in their old relationships or an enhanced capacity to establish positive new relationships.

3. After firewalking, 65% note positive new behaviors in their lives, including improved relationships, less time urgency, improved diets, new jobs, more confidence in public speaking, and taking up activities which had previously been avoided due to their fear.

4. Individuals who allowed themselves to experience a full range of emotions while firewalking, from terror to ecstasy, reported more long-range positive impact on their lives than those who felt little emotion during their firewalk.

5. People who reported no positive, long range, life-altering impact as a result of firewalking nevertheless enjoyed the firewalking experience and recommended it to others.

6. Firewalkers often describe their experience using some of the terms typically used to define peak performance.

We defined "change" as a shift or alteration which could be reflected in our behavior, or relationships, or in our "inner perceptions"—our thoughts, emotions, fears, attitudes, and beliefs. The data reveal that most individuals who have challenged their limits by firewalking believe they have changed and can offer examples to support their belief.

Yet, one question which arises out of this research on the

perception of change is one of generalization. Richard Gunther[1] felt he had profoundly changed following his firewalk experience and generalized beyond it to: "What are we humans capable of being and of doing?"

Are we capable of transcending limiting beliefs such as "War always was and always will be" and "Nature is there for us to conquer" to find a nurturing and sustainable way to live? If individuals can experience meaningful, positive change as a result of a limit-challenging experience such as firewalking, can humanity challenge its limits and rise to a more meaningful, positive way of living on the Earth?

Notes and References

Preface

1. Pearce, 1971/1973, p. 112.
2. Hopkins, 1913/1951.
3. Blake, 1985; Sky, 1989; Vilenskaya, 1985a, 1985b, 1985c, 1986, 1988, 1989.
4. Ianuzzo, 1983.
5. Hopkins, 1913/1951.
6. "The Mystery of Firewalking," 1978.
7. Armstrong, 1970; Cassoli, 1958; Christodoulou, 1978; Danforth, 1978; Frazer, 1900/1955; Gaddis, 1967; Gibson, 1952; Godwin, 1968; Gunther & Gunther, 1983; Heinze, 1985; Henry, 1893; Hopkins, 1913/1951; Ianuzzo, 1982, 1983; Kane, 1982; Kenn, 1949; Lang, 1897, 1900; Langley, 1901, Lodge, 1948; Marden, 1958; Menard, 1949; McClenon, 1983a, 1983b; Sayce, 1933; Schwabe, 1901; Shaw, 1975; Stowell & Mahaluxmivala, 1928; Thomas, 1934; White, 1934.

Chapter 1

1. Guberman, 1969; Slavchev, 1971/1983.
2. Maisyuk, 1982/1983.
3. *Ibid.*, p. 107.
4. Cotterell, 1979/1980; Gaddis, 1967, pp. 115-116.
5. Parrinder, 1976, p. 117.

6. *Ibid.*, p. 156.
7. Crawley, 1913/1951, p. 30.
8. *Rig Veda*, X.191.1; 191.4; in Le Mee, 1975, pp. 210, 216.
9. Cotterell, 1979/1980, p. 82.
10. Holmberg, 1964, pp. 235-236; Simcenko, 1978, pp. 510-511.
11. Simcenko, 1978, p. 510.
12. Vasiljev, 1978, p. 435.
13. Holmberg, 1964, pp. 235-236, 453-455; Simcenko, 1978, pp. 510-511.
14. Troshchansky, 1902, p. 28.
15. Holmberg, 1964, p. 455.
16. Mullins, 1985, p. 32.
17. Luomala, 1987, p. 218.
18. Bray, 1967/1985, p. 15.
19. Gutmanis, 1976/1979, p. 9.
20. Emerson, 1965.
21. John Tanner, *Narrative of Captivity and Adventures among the Indians of North America*, quoted in Emerson, 1965, p. 108.
22. Tanner, quoted in Emerson, 1965, p. 236.
23. Emerson, 1965, p. 53.
24. *Ibid.*, p. 110.
25. Blavatsky, 1966, p. 40.
26. *Toward the Light: A Message to Mankind from the Transcendental World*, p. 3.
27. Poignant, 1967, p. 29.
28. Blavatsky, 1966, p. 40.
29. *Ibid.*, pp. 41-42.
30. Evans-Wentz, 1960, p. 206
31. *Ibid.*, p. 85.
32. *Ibid.*, p. 28.
33. Cotterell, 1979/1980, p. 63.
34. Kiefer, 1988, pp. 85-86.
35. Krishna, 1971, p. 87.
36. Kiefer, 1988, pp. 2-3.
37. Muktananda, 1974, p. 63.
38. Eliade, 1964/1972, pp. 60-61; Sannella, 1987, pp. 44-45.
39. *The Bhagavad Gita*, 1962, 14:5-7,11; pp. 103-104.
40. *Ibid.*, 11:9-10,12-15,17; pp. 89-90.

41. Long, 1948/1976, p. 122.
42. Sannella, 1987, p. 46.
43. Edsman, 1987, p. 345.
44. Da Love-Ananda, 1980, p. 27.
45. Sannella, 1987, p. 122.
46. Andrade, 1975, pp. 174-175; 1988, pp. 32-88.
47. Gaddis, 1967, pp. 181-201; Gowan, 1980, pp. 121-122; Morris, 1974; Persinger & LaFreniere, 1977, p. 106.
48. Lisovenko, 1987; Ivchenko & Lisovenko, 1987; Dorofeyev, 1987; Vilenskaya, 1988a.
49. Tweedie, 1979, p. 62.
50. *Ibid.*, p. 68.
51. Eliade, 1968, p. 147.
52. *Ibid.*, p. 148.

Chapter 2

1. Hopkins, 1913/1951.
2. Lang, 1900, p. 14.
3. Coe, 1957.
4. Lang, 1900, p. 12.
5. Rooke, 1936.
6. Thurston, 1952, pp. 171, 222-23.
7. Gaddis, 1967, p. 117.
8. Dutt, 1944/1972, pp. 152-153.
9. Benedict, 1934; Eliade, 1964/1972, pp. 54, 112, 206, 315, 333, 372, 376, 442, 456; Gibson, 1952; Holmberg, 1964, p. 283; Parsons, 1939; Stevenson, 1904.
10. Grim, 1983, p. 67.
11. Belo, 1960; Passeron, 1983.
12. Oesterreich, 1921/1974.
13. Kiev, 1968; Metraux, 1972.
14. Eliade, 1966; Lane, 1842.
15. Thomson, 1894.
16. Hocken, 1898.
17. Roth, 1933.
18. Sebi Breci, 1982, p. 68.
19. Gudgeon, 1899.

20. cited in Lang, 1900, p. 4.
21. Kenn, 1949, p. 12.
22. Henry, 1893.
23. Kenn, 1949; Long, 1948/176.
24. Sayce, 1933.
25. Thurston, 1952, pp. 187-189.
26. Pathak, 1970, p. 93.
27. cited in Lang, 1900, p. 11.
28. Godwin, 1968; McClenon, 1983a.
29. Puharich, 1962, pp. 87-88.
30. Gaddis, 1967; Long, 1948/1976.
31. Feinberg, 1959.
32. Grosvenor & Grosvenor, 1966.
33. Godwin, 1968.
34. Perera, 1971, p. 20.
35. Godwin, 1968.
36. e.g., Cassoli, 1958; Christodoulou, 1978; Danforth, 1978; Dimantoglou, 1952, 1953; Gault, 1954; Krechmal, 1957; Manganas, 1983; Tanagras, 1953, 1956.
37. Calicoat, 1986; Danforth, 1978; Ianuzzo, 1983.
38. Cassoli, 1958.
39. cited in Ianuzzo, 1983, p. 7.
40. Danforth, 1978; Lodge, 1948.
41. Slavchev, 1971/1983.
42. Gaddis, 1967, pp. 133-155.
43. Godwin, 1968, pp. 145-171; Gowan, 1980, pp. 149-160; Hansen, 1982; Ianuzzo, 1982, 1983; Mead, 1964, pp. 362-363; Steffy-Channon, 1989; Truzzi, 1983.
44. Babb, 1974; Heinze, 1984, 1985.
45. Heinze, 1985, p. 49.
46. Ho Ku-Li, 1972.
47. Bach, 1952.
48. *Ibid.*, pp. 89-90.
49. Smith, 1984, p. 11.
50. Worrall, 1972, p. 51.
51. Crooks, 1889-1890; Earl of Dunraven, 1924; Home, 1921.
52. Zorab, 1976.
53. Price, 1936, 1939.
54. Price, 1936.

55. Ingalls, 1939; Price, 1936.
56. Price, 1936.
57. Brown, 1938; Price, 1937, 1939.
58. Price, 1939, p. 254.
59. *Ibid.*, pp. 250-262.
60. *Ibid.*, p. 261.
61. Mishlove, 1975, pp. 157-160.
62. Kenn, 1949, pp. 5-8.
63. "Argentine Institute," 1961.
64. Doherty, 1982.
65. Coe, 1957, p. 107.
66. Coe, 1978.
67. Danforth, 1978.
68. Cassoli, 1958; Lodge, 1948; Tanagras, 1953, 1956.
69. Ballis, Beaumanoir, & Xenakis, 1979; Xenakis, Larbig, & Tsarouchas, 1977.
70. Manganas, 1983, p. 81.
71. Manganas, 1983; Manganas & Zachariades, 1983.
72. Manganas, 1983, p. 82.
73. *Ibid.*
74. Kane, 1976, 1979, 1982.
75. Kane, 1982, pp. 372-373.
76. *Ibid.*, p. 376.
77. Schwarz, 1960, pp. 415-416.
78. Green & Green, 1973, p. 146.
79. Mundy, 1971.
80. Heinze, 1985.
81. Breci, 1982, p. 67.
82. *Ibid.*, p. 68.
83. Horn, 1953, p. 21.
84. Manganas, 1983.
85. *Ibid.*
86. Danforth, 1978, p. 35.
87. Danforth, 1978; Manganas, 1983.
88. Lang, 1900; Mundy, 1971.
89. Long, 1948/1976, pp. 31-37.
90. Kenn, 1949, pp. 20-22.
91. *Ibid*, pp. 29-30.
92. *Ibid.*, p. 33

93. e.g., Long, 1948/1976, p. 401.
94. Coe, 1957, 1978; Cooley, 1957; Komar, 1979.
95. Blake, 1985; Vilenskaya, 1983, 1984a, 1985a, 1985b, 1985c, 1988b, 1989.
96. Blake, 1985, p. 84.
97. Vilenskaya, 1985a.
98. James McClenon, personal communication, 1986.
99. Garrison, 1985; Griffin, 1985; Kotzsch, 1985; Vilenskaya, 1985b.
100. Blake, 1985, p. 63.
101. Vilenskaya, 1985c.
102. Calicoat, 1986.
103. *Ibid.*, p. 2.
104. *Ibid.*
105. *Ibid.*, pp. 2-3.
106. *Ibid.*, p. 3.
107. *Ibid.*
108. Feinberg, 1959; Komar, 1979; McClenon, 1983b.
109. Lang, 1900, p. 11.
110. Benson, 1984; Evans-Wentz, 1958.
111. Eliade, 1964/1972, pp. 112-113, 476.
112. Schwarz, 1960.
113. Kane, 1982.
114. Schwarz, 1960.
115. *Ibid*, p. 406.
116. Price, 1936.
117. Price, 1939.
118. Lang, 1900, p. 12.
119. Danforth, 1978, p. 124.
120. Danforth, 1978.
121. Megas, 1961, p. 499.
122. Danforth, 1978, pp. 235-236, 246.
123. Manganas, 1983, p. 80.
124. Danforth, 1978, p. 111.
125. Pathak, 1970, p. 92.
126. Kane, 1976, 1982; Schwarz, 1960.
127. Schwarz, 1960, p. 409.
128. Weil, 1983, p. 249.

129. Pierce, 1985; Weil, 1983; Blake, 1985; Vilenskaya, 1984a, 1985a, 1985b, 1985c.
130. cited in Garrison, 1985.
131. Smith, 1984.
132. Manganas, 1985.
133. Danforth, 1978, p. 134.
134. *Ibid.*, pp. 137-138.
135. *Ibid.*, p. 138.
136. Blake, 1985; Cohen, n.d., Kotzsch, 1985; Vilenskaya, 1983, 1984a, 1989.
137. Vilenskaya, 1984a.
138. Vilenskaya, 1985a, p. 62.
139. Blake, 1985, p. 83.
140. Gunther & Gunther, 1983; Smith, 1984.
141. Gunther & Gunther, 1983, p. 102.
142. Stillings, 1985b, p. 54.
143. Gunther & Gunther, 1983.

Chapter 3

1. Feinberg, 1959.
2. Gaddis, 1967; Gunther & Gunther, 1983; McClenon, 1983.
3. Gaddis, 1967; McClenon, 1983a, 1983b; Price, 1936, 1939; Stillings, 1985a, 1985b; Vilenskaya, 1983, 1984a, 1985a, 1985b.
4. Coe, 1957; Doherty, 1982; Walker, 1977; & Xenakis, Larbig, & Tsarouchas, 1977.
5. Weil, 1983.
6. Chari, 1960.
7. Coe, 1957; Darling, 1935; Kenn, 1949; Price, 1936, 1937, 1939.
8. Hocken, 1898; cited in Lang, 1900, p. 9.
9. Evaggelou, 1971, p. 159.
10. Cohen, 1971, p. 122.
11. Brown, 1938; Fonseka, 1971; Mishlove, 1975, pp. 157-160; Price 1936, 1939; Vilenskaya, 1983, 1984a.
12. Blacker, 1975, pp. 248-251; Calicoat, 1986; Ianuzzo, 1983; Sky, 1989; Vilenskaya, 1985a, 1985b, 1985c.

13. Leikind & McCarthy, 1985.
14. Blake, 1985, p. 72.
15. Roth, 1933; Fulton, 1902; Langley, 1901; Price, 1936, 1939; Leikind & McCarthy, 1985.
16. Coe, 1957; Walker, 1977.
17. Fonseka, 1971; Frazer, 1900/1955.
18. Freeman, 1974; Gudgeon, 1899; McClenon, 1983a.
19. Kenn, 1949; Ianuzzo, 1983.
20. Hopkins, 1913/1951; Coe, 1978.
21. Danforth, 1978.
22. Fulton, 1902.
23. Roth, 1933.
24. Kenn, 1949, pp. 4-6.
25. *Ibid.*, p. 6.
26. *Ibid.*, pp. 4-8, 11.
27. Darling, 1935; Ingalls, 1939; Price, 1936, 1937, 1939.
28. Ingalls, 1939, p. 176.
29. *Ibid.*, p. 177.
30. *Ibid.*
31. Price, 1936
32. Kenn, 1949.
33. Stillings, 1985a, 1985b, 1986.
34. Price, 1936.
35. Ingalls, 1939, pp. 177-178.
36. McClenon, 1983a, 1983b; Mishlove, 1975.
37. Ingalls, 1939, p. 174.
38. Price, 1936, 1939.
39. Fonseka, 1971.
40. Coe, 1978.
41. Freeman, 1974; Hopkins, 1913/1951.
42. Baker, 1985; Garrison, 1985.
43. Leikind and McCarthy, 1985,
44. Coe, 1957.
45. cited in Doherty, 1982, p. 68.
46. Kane, 1982.
47. Coe, 1957; Walker, 1977.
48. Coe, 1957; Ingalls, 1939.
49. Stillings, 1985b.
50. McClenon, 1983a, p. 27.

51. e.g., Price, 1939.
52. McClenon, 1983a.
53. *Guinness Book of World Records, 1988*, p. 33; *Guinness Book of World Records, 1989*, p. 31.
54. Ingalls, 1939, p. 175.
55. cited in Leikind & McCarthy, 1985, p. 31.
56. Walker, 1977, p. 131.
57. Doherty, 1982.
58. Kane, 1982.
59. Vilenskaya, 1984a; Xenakis, Larbig, & Tsarouchas, 1977.
60. Ballis, et al., 1979.
61. "The Mystery of Firewalking," 1978.
62. e.g., Darling, 1935; Feigen, 1969; Freeman, 1974; Kane, 1982; Kenn, 1949; McClenon, 1983b.
63. Feinberg, 1959, p. 75.
64. Darling, 1935; Freeman, 1974; Kane, 1982; Kenn, 1949; McClennon, 1983a.
65. Hadfield, 1917, p. 678.
66. Chapman, Goodell, & Wolff, 1959; Ullman, 1947.
67. Blake, 1985; Coe, 1978; Gaddis, 1967; Ianuzzo, 1983; Kane, 1982.
68. Blake, 1985, p. 77.
69. Stillings, 1985b.
70. cited in Vilenskaya, 1984, p. 113.
71. Coe, 1957.
72. James McClenon, personal communication, 1986.
73. Gaddis, 1967; Ianuzzo, 1983.
74. Zorab, 1976.
75. Weil, 1983, p. 249.
76. Weil, 1980, p. 253; 1983, p. 254.
77. e.g., Ader, 1981; Borysenko, 1984; Locke, & Colligan, 1986; Locke, & Horning-Rohan, 1983; Oubre, 1986; Prince, 1982a, 1982b; Rogers, Dubey, & Reich, 1979.
78. Achterberg, 1985; Geschwind & Behan, 1982.
79. Stillings, 1985b, p. 58.
80. Leikind & McCarthy, 1985.
81. Stillings, 1985b, p. 58.
82. Breci, 1982; Danforth, 1978; Godwin, 1968; Kane, 1982; Manganas, 1983.

83. Pathak, 1970.
84. Danforth, 1978, p. 124.
85. *Ibid.*, pp. 137-138.
86. *Ibid.*, p. 281.
87. Kane, 1979, 1982; Schwarz, 1960.
88. Kane, 1982, pp. 376-377.
89. Weil, 1983.
90. Weil, 1983; Pearce, 1971/1973, 1985.
91. Weil, 1983, p. 253.
92. *Ibid.*, p. 250.
93. Evaggelou, 1971.
94. LeShan, 1975, 1976; Pearce, 1971/1973, 1977, 1985.
95. Mir & Vilenskaya, 1986, p. 191.
96. Schmeidler, 1973, 1984.
97. Manganas, 1983.
98. Stillings, 1985a, 1985b, 1986.
99. Doherty, 1982, p. 69.
100. Pearce, 1971/1973, 1985.
101. Kane, 1976, 1982.
102. Stillings, 1985a, p. 17.
103. Gudgeon, 1899; Kenn, 1949; Menard, 1949; Ross, 1966.
104. Pearce, 1985, pp. 80-81.
105. *Ibid.*, p. 104.
106. LeShan, 1976, p. 24.
107. Breci, 1982, p. 68.
108. Kane, 1982, p. 382.

Chapter 4

1. Maisyuk, 1984, p. 47.
2. e.g., Bandler, & Grinder, 1975, 1976, 1979.
3. Blake, 1985, p. 86.
4. Blake, 1985, p. 83; Weil, 1983, p. 253.
5. Stillings, 1985b.
6. Griffin, 1985, p. 44.
7. Robbins, 1986.
8. Foreword to Makrakis, 1982, pp. 9-11.
9. Christodoulou, 1978, p. 170.

10. Makrakis, 1982, p. 55.
11. Christodoulou, 1978, p. 171.
12. Villoldo, & Krippner, 1987, p. 77.
13. e.g., Roberts, 1974/1978; *Course in Miracles*, 1975/1985; *Right Use of Will*, 1984, pp. 8-9.
14. Roberts, 1974/1978, p. 10.
15. *Course in Miracles*, Workbook for Students, p. 86.
16. LeShan, 1976, pp. 10-11.
17. Kozulin, 1984, pp. 95-96; Uznadze, 1966a, 1966b.
18. Kozulin, 1984, p. 95.
19. Uznadze, 1966a, p. 150.
20. *Ibid.*, p. 152.
21. Coon, 1980, p. 411.
22. e.g., Ullman, Krippner, & Vaughan, 1973; Vilenskaya, 1984b.
23. Morozova, Ilyina & Dashevskaya, 1982, p. 92.
24. Kolodny, 1986; Vilenskaya, 1981; Volchenko, Dulnev, Krylov, Kulagin, & Pilipenko, 1984.
25. this book, Chapter IV, Section 3, p. 105.
26. Clifton, 1962, p. 75.
27. Kenn, 1949.
28. Villoldo, & Krippner, 1987, p. 77.
29. *Ibid.*
30. Weil, 1983, p. 249.
31. Sidenbladh, 1983.
32. Manganas, 1983, p. 80.
33. Aron & Aaron, 1986; Borland & Landrith, 1975; Dillbeck, Bauer, & Seferovich, 1978; Dillbeck, Cavanaugh, Glenn, Orme-Johnson, & Mittlefehldt, 1987; Giles, 1978; Hatchard, 1978; Landrith, 1978.
34. Clifton, 1962, p. 84.
35. Sky, 1989, back cover.

Chapter 5

1. Danforth, 1978; Kane, 1982; Vilenskaya, 1983, 1984a.
2. Coe, 1957; Doherty, 1982; Walker, 1977; Xenakis, Larbig, and Tsarouchas, 1977.
3. Blake, 1985.

4. Barker, 1971-1972, pp. 164-165.
5. Keen, 1975, p. 117.
6. Blake, 1985; Coe, 1978; Ianuzzo, 1983; Kane, 1982.
7. Tart, 1969, p. 3; 1972, p. 76.
8. Ludwig, 1969, pp. 13-16.
9. Blake, 1985, p. 77.
10. Leikind & McCarthy, 1985.
11. Privette, 1981a, 1981b, 1982a, 1982b, 1983; Garfield & Bennett, 1984; Waller, 1984.
12. Privette, 1981b, p. 51.
13. Privette, 1983, p. 1361.
14. Garfield and Bennett, 1984.
15. e.g., Gallwey & Kriegel, 1977; Leonard, 1975; McCluggage, 1977; Millman, 1979; Murphy & White, 1978; Spino, 1976.
16. Garfield & Bennett, 1984.
17. Vilenskaya, 1983, p. 94.
18. Vilenskaya, 1985a, p. 91.
19. *Ibid.*
20. Vilenskaya, 1983, p. 93.
21. Murphy & White, 1978, p. 144.
22. Privette, 1983, p. 1364.
23. Waller, 1984, p. 17.
24. e.g., Privette, 1981a, 1981b, 1982a, 1982b, 1983; Waller, 1984, 1988.
25. Privette, 1982a, 1982b, 1983.
26. Waller, 1988.
27. Lofland, 1971, p. 12.
28. Kerlinger, 1973.
29. Kidder, 1981, p. 157.
30. Polkinghorne, 1983, p. 267.
31. Lofland, 1971, p. 6.
32. Cannell, 1968, p. 530.
33. White, 1977, p. 57.
34. Kruger, 1979, p. 136.
35. Gorden, 1969, p. 36.
36. Fenlason, Beals, and Abrahamson, 1962, p. 129.
37. Lofland, 1971, p. 76.
38. Rogers, 1942.
39. Sellitz, Wrightsman, & Cook, 1976.

40. Golden, 1976, p. 26.
41. Kidder, 1981, p. 147.
42. Epstein, 1980.
43. Kidder, 1981; Galtung, 1967.
44. Neufield, 1977.
45. Golden, 1976, p. 27.
46. Johnson, 1975, p. 11.
47. McClelland & Atkinson, 1948; quoted in Steffy-Channon, p. 76.
48. Bruner, Goodnow, & Austin, 1956.
49. Whorf, 1956; quoted in Steffy-Channon, p. 77.
50. Cicourel, 1964.
51. Johnson, 1975, p. 12.
52. Giorgi, 1971b, p. 25; Keen, 1975, p. 155; Kruger, 1979, p. 117.
53. Golden, 1976, p. 24.
54. Kidder, 1981.
55. Krausz & Miller, 1974, pp. 49-50.
56. Goode & Hatt, 1952, pp. 48-49.
57. Kidder, 1981.
58. Gorden, 1969, p. 53.
59. Kruger, 1979, p. 126.
60. Kerlinger, 1973, p. 471.
61. *Ibid.*
62. Ross, 1974, p. 68.
63. Gorden, 1969, p. 54.
64. Kidder, 1981, p. 148.
65. *Ibid.*, p. 150.
66. Gorden, 1969, p. 55.
67. Stevick, 1971, p. 135.
68. Colaizzi, 1978, p. 62.
69. Stevick, 1971, p. 135.
70. in Polkinghorne, 1983, p. 39.
71. *Ibid.*
72. Polkinghorne, 1983, p. 279.
73. Golden, 1976, p. 16.
74. Giorgi, 1971a, p. 14.
75. Keen, 1975.
76. Fischer & Wertz, 1979, p. 157.

77. Giorgi, 1975, p. 101.
78. *Ibid.*, p. 72.
79. Goode & Hatt, 1952, pp. 48-49.
80. Kerlinger, 1973.
81. Kruger, 1979, p. 126.

Chapter 6

1. Stevick, 1971, p. 136.
2. Golden, 1976, p. 79.
3. Privette, 1981b, p. 51.
4. Garfield & Bennett, 1984.
5. *Ibid.*
6. Privette, 1983, p. 1361.

Chapter 7

1. Bruner, Goodnow, & Austin, 1956.
2. Valle & King, 1978.
3. Sellitz, Wrightsman, & Cook, 1976, p. 472.
4. e.g., Eliade, 1964/1972; Oesterreich, 1921/1974; Metraux, 1972.
5. Danforth, 1978.
6. Coe, 1957.
7. Lang, 1900, p. 12.
8. Danforth, 1978, p. 281.
9. Kenn, 1949.
10. LeShan, 1976.
11. Pearce, 1971, 1977, 1985.
12. Ring, 1984.
13. *Ibid.*
14. Davis, 1985.
15. Polkinghorne, p. 46.

Conclusions

1. Gunther & Gunther, 1983.

Bibliography

Achterberg, J. (1985). *Imagery in healing: Shamanism and modern medicine*. Boston, MA: New Science Library/Shambala.

Ader, R. (Ed.) (1981). *Psychoneuroimmunology*. New York: Academic Press.

Andrade, H.G. (1975). The Suzano poltergeist. *Proceedings of the Second International Congress on Psychotronic Research* (pp. 174-175). Monte Carlo.

Andrade, H.G. (1988). *Poltergeist: Algumas de suas ocorrencias no Brasil* [Poltergeist: Some Occurrences in Brazil]. São Paulo, Brazil: Editora Pensamento.

Argentine institute studies "firewalking." (May-June, 1961). *Newsletter of the Parapsychology Foundation*, p. 3.

Armstrong, L. (1970). Fire-walking at San Pedro Manrique, Spain. *Folk-lore, 81*, 198-214.

Aron, E., & Aaron, A. (1986). *The Maharishi effect: A revolution through meditation*. Wapole, NH: Stillpoint.

Babb, L.A. (1974). *Walking on flowers in Singapore, a Hindu festival cycle*. Singapore: University of Singapore, Department of Sociology, Working Paper No. 27.

Bach, M. (1952). *Strange altars*. Indianapolis, IN: Bobbs-Merrill Co.

Baker, B. (1985, April 21). A skeptical view: Doubting academics waging a flamboyant battle to debunk society's fascination with popular theories. *Los Angeles Times*.

Ballis, T., Beaumanoir, A., & Xenakis, C. (1979). Anastenaria. *Iatriki Epitheorisi ton Enoplon Dinameon* [Hellenic Armed Force Medical Review], *13*, 245-250 [in Greek].

229

Bandler, R., & Grinder, J. (1975). *Structure of magic*, Vol. I. Palo Alto, CA: Science and Behavior Books.
Bandler, R., & Grinder, J. (1976). *Structure of magic*, Vol. II. Palo Alto, CA: Science and Behavior Books.
Bandler, R., & Grinder, J. (1979). *Frogs into princes*. Moab, UT: Real People Press.
Barker, E.N. (1971-1972). Humanistic psychology and scientific method. *Interpersonal Development*, 2, 137-172.
Belo, J. (1960). *Trance in Bali*, Columbia University Press.
Benedict, R. (1934). *Patterns of culture*. Boston: Houghton Mifflin.
Benson, H. (1984). *Beyond the relaxation response*. New York: Times Books.
The Bhagavad Gita. (1962). Translated from the Sanskrit with an introduction by Juan Mascaro. New York: Penguin.
Blacker, C. (1975). *The Catalpa bow: A study of shamanistic practices in Japan*. London: George Allen & Unwin.
Blake, J. (1985). Attribution of power and the transformation of fear: An empirical study of firewalking. *Psi Research*, 4(2), 64-90.
Blavatsky, H. (1966). *An abridgement of the Secret Doctrine*, edited by Elizabeth Preston and Christmas Humphreys. London: Theosophical Publishing House.
Borland, C., & Landrith, G. (1975). *Improved quality of city life: Decreased crime rate*. MERU Report 7502. Weggis, Switzerland: Department of Sociology, Center for the Study of Higher States of Consciousness, Maharishi European Research University.
Borysenko, J. (1984). Psychoneuroimmunology: Behavioral factors and the immune response. *ReVision*, 7(1), 56-65.
Bray, D. K. (1985). *Lessons for a kahuna*. Kailua-Kona, Hawaii. (Original work published in 1967.)
Breci, S. (1982, October). Fire walking has its pitfalls. *Fate*, pp. 67-69.
Brown, G.B. (1938). A report on three experimental fire-walks by Ahmed Hussain and others. *Bulletin IV*. University of London, Council for Psychical Investigation.
Bruner, J.S., Goodnow, J.J., & Austin, G.A. (1956). *A study of thinking*. New York: John Wiley.
Calicoat, B. (1986, Spring). The ultimate fear management workshop. *The Huna Work*, No. 284, pp. 1-3.

Cannell, C.F. (1968). Interviewing. In G. Lindzey & E. Aronson (Eds.). *The handbook of social psychology* (2nd ed.), Vol. II. Reading, MA: Addison-Wesley.

Cassoli, P. (1958). La pirobazia in Grecia (Le Anastenaria). *Minerva Medica, 77*, 3679-3686.

Chapman, L., Goodell, H., & Wolff, H. (1959). Increased inflammatory reaction induced by central nervous system activity. *Transactions of the Association of American Physicians, 72*, 84-110.

Chari, C.T.K. (1960). Parapsychological studies and literature in India. *International Journal of Parapsychology, 2*(1), 24-32.

Christodoulou, S.P. (1978). *Continuity and change among the Anastenaria, a firewalking cult in Northern Greece.* Unpublished doctoral dissertation, Department of Anthropology, State University of New York at Stony Brook.

Cicourel, A.V. (1964). *Method and measurement in sociology.* New York: Free Press.

Clifton, R.S. (1962, June). I walked on the fiery coals. *Fate*, pp. 75-84.

Coe, M.R., (1957). Fire-walking and related behaviors. *Psychological Record, 7*(2), 101-110.

Coe, M.R. (1978, June). Safely across the fiery pit. *Fate*, pp. 84-86.

Cohen, A. (n.d.) [1987]. *The healing of the planet Earth.* Somerset, NJ: Author.

Cohen, D. (1971). *Masters of the occult.* New York: Dodd, Mead & Company.

Colaizzi, P.F. (1978). Psychological research as the phenomenologist views it. In R.S. Valle & M. King (Eds.), *Existential-phenomenological alternatives for psychology* (pp. 48-71). New York: Oxford University Press.

Cooley, D.G. (1957, August). Secret of the firewalkers. *True*, pp. 39-85.

Coon, D. (1980). *Introduction to psychology.* St.Paul, MN: West Publishing.

Cotterell, A. (1980). *A dictionary of world mythology.* New York: G.P. Putnam's Sons. (Original work published 1979).

A course in miracles (1985). Tiburon, CA: Foundation for Inner Peace. (Original work published 1975).

Crawley, A.E. (1951). Fire, Fire-Gods. In J. Hastings (Ed.), *Encyclopedia of religion and ethics*, Vol. 6 (pp. 26-30). New York: Charles Scribner's Sons. (Original work published 1913).

Crooks, W. (1889-1890). Notes on seances with D.D. Home. *Proceedings of the Society for Psychical Research*, 6, 98.

Da Love-Ananda [Da Free John] (1980). *Compulsory dancing*. Clearlake, CA: Dawn Horse Press.

Danforth, L.M. (1978). *The Anastenaria: A study in Greek ritual therapy*. Unpublished doctoral dissertation, Princeton University, Princeton, NJ.

Darling, C.R. (1935). Fire-walking. *Nature*, 136, 521.

Davis, L. (1985). How the Unidentified Flying Object Experience (UFOE) compares with the Near-Death Experience (NDE) as a vehicle for the evolution of human consciousness. Unpublished Master's thesis, John F. Kennedy University, Orinda, CA.

Dillbeck, M.C., Bauer, T.W., & Seferovich, S.I. (1978). *The transcendental meditation program as a predictor of crime rate changes in the Kansas City metropolitan area*. (Unpublished paper. Available from the International Center for Scientific Research, Maharishi International University, Fairfield, Iowa 52556.)

Dillbeck, M.C., Cavanaugh, K.L., Glenn, T., Orme-Johnson, D.W., & Mittlefehldt, V. (1987). Consciousness as a field: The Transcendental Meditation and TM-Sidhi program and changes in social indicators. *Journal of Mind and Behavior*, 8, 67-103.

Dimantoglou, M.J. (1952). Pyrovassie et incombustibilite. *Revue Metapsychique*, 22, 82-89.

Dimantoglou, M.J. (1953). La pyrobatie en Grece. *Revue Metapsychique*, 23, 9-19.

Doherty, J. (1982, August). Hot feat: Firewalkers of the world. *Science Digest*, pp. 67-71.

Dorofeyev, G. (1987). [Miracles ... under investigation]. *Sotsialisticheskaya Industriya* [Socialist Industry] (Moscow), May 31 [in Russian].

Dutt, R.C. (1972). *The Ramayana* (Condensed into English Verse). Bombay, India: Jaico Publishing House. (Original work published 1944).

Earl of Dunraven. (1924). Experiences in spiritualism with D.D. Home. *Proceedings of the Society for Psychical Research, 35,* 1-285.

Edsman, C.-M. (1987). Fire. In M. Eliade (Ed.), *The Encyclopedia of Religion* (Vol. 5, pp. 340-346). New York: Macmillan.

Eliade, M. (1972). *Shamanism: Archaic techniques of ecstasy.* Princeton: Princeton University Press. (Original work published 1964).

Eliade, M. (1968). *Myths, dreams and mysteries.* London: Collins.

Emerson, E.R. (1965). *Indian myths: Legends, traditions, and symbols of the aborigines of America.* Minneapolis, MN: Ross & Haines.

Epstein, S. (1980). The stability of behavior II: Implications for psychological research. *American Psychologist, 35*(9), 790-806.

Evans-Wentz, W.Y. (1958). *Tibetan yoga and secret doctrines.* Oxford University Press.

Evans-Wentz, W.Y. (1960). *The Tibetan book of the dead.* 3rd edition. Oxford: Oxford University Press. (Original work published 1927).

Evaggelou, I. (1971). [The Anastenaria and the phenomenon of akaia (non being burned) of the people walking on fire]. In *I goiteta tou mistiriou* [The fascination of mystery]. Athens: Dodoni [in Greek].

Feigen, G.M. (1969, July 12). Bucky Fuller and the firewalk. *Saturday Review,* pp. 22-23.

Feinberg, L. (1959, May). Fire walking in Ceylon. *Atlantic Monthly,* pp. 73-76.

Fenlason, A., Beals, G., & Abrahamson, A. (1962). *Essentials in interviewing* (Rev. ed.). New York: Harper & Row.

Fischer, C.T., & Wertz, F.J. (1979). Empirical phenomenological analysis of being criminally victimized. In A. Giorgi, R. Knowles, & D.L. Smith (Eds.), *Duquesne studies in phenomenological psychology: Vol. III* (pp. 135-158). Pittsburgh, PA: Duquesne University Press.

Fonseka, C. (1971, June). Fire-walking: A scientific investigation. *Ceylon Medical Journal,* pp. 104-109.

Frazer, J.G. (1955). *The golden bough* (3rd ed.). London: Macmillan. (Original work published 1900)

Firewalking

Freeman, J.M. (1974). Trial by fire. *Natural History*, *83*(1), 54-62.

Fulton, R. (1902). An account of the Fiji fire-walking ceremony, or Vilavilairevo with a probable explanation of the mystery. *Transactions and Proceedings of the New Zealand Institute*, *35*, 187-201.

Gaddis, V.H. (1967). *Mysterious fires and lights*. New York: David McKay.

Gallwey, T., & Kriegel, B. (1977). *Inner skiing*. New York: Random House.

Galtung, J. (1967). *Theory and methods of social research*. New York: Columbia University Press.

Garfield, C.A., & Bennett, H. (1984). *Peak performance: Mental training techniques of the world's greatest athletes*. Los Angeles: Jeremy Tarcher.

Garrison, P. (1985, April). Kindling courage. *Omni*, pp. 44-48, 84-85.

Gault, A.A. (1954). The Anastenaria: Thracian fire-walking festival. *Thracian Archives*, *36*.

Geschwind, N., & Behan, P. (1982). Left-handedness: Association with immune disease, migraine, and developmental learning disorder. *Proceedings of the National Academy of Sciences*, *79*, 5097-5100.

Gibson, E.P. (1952). The American Indian and the fire walk. *Journal of the American Society for Psychical Research*, *46*, 149-153.

Giles, S. (1978). Analysis of crime trend in 56 major US cities. *Scientific Research on the Transcendental Meditation Program: Collected Papers*, Vol. II (Rheinweiler, West Germany: MERU Press).

Giorgi, A. (1971a). Phenomenology and experimental psychology: I. In A. Giorgi, W.F. Fisher, & R. von Eckartsberg (Eds.), *Duquesne studies in phenomenological psychology: Vol. I* (pp. 6-16). Pittsburgh, PA: Duquesne University Press.

Giorgi, A. (1971b). Phenomenology and experimental psychology: II. In A. Giorgi, W.F. Fisher, & R. von Eckartsberg (Eds.), *Duquesne studies in phenomenological psychology: Vol. I* (pp. 17-29). Pittsburgh, PA: Duquesne University Press.

Giorgi, A. (1975). An application of phenomenological methods in psychology. In A. Giorgi, C.T. Fischer, & E.L. Murray (Eds.). *Duquesne studies in phenomenological psychology: Vol. II* (pp. 8-103). Pittsburgh, PA: Duquesne University Press.

Godwin, J. (1968). *This baffling world.* New York: Hart, 1968.

Golden, P.M. (Ed.) (1976). *The research experience.* Itasca, IL: Peacock.

Goode, W.J., & Hatt, P.K. (1952). *Methods in social research.* New York: McGraw-Hill.

Gorden, R.L. (1969). *Interviewing: Strategy, techniques, and tactics.* Homewood, IL.: Dorsey Press.

Gowan, J.C. (1980). *Operations of increasing order.* Westlake Village, CA: Author.

Green, A., & Green, A. (1973). The ins and outs of mind-body energy. *Science Year 1974, World Book Science Annual.* Chicago: Field Enterprises.

Griffin, N. (1985, March). The charismatic kid. *Life,* pp. 41-48.

Grim, J.A. (1983). *The shaman: Patterns of Siberian and Ojibway healing.* Oklahoma University Press: Norman.

Grosvenor, D.K., & Grosvenor, G.M. (1966, April). Ceylon. *National Geographic,* pp. 447-497.

Guberman, I. (1969). [Way beyond the horizon]. *Nauka i Religiya* (Science and Religion), No. 8, pp. 51-55 [in Russian].

Gudgeon, W.E. (1899). Te Umu-Ti, or fire-walking ceremony. *Journal of the Polynesian Society,* 8(29), 58-60.

Guinness book of world records, 1988. (1987). New York: Sterling Publishing Co.

Guinness book of world records, 1989. (1988). New York: Sterling Publishing Co.

Gunther, R., & Gunther, D. (1983). If we can walk on red-hot coals, we can do anything. *Psi Research,* 2(4), 101-102.

Gutmanis, J. (1979). *Kahuna La'au Lapa'au: The practice of Hawaiian herbal medicine.* Honolulu, HI: Island Heritage/ Honolulu Publishing. (Original work published 1976.)

Hadfield, J.A. (1917). The influence of hypnotic suggestion on inflammatory conditions. *Lancet,* 2, 678-679.

Hansen, G.P. (1982). *References on firewalking.* Unpublished bibliography, the Foundation for Research on the Nature of Man, P. O. Box 6847, College Station, Durham, NC, 27708.

Hatchard, G. (1978). *Influence of Transcendental Meditation Program on crime rate in suburban Cleveland.* (Unpublished paper. Available from the International Center for Scientific Research, Maharishi International University, Fairfield, Iowa 52556.)

Heinze, R.-I. (1984). *Trance and healing in Southeast Asia today.* Berkeley: Independent Scholars of Asia.

Heinze, R.-I. (1985). "Walking on flowers" in Singapore. *Psi Research, 4*(2), 46-50.

Henry, T. (1893). Fire-walking in Tonga. *Journal of the Polynesian Society, 2*(2), 105-108.

Ho Ku-Li. (1972, January). Firewalking in Hsinchuang. *Echo of Things Chinese* (Taipei, Taiwan), pp. 18-24.

Hocken, T.M. (1898). An account of the Fiji fire ceremony. *Transactions and Proceedings of the New Zealand Institute, 31,* 667-673.

Holmberg, U. (1964). *Finno-Ugric and Siberian mythology.* In C.J.A. MacCulloch (Ed.), *The mythology of all races,* Vol. 4, New York: Cooper Square Publishers.

Home, Mme. D. (1921). *D.D. Home: His life and mission.* London: Kegan Paul, Trench, Trubner.

Hopkins, E.W. (1951). Fire-walking. In J. Hastings (Ed.), *Encyclopedia of religion and ethics,* Vol. 6 (pp. 30-31). New York: Charles Scribner's Sons. (Original work published 1913)

Horn, J.T. (1953, February). I was a firewalker! *Travel,* pp. 20-22.

Ianuzzo, G. (1982). Fire-immunity and fire-walks: Some historical and anthropological notes. *European Journal of Parapsychology, 4,* 271-275.

Ianuzzo, G. (1983). "Fire-immunity": Psi ability or psychophysiological phenomenon. *Psi Research, 2*(4), 68-74.

Ingalls, A.G. (1939). Fire-walking. *Scientific American, 160,* 135-138, 173-178.

Ivchenko, L., & Lisovenko, N. (1987). ["Wonder" in Yenakiyevo: What scientists think about it]. *Izvestiya* [News] (Moscow), May 27, No. 147 [in Russian].

Johnson, J.M. (1975). *Doing field research.* New York: Free Press.

Kane, S.M. (1976, November). *Holiness fire handling: A psychophysiological analysis.* Paper presented at the 75th Annual

Meeting of the American Anthropological Association, Washington, DC.

Kane, S.M. (1979). *Snake handlers of Southern Appalachia*. Unpublished doctoral dissertation, Princeton University, Princeton, NJ.

Kane, S.M. (1982). Holiness ritual fire handling: Ethnographic and psychophysiological considerations. *Ethos, 10*, 369-384.

Keen, E.E. (1975). *A primer in phenomenological psychology*. New York: Holt, Rinehart & Winston.

Kenn, C.W. (Arii-Peu Tama-Iti) (1949). *Fire-walking from the inside*. Los Angeles: Franklin Thomas.

Kerlinger, F.N. (1973). *Foundations of behavioral research* (2nd ed.). New York: Holt, Rinehart & Winston.

Kidder, L.H. (1981). *Sellitz, Wrightsman, and Cook's research methods in social relations* (4th ed.). New York: Holt, Rinehart & Winston.

Kiefer, G. (Ed.) (1988). *Kundalini for the New Age: Selected writings by Gopi Krishna*. New York: Bantam,

Kiev, A. (1968). The psychotherapeutic value of spirit-possession in Haiti. In R. Prince (Ed.), *Trance and possession states* (pp. 143-148). Montreal: R.M. Bucke Memorial Society.

Kolodny, L. (1986, August). ["What can a journalist do?..."] *Zhurnalist* [Journalist], No. 8, pp. 42-44 [in Russian].

Komar, with Steiger, B. (1979). *Life without pain*. New York: Berkeley.

Kotzsch, R.E. (1985, April). Fire-walking. *East West Journal*, pp. 40-45.

Kozulin, A. (1984). *Psychology in Utopia: Toward a social history of Soviet psychology*. Cambridge, MA: The MIT Press.

Krausz, E., & Miller, S.H. (1974). *Social research design*. London: Logman.

Krechmal, A. (1957, October). Firewalkers of Greece. *Travel, 108*, 46-47.

Krishna, G. (1971). *Kundalini: Evolutionary energy in man*. Berkeley: Shambhala.

Kruger, D. (1979). *An introduction to phenomenological psychology*. Pittsburgh, PA: Duquesne University Press.

Landrith, G. (1978). *The Maharishi Effect and invincibility: The influence of the TM Program on the variables of crime, automobile accidents and fires.* (Unpublished paper. Available from the International Center for Scientific Research, Maharishi International University, Fairfield, Iowa 52556.)

Lane, E.W. (1842). *An account of the manners and customs of the modern Egyptians.* London: Charles Knight.

Lang, A. (1897). *Modern mythology.* New York: Longmans, Green.

Lang, A. (1900). The fire walk. *Proceedings of the Society for Psychical Research, 15,* Part 36, 2-15.

Langley, S.P. (1901). The fire walk ceremony in Tahiti. *Nature, 64,* 397-399.

Leikind, B.J., & McCarthy, W.J. (1985). An investigation of firewalking. *Skeptical Inquirer, 10*(1), 23-34.

Le Mee, J. (1975). *Hymns from the Rig-Veda.* New York: Alfrd A. Knopf.

Leonard, G. (1975). *The ultimate athlete.* New York: Viking.

LeShan, L. (1975). *The medium, the mystic, and the physicist.* New York: Ballantine Books.

LeShan, L. (1976). *Alternate realities.* New York: M. Evans.

Lisovenko, N. (1987). [Fire ... "as you like it!"] *Izvestiya* [News], (Moscow), April 11, No. 101, p. 4 [in Russian].

Locke, S.E., & Colligan, D. (1986, March). Mind cures. *Omni,* pp. 51-54, 112-114.

Locke, S.E., & Horning-Rohan, M. (1983). *Mind and immunity: Behavioral immunology, An annotated bibliography 1976-1982.* New York: Institute for the Advancement of Health.

Lodge, O.C. (1948). Fire dances in Bulgaria—1939. *Slavonic and East European Review, 26*(67), 467-483.

Lofland, J. (1971). *Analyzing social settings.* Belmont, CA: Wadsworth.

Long, M.F. (1976). *The secret science behind miracles.* Los Angeles, CA: DeVorss & Co. (Original work published 1948).

Ludwig, A.M. (1969). Altered states of consciousness. In C.T. Tart (Ed.), *Altered states of consciousness: A book of readings* (pp. 9-22). New York: John Wiley.

Luomala, K. (1987). Hawaiian religion. In M. Eliade (Ed.), *The encyclopedia of religion* (Vol. 6, pp. 214-219). New York: Macmillan.

Maisyuk, A. (1983). Know yourself. *Psi Research*, 2(1), 106-109. (Original work published 1982)

Maisyuk, A. (1984, July). [What are humans capable of?] *Tekhnika-Molodezhi* [Technology for Youth], pp. 44-47 [in Russian].

Makrakis, B. (1982). *Fire dances in Greece*. Crete, Greece: Author, 1982.

Manganas, V. (1983). Fire dancing in Greece. *Psi Research*, 2(4), 80-83.

Manganas, V. (1985). Fire dancing in Greece (Letter to the editor). *Psi Research*, 4(3/4), 220.

Manganas, V., & Zachariades, N. (1983). Corona discharge photography in psychiatry. *Psychoenergetics: The Journal of Psychoenergetic Systems*, 4, 391-400.

Marden, L. (1958). The island called Fiji. *National Geographic*, 94(10), 526-557.

McClenon, J. (1983a). Firewalking at Mount Takao. *Archaeus*, 1(1), 25-28.

McClenon, J. (1983b). Firewalking in Sri Lanka. *Psi Research*, 2(4), 99-100.

McCluggage, D. (1977). *The centered skier*. Vermont Crossroads: Vermont Crossroads Press.

Mead, M. (1964). *Continuities in cultural evolution*. New Haven: Yale University Press.

Megas, G. (1961). [The custom of Anastenaria]. *Laographia*, [Folklore], 19, 475-534 [in Greek].

Menard, W. (1949). Firewalkers of the South seas. *Natural History*, 58, 8-15, 48.

Metraux, A. (1972). *Voodoo in Haiti*. New York: Schocken.

Millman, D. (1979). *Whole body fitness: Training body, mind, and spirit*. New York: Clarkson N. Potter.

Mir, M., & Vilenskaya, L. (1986). *The golden chalice*. San Francisco: H.S. Dakin.

Mishlove, J. (1975). *The roots of consciousness*. New York: Random House.

Morozova, E.V., Ilyina, A.P., & Dashevskaya, E.B. (1982). Plants as detectors of the biofield. *Psi Research*, 1(3), 92.

Morris, F. (1974, July). Exorcising the devil in California. *Fate*, pp. 36-46.

Muktananda, Swami. (1974). *The play of consciousness.* Campbell, CA: Shree Gurudev Ashram,

Mullins, J. (1985). *Hawaii's volcanoes: Legends and facts.* Honolulu, HI: Aloha Graphics and Sales.

Mundy, J. (1971, January-February). Faith and fire-walking. *Realist*, pp. 22-23.

Murphy, M., & White, R. (1978). *The psychic side of sports.* Reading, MA: Addison-Wesley.

The mystery of firewalking. (1978). *Human Behavior*, 7(3), 51.

Neufield, R.W.J. (1977). *Clinical quantitative methods.* New York: Grue & Stratton.

Oesterreich, T.K. (1974). *Possession and exorcism.* New York: Causeway Books. (Original work published 1921.)

Oubre, A. (1986). Shamanic trance and the placebo effect: The case for a study in psychophysiological anthropology. *Psi Research*, 5(1/2), 116-144.

Parrinder, G. (1976). *Mysticism in the world's religions.* New York: Oxford University Press.

Parsons, E.C. (1939). *Pueblo Indian religion.* Chicago: University of Chicago Press.

Passeron, A. (1983). Bali: Trances and dances. *Revue Metapsychique*, 17(1-4), 9-16.

Pathak, R. (1970, June). The India devtia: Fire-walking deity. *Fate*, pp. 90-99.

Pearce, J.C. (1973). *The crack in the cosmic egg.* New York: Pocket Books. (Original work published 1971).

Pearce, J.C. (1977). *Magical child.* New York: Dutton.

Pearce, J.C. (1985). *Magical child matures.* New York: Dutton.

Perera, V. (1971, May). Foreign notes: The firewalkers of Udappawa. *Harper's*, pp. 18, 20, 21.

Persinger, M.A., & LaFreniere. (1977). *Space/time transients.* Chicago: Nelson Hall.

Poignant, R. (1967). *Oceanic mythology.* London/New York/Sidney/Toronto: Paul Hamlyn.

Polkinghorne, D.E. (1983). *Methodology for the human sciences: Systems of inquiry.* Albany, NY: State University of New York Press.

Price, H. (1936). A report on two experimental fire-walks. *Bulletin II.* University of London, Council for Psychical Investigation.

Price, H. (1937). Fire-walking. *Nature*, *139*, 928-929.

Price, H. (1939). *Fifty years of psychical research*. London: Longmans, Green.

Prince, R. (1982a). The Endorphins: A review for psychological anthropologists. *Ethos*, *10*(4), 303-316.

Prince, R. (1982b). Shamans and endorphins: Hypotheses for a synthesis. *Ethos*, *10*(4), 409-423.

Privette, G. (1981a). Dynamics of peak performance. *Journal of Humanistic Psychology*, *21*(1), 57-67.

Privette, G. (1981b). The phenomenology of peak performance in sports. *International Journal of Sport Psychology*, *12*, 51-60.

Privette, G. (1982a). Experiential correlates of peak intellectual perfomance. *Psychological Reports*, *51*, 323-330.

Privette, G. (1982b). Peak performance in sports: A factorial topology. *International Journal of Sport Psychology*, *13*, 242-249.

Privette, G. (1983). Peak experience, peak performance, and flow: A comparative analysis of positive human experiences. *Journal of Personality and Social Psychology*, *45*(6), 1361-1368.

Puharich, A. (1962). *Beyond telepathy*. Garden City, NY: Doubleday.

Right use of will: Healing and evolving the emotional body. (1984). Albuquerque, NM: One World Publications.

Ring, K. (1984). *Heading toward Omega*. New York: William Morrow.

Robbins, A. (1986). *Unlimited power*. New York: Fawcett Columbine.

Roberts, J. (1974). *The nature of personal reality*. New York: Bantam.

Rogers, C. (1942). *Counseling and psychotherapy*. New York: Houghton Mifflin.

Rogers, M.P., Dubey, D., & Reich, P. (1979). The influence of the psyche and the brain on immunity and disease susceptibility: A critical review. *Psychosomatic Medicine*, *41*, 147-165.

Rooke, G.H. (1936). Indian occultism: The rope-trick and other phenomena. *Asiatic Review*, *32*, 257-284.

Ross, I. (1966, April). I joined the firewalkers. *Fate*, pp. 46-50.

Ross, R. (1974). *Research: An introduction*. New York: Barnes & Noble.

Roth, K. (1933). The fire-walk in Fiji. *Man*, *33*, 44-49.

Firewalking

Firewalking*Firewalking*

Firewalking

*Firewalking**Firewalking*

Sannella, L. (1987). *The Kundalini experience*. Lower Lake, CA: Integral Publishing.

Sayce, R.V. (1933). Fire-walking ceremony in Natal. *Man, 33*, 2.

Schmeidler, G.R. (1973). PK effects upon continuously recorded temperature. *Journal of the American Society for Psychical Research, 67*, 326-338.

Schmeidler, G.R. (1984). Further analysis of PK with continuous temperature recordings. *Journal of the American Society for Psychical Research, 78*, 355-362.

Schwabe, M.J.S. (1901). Fire-walking in Mauritius. *Journal of the Society for Psychical Research, 10*, 154-155.

Schwarz, B.E. (1960). Ordeal by serpents, fire and strychnine. *Psychiatric Quarterly, 34*, 405-429.

Sellitz, C., Wrightsman, L.S., & Cook, S.W. (1976). *Research methods in social relations* (3rd ed.). New York: Holt, Reinhart & Winston.

Shaw, W. (1975). *Aspects of Malaysian magic*. Kuala Lumpur, Malaysia: Muzium Negara.

Simcenko, Yu.B. (1978). Mother cult among the North-Eurasian peoples. In V. Dioszegi & M. Hoppal (Eds.), *Shamanism in Siberia* (pp. 503-513). Budapest: Akademiai Kiado.

Sky, M. (1989). *Dancing with the fire*. Santa Fe, NM: Bear & Company.

Slavchev, S. (1983). Fire dancing. *Psi Research, 2*(4), 77-79. (Original work published 1971).

Smith, A. (1984, January). Walking on fire. *Esquire*, pp. 11-12.

Spino, M. (1976). *Beyond jogging: The innerspaces of running*. Millbrae, CA: Celestial Arts.

Steffy-Channon, J. (1989). *An investigation of the changes perceived by individuals after their firewalking experience*. Unpublished doctoral dissertation, Saybrook Institute, San Francisco, CA.

Stevenson, M.C. (1904). The Zuni Indians: Their Mythology, Esoteric Societies, and Ceremonies. *23rd Annual Report of the Bureau of American Ethnology*, pp. 1-634.

Stevick, E.L. (1971). An empirical investigation of the experience of anger. In A. Giorgi, R. Knowles, & D.L. Smith (Eds.), *Duquesne studies in phenomenological psychology: Vol. I* (pp. 132-148). Pittsburgh, PA: Duquesne University Press.

Stillings, D. (1985a). Fire walk. *Artifex*, *4*(1), 15-17.

Stillings, D. (1985b). Observations on firewalking. *Psi Research*, *4*(2), 51-60.

Stillings, D. (1986, February). I walked on fire. *Fate*, pp. 56-61.

Stowell, V.E., & Mahaluxmivala, P.D. (1928). The fire-walk. *Journal of the Society for Psychical Research*, *24*, 278-284.

Tanagras, A. (1953). L'incombustibilite dans les Balcanes. *Metapsichica*, *8*.

Tanagras, A. (1956, April). Firewalkers of modern Greece. *Tomorrow*, pp. 73-79.

Tart, C.T. (1969). Introduction. In C.T. Tart (Ed.), *Altered states of consciousness: A book of readings* (pp. 1-6). New York: John Wiley.

Tart, C.T. (1972). The changing scientific attitude in psychology. In C. Muses & A.M. Young (Eds.), *Consciousness and reality* (pp. 73-85). New York: Outerbridge & Lazard.

Thomas, E.S. (1934). The fire walk. *Proceedings of the Society for Psychical Research*, *42*, 292-309.

Thomson, B. (1894). *South sea yarns*. Edinburgh & London: William Blackwood & Sons.

Thurston, H. (1952). *The physical phenomena of mysticism*. London: Burns Oates.

Toward the Light: A message to mankind from the transcendental world. (1979). Copenhagen/New York: Michael Agerskov Toward the Light Publishing House. (The original in Danish was published in 1920).

Troshchansky, V.F. (1902). *Evolyutsiya chernoy very u yakutov* [Evolution of black beliefs in Yakuts]. Kazan: Kazanskoye Knizhnoye Izdatelstvo [in Rissian].

Truzzi, M. (1983), A bibliography on fire-walking. *Zetetic Scholar*, No. 11, 105-108.

Tweedie, I. (1979). *The chasm of fire*. Tisbury, England: Element Books.

Ullman, M. (1947). Herpes simplex and second degree burn induced under hypnosis. *American Journal of Psychiatry*, *103*, 828-830.

Ullman, M., Krippner, S., & Vaughan, A. (1973). *Dream telepathy*. London: Turnstone Books.

Uznadze, D. (1966a). *Psikhologicheskiye issledovaniya* [Psychological studies]. Moscow: Nauka [in Russian].

Uznadze, D. (1966b). *The psychology of set*. New York: Consultants Bureau.

Valle, R.S., & King, M. (1978). In introduction to existential-phenomenological thought in psychology. In R.S. Valle & M. King (Eds.), *Existential-phenomenological alternatives for psychology*. New York: Oxford University Press.

Vasiljev, V.I. (1978). Animistic notions of the Enets and the Yenisei Nenets. In V. Dioszegi & M. Hoppal (Eds.), *Shamanism in Siberia* (pp. 429-437). Budapest: Akademiai Kiado.

Vilenskaya, L. (1981). Psycho-physical effects by N. Kulagina: Remote influence on surrounding objects. *Parapsychology in the USSR* (Vol. III, pp. 12-25). San Francisco: Washington Research Center.

Vilenskaya, L. (1983). An eyewitness report: Firewalking in Portland, Oregon. *Psi Research*, 2(4), 85-98.

Vilenskaya, L. (1984a). Firewalking: A new fad, a scientific riddle, or an excellent tool for healing, spiritual growth and psychological development? *Psi Research*, 3(2), 102-118.

Vilenskaya, L. (1984b). Psi research in the Soviet Union: Are they ahead of us? In R. Targ, & K. Harary, *The mind race: Understanding and using psychic abilities* (pp. 247-260). New York: Villard/Random House.

Vilenskaya, L. (1985a). Firewalking: Renewing an old tradition to raise consciousness. In R.-I. Heinze, (Ed), *Proceedings of the Second International Conference on Shamanism* (pp. 58-65). Berkeley: Independent Scholars of Asia.

Vilenskaya. L. (1985b). Firewalking and beyond, *Psi Research*, 4(2), 91-109.

Vilenskaya, L. (1985c, August). Psi in mental healing, with observations from firewalking. Paper presented at the panel discussion "States of Mind in Psychic Healing," the 28th Convention of the Parapsychological Association, Medford, MA (Abstract published in: Debra H. Weiner & Dean I. Radin, Eds., *Research in Parapsychology 1985*, p. 158).

Vilenskaya, L. (1986). A few additional words: My story. In M. Mir & L. Vilenskaya (Eds), *The golden chalice* (pp. 167-176), San Francisco, CA: H.S. Dakin.

Vilenskaya, L. (1988a, April). Poltergeist cases in the Soviet Union. *ASPR Newsletter, 14*(2), 10-11.

Vilenskaya, L. (1988b). Epilogo: Seis anos depois [Epilogue: Six years later]. In S. Krippner, *Possibilidades humanas* [Human possibilities] (pp. 357-373). Rio de Janeiro: Francisco Alves [in Portuguese].

Vilenskaya, L. (1989). Symbolism of fire, firewalking and individual belief systems: Do we create our own reality? In R.-I. Heinze (Ed), *Proceedings of the Sixth International Conference on Shamanism* (pp. 107-132). Berkeley: Independent Scholars of Asia.

Villoldo, A., & Krippner, S. (1987). *Healing states.* New York: Simon & Schuster.

Volchenko, V.N., Dulnev, G.N., Krylov, K.I., Kulagin, V.V., & Pilipenko, N.V. (1984). Measurements of extreme values of physical fields of the human operator. In *Tekhnicheskie Aspekty Refleksoterapii i Sistemy Diagnostiki* [Technical Aspects of the Reflex Therapy and Diagnostic System] (pp. 53-59), Kalinin: Kalinin State University [in Russian; English translation in: *Psi Research, 3*(3/4), Sep./Dec. 1984, 66-73].

Waller, S. (1984). *Alignment of psychology and physiology presents the most holistic research in the peak performance field.* Unpublished manuscript, Saybrook Institute, San Francisco.

Waller, S. (1988). *Altered states of consciousness in sports peak performance*, Saybrook Institute, San Francisco.

Walker, J. (1977). The amateur scientist: Drops of water dance on a hot skillet and the experimenter walks on hot coals. *Scientific American, 237,* 126-131.

Weil, A. (1980). *The marriage of the sun and moon.* Boston: Houghton Mifflin.

Weil, A. (1983). *Health and healing: Understanding conventional and alternative medicine.* Boston: Houghton Mifflin.

White, R.W. (1977). *Lives in progress.* New York: Holt, Rinehart & Winston.

White, S.M. (1934). A "fire walking" ceremony in Fiji. *Journal of the Society for Psychical Research, 28,* 170-175.

Worrall, A. (1972, June). I achieved fire immunity. *Fate*, pp. 47-51.

Worrall, A., & Worrall, O. (1968). *The miracle healers.* New York: New American Library.

Firewalking

Xenakis, C., Larbig, W., & Tsarouchas, E. (1977). Zur Psychophysiologie des Feuerlaufers [To psychophysiology of firewalkers]. *Archiv für Psychiatrie und Nervenkrankheiten*, *223*, 309-322.

Zorab, G. (1976). *D.D. Home il medium*. Milan: Armenia.

𝓙𝓷𝓭𝓮𝔁

247

Index

preparation to 9, 13-16, 19, 56-
60, 98-99, 105, 108
review of studies of 50-56, 72-80
workshops xiv, xv, 10, 13, 60-
62, 67, 94-95, 97-100, 125,
136-137, 139, 146-148,
160, 164-167, 209-212
Flouris, George 104
Fonseka, C. 77
Free Pentecostal Holiness Church 54,
56, 64, 65, 85
Free University of Berlin 112
Fulton, R. 75

Gaddis, Vincent H. 47
Garfield, Charles A. 127, 129, 185,
186
Goodell, H. 81
Gorden, R.L. 133
Greece x, xv, xvi, 4, 46, 53-54, 65,
66, 80, 85, 103-112, 120, 205
Greek Society for Psychical Research
108
Grim, John A. 41
Grinder, John 98
Grosvenor, Gilbert M. 45
Guberman, Igor 3
Gudgeon, W.E. 43
Guinness Book of World Records 79
Gunther, Daniel 49, 113
Gunther, Richard 48-49, 67, 68, 213
Gurdjieff, Georges 96

Hadfield, J. Arthur 81
Haggard, Andrew 44
Haiti xiv, xv, 41, 48
Hawaii ix, 43, 51, 59, 75, 205
Hawaiians, *see also* Hawaii 21, 25,
33, 117
healing 65-66, 82, 118-119, 197
Heinze, Ruth-Inge xvi, 47
Henry, T. 43
Hindu 23-24, 26, 29
Hocken, T.M. 42, 73
Home, Daniel Dunglas 49
Horn, J.T. 57

human possibilities 1-2, 7-9, 19-20,
213
Huna (ancient Hawaiian spiritual
teaching); *see also* kahunas and
Hawaiians 62
Hussain, Ahmed 50, 76
hypotheses concerning firewalking x,
5, 71-90, 155-157, 176-179
calloused feet x, 5, 74-75
deception 73-74, 176
electrostatic cooling 87
Leidenfrost effect 78-80, 101,
196
low thermal conductivity 74, 75,
77-78
mind over matter 87-89, 156,
177-178, 195, 205-206
perspiration on the feet x, 5, 78-
80, 119, 155
power of belief (faith) 40, 59,
60, 61, 84-86, 90, 101, 105,
117, 156, 166, 177, 195,
205
physiological regulation 51, 64,
83, 110, 155
superconductivity 5, 87, 119

immunity to pain 63-64
to cold 36, 64
India ix, xv, 3, 29, 39, 43-44, 65, 76,
85
Indonesia xv, 3, 41
Ingalls, A.G. 79
Iowa State College 45
Ivanova, Barbara 121, 122

Japan ix, xv, 3, 44-45, 57, 61
Jews 22

kahunas (Hawaiian shamans) ix, 51,
59-60
Kamensky, Yuri 1
Kane, Steven M. 54-56, 78, 90
Karger, Friedbert 52, 78, 80
Keen, E.E. 136
Kellogg 4

Index

Russian, Russians, *see also* Soviet Union 2, 27, 31

St. Constantine ix, 6, 46, 58, 65, 66, 85, 105, 106, 108, 110
St. Helen 6, 58, 105, 108, 110
St. Peter Igneus (Peter Aldobrandini) 40
St. Polycarp 40
Saybrook Institute ix
Sayce, R. V. 43
Schmeidler, Gertrude R. 87
Schwarz, Bertold E. 56
Schwarz, Jack 56
Sellitz, C. 189
shamanism and shamans ix, xi, 31, 36, 41, 64
Sharankov 4
Singapore xv, 47, 57
Sky, Michael 121
Slavchev, Svyatoslav 5, 47
Slavs 2, 21
snake handlers 54, 64
South Africa xv, 43
Soviet Union 1, 2, 7, 9, 34, 35, 95, 114, 116
Spain xv, 40
Spencer, Edmund 91
spontaneous combustion 34-35
Sri Lanka xv, 45, 79, 80
State-Trait Anxiety Inventory 67
Stephenson, E.G. 44
Stillings, Dennis 68, 76, 82, 84, 87, 101
"supernatural" knowledge, *see also* clairvoyance and extrasensory perception 65, 205
Swann, Ingo 87

Tahiti 4, 57
Taiwan 47
Tanagras, A. 108
Tanner, John 26
Te Umu-Ti (firewalking ceremony) 43
Tekhnika-Molodezhi (Technology for Youth) 7

telekinesis, *see* psychokinesis
telepathy, *see also* extrasensory perception 1
Thailand xiv, xv
Thematic Apperception Test (TAT) 115-116
Thomson, Basil 42
Tibet ix, 174
The Tibetan Book of the Dead 28
trance, *see* altered states of consciousness
Transcendental Meditation (TM) 120
Trinidad xiv, xv
Tweedie, Irina 35

UFO experience 208
Ullman, Montague 81
University of California 48
University of Hawaii 51, 75
University of London Council for Psychical Investigation 50, 76
University of Tubingen ix
Unlimited Power 102
USSR Academy of Sciences 35, 116
Uznadze, Dmitri 114-115

Valle, R.S. 187
Villoldo, Alberto 118

Walker, Jearl 79
Waller, S. 127, 129
Weil, Andrew 65, 66, 83, 86, 101, 119, 155
White, Rhea A. xvi, 129
White, R.W. 130
Wolff, H. 81
Worrall, Ambrose 49

Xenakis, Christos 112

Yakuts (an ethnic group) 21, 25
Yukagirs (an ethnic minority in the USSR) 24, 25
yoga 8, 12, 29, 32, 54, 79

Zorab, George 49
Zoroastrianism 23